The Lamb of God Victorious!

The Keeping of the Revelation Promise

D Robert Pike, Ph.D.

Other Books by Rob Pike

God's Promise of Redemption
a story of fulfilled prophecy

God's Purpose for Hell
a compelling probe of God's love for the lost

Jehovah's Witnesses -
Modern Day Arians or Not

The Great American Divide
How we got here and what we can do about it

Find them at your favorite book store or at Amazon.com

Visit Rob's website at:

www.truthinliving.net

TruthinLiving Publishing, North Port, FL

 ISBN: 9781723173288

DEDICATION

I wish to dedicate this book to Jesus Christ, God the Father, and the Holy Spirit. I am your servant and the work of your hands. Thank you dear God for the insights that you have provided me through the work of the Holy Spirit and also from your precious saints from whom I have learned much concerning the Revelation which you gave to your servant and Apostle John. May I honor you with this work? I ask this in the precious name of Jesus. AMEN!

In the production of this volume, Rick Meyers excellent resource was used.
e-Sword Version 10.2.1
Copyright 2000-2013
www.e-sword.net/support.html

CONTENTS

ACKNOWLEDGMENTS

As always, I first of all thank God for giving me the ability to do the research and write this book. I also want to thank my loving wife Ida for her continued support of my work. My special thanks go out to Stephen King and Julie McAllen who were kind enough to proofread my book for me and give me extremely valuable feedback.

Foreword

As Dr. Pike says in his introduction, the book of Revelation continues to be a source of fascination for virtually all Bible students. Unfortunately, generation after generation of so-called prophecy experts have assured us that this is it, the end is near! Our generation "must" be the last generation. And yet, generations come and generations go, and every one of those prognosticators have failed.

Why? Is it, as the skeptics claim, because the Bible is not inspired? Is it because Jesus and His apostles were, in the final analysis, the first in a long, sordid line of failed prophets, zealous, but wrong? Is the fault with an uninspired Bible? Or, is it just possible that all modern "Bible prophecy experts" are the ones at fault - deeply at fault? Why are men always so ready to blame the Bible, *when the fault is with the Bible readers and interpreters* failing to honor what the book actually says?

In this more than welcome book, Dr. Robert Pike offers an extremely sensible, logical, and most of all textual and contextual analysis of the Apocalypse. Now, if you are looking for another sensationalistic prediction that the end is just around the corner, you will not find it here. But, if you want to read a serious, though certainly not ponderous, exegesis of the book of Revelation, this is the book for you.

Dr. Pike avoids that sensationalism by focusing on the reality - the undeniable but mostly overlooked reality - that the book of Revelation tells us, repeatedly, emphatically, explicitly and undeniably, that the fulfillment of the vision was to take place soon. This fact alone falsifies the modern day "newspaper exegesis" that dominates evangelical Christianity and its view of Revelation. After all, if the book was written in the first century and was to be (and was) fulfilled shortly, that means it did not predict the "*The 1980's: Countdown to Armageddon*!", or "*88 Reasons Why the Rapture Will Be in 1988*!"

There is a great deal in Dr. Pike's book that impresses me, but, let me mention three of the most outstanding.

First, and most important, Dr. Pike does a great job of showing how the Old Testament serves as the source for much of the Revelation and demonstrates the incredible importance of allowing those OT sources to guide our understanding of the book. He does this particularly with the book of Daniel which, by universal consent, played a major role in John's thought. In similar vein, he shows how the Olivet Discourse is crucial for understanding Revelation. You will be amazed at the richness - and persuasive power - of this evidence. This is some great material!

Second. Pike shares with his readers how the book of Revelation can be shown from the historical sources to have been fulfilled shortly. He does this by sharing numerous citations from Josephus, highly respected first century Jewish Historian, who was literally an eyewitness to the fulfillment of much of

Revelation! Unfortunately, this wealth of reliable historical information may come as a huge surprise to many Bible students who have not been encouraged to read the ancient sources. But, I can assure you that you will be amazed at what Josephus has to say. The correlations between the text of Revelation and Josephus are simply amazing!

Third, in passage after passage, after showing the historical fulfillment of John's vision, Dr. Pike shows what that fulfillment means to us today. What does the fulfillment of Revelation mean for the believer in Christ, the Triumphant King of kings, mean for us? And, what does it mean for the unbeliever who rejects the King of kings? This is the "practical" side of this book, and if you are a true follower of the King, you will rejoice and take tremendous comfort in following and in knowing: "The Lamb of God Victorious!"

I am more than honored to recommend this book.

Don K. Preston (D. Div.)
President
Preterist Research Institute
www.bibleprophecy.com

Prologue

The book of Revelation is likely regarded by most people as the most captivating book in the Bible. It has been the object of fascination by Bible students for centuries. Having been raised by my parents who were Jehovah's Witnesses, I was soon indoctrinated with a view of Revelation which included the idea that there would be a destruction of everyone on the planet with the exception of Jehovah's Witnesses in a global event called "the battle of Armageddon." The anticipation of this event subsequently ruled my thinking for all of life until I reached my early thirties.

The anticipation of a global disaster brought on by God still rules the life of everyone associated with that organization as well as many others who label themselves as Christian. Regarding this, I will only say that if those members of Jehovah's Witnesses would do the math, they would realize the folly of their teaching. It would mean that the sacrificial death of Christ happened for just over .012% of the population of the earth. In other words 99.98% of the population of the earth would be destroyed in the battle of

Armageddon. How ridiculous! Doesn't this teaching cut off at the knees the power of the blood of Christ?

Once I realized the fallacy of the teachings of Jehovah's Witnesses on this matter, I sought to find another explanation. I soon settled on an approach that was somewhat similar to my earlier training which has likewise proven to be false. I will now refer to this as "The Hal Lindsey approach." The basic premise of this was also that we were on the verge of the fulfillment of the book of Revelation based upon the timing of the establishment of the Israeli state in 1948. Notice what Lindsey states in his book, "The Late Great Planet Earth:"

> The one event which many Bible students in the past overlooked was this paramount sign: Israel had to be a nation again in the land of its forefathers.
>
> Israel a nation – a dream for so many years made a reality on 14 May 1948 when David Ben-Gurion read the declaration of Independence announcing the establishment of a Jewish nation to be known as the State of Israel.
>
> In 1949, Prime Minister Ben-Gurion said that Israel's policy "consists of bringing all Jews to Israel . . . we are still at the beginning."[i]

With this event having taken place, Lindsey goes on to show that this was the basis for an end times scenario to play out which would culminate in a great holocaust known as the battle of Armageddon. But Christians would be rescued from this horrible event by being snatched away, or "raptured." Notice what Lindsey says:

> The word "rapture" means to snatch away or take out. But whether we call this event "the Rapture" or the "translation" makes no difference – the important thing is that it will happen.

> It will happen! Someday, a day only God knows, Jesus Christ is coming to take away all those who believe in Him. He is coming to meet all true believers in the air. Without the benefit of science, space suits, or interplanetary rockets, there will be those who will be transported into a glorious place more beautiful, more awesome, than we can possibly comprehend. Earth and all its thrills, excitement, and pleasures will be nothing in contrast to this great event.
>
> It will be the living end. The ultimate trip.[ii]

Those words were written by Lindsey and published in 1970. He believed that the generation that saw the 1948 establishment would also see this event called "the Rapture."

In 1988, Edgar C. Whisenant, a retired engineer from NASA, published a popular book entitled **"88 reasons why the rapture will be in 1988."** Whisenant was a well-educated man. He held five degrees in technical fields, and was an electrical engineer by trade. His name is among those listed on the plaque of people who worked on the first manned moon mission. His background also includes being an instructor at the Naval Academy (Annapolis).

As a strong believer in dispensational eschatology, Whisenant set out to find the end-time solution. Since I have a background in engineering, I can relate to his methodology, but it is obvious in view of the complete failure of all 88 of the reasons he proposed that he was way off the mark. He was a very sincere Christian who loved God and believed in his heart that this work was what God would have him to do. However sincere Mr. Whisenant was, it was soon apparent that his predictions were errant and completely off base.

As the title suggests, this book was a collection of reasons why he believed that the rapture of the church was imminent. Here is one of the reasons (reason #7) that he listed as why this would happen in 1988. It was based on a three generation premise. Here are the first two generations he references:

> Three wicked generations of 40 years each were given in the Bible. The first 40-year wicked generation was the 40-year wicked generation to die off in the desert in the days of Moses, and they never reached the Promised Land. The second wicked generation of 40 years was given to Israel by Jesus from 30 A.D. to 70 A.D. Jesus said in Matt. 23:33–36—in speaking to the teachers of the law (the scribes) and to the Pharisees (the preachers of Jesus' day)—"You snakes! You brood of vipers! How will you escape being condemned to hell? (34)
>
> Therefore I am sending you prophets and wise men and teachers. Some of them you will kill and crucify; others you will flog in your synagogues and pursue from town to town. (35) And so upon you will come all the righteous blood that has been shed on earth, from the blood of righteous Abel to the blood of Zechariah son of Berakiah, whom you murdered between the temple and the altar. (36) I tell you the truth, all this (the righteous blood of history) will come upon this generation." (From 30 A.D. to 70 A.D. was the second wicked 40-year generation.) Israel was destroyed in 70 A.D. by the Roman Armies and scattered throughout the world to this day. Now Jesus had made the above statement to the teachers of the law and to the Pharisees after he had been welcomed into Jerusalem on the foal of a donkey, but before his crucifixion.
>
> Therefore, the above statement was made about 4 April 30 A.D. and was completed 40 years later in 70 A.D. when Israel was conquered by Rome, the national of Israel was destroyed as a nation, and the Jew scattered throughout the known world. So here there is no question that a wicked generation is 40 years long.[iii]

Whisenant is correct in the fact that the two generations of Israelites mentioned are wicked generations. However, there were certainly many more generations of Israelites who were terribly wicked. God warned them continually from the mouths of the prophets in the Old Testament of their wicked ways. They ignored most of the warnings including the warnings that resulted in the complete destruction of Jerusalem in 586 BC at the hands of the Assyrian army.

But now is where Whisenant really goes "off the rails" so to speak. Notice what he says here in the next section:

> Now let's look at the third time that the 40-year wicked generation is spoken of in the Bible. In the Olivet Discourse, Jesus said to his disciples (Matt. 24:32), "Now learn this lesson from the fig tree: as soon as its twigs get tender and its leaves come out, you know that summer is near. (33) Even so, when you see all these things, (wars and rumors of wars, nation rising against nation and kingdom against kingdom, famines and earthquakes in various places, all these are the beginning of birth pains.) I (Jesus) tell you the truth, this wicked generation (1948–1988) will certainly not pass until all these things have happened. (35) Heaven and earth will pass away, but My words will never pass away."
>
> This last generation spoken of above started on 14 May 1948, the day Israel became a nation. Israel is the time clock of God throughout history. Israel is the blooming fig tree, (Jer. 24:4–8) and the last generation will end 40 wicked Gentile years later on 14 May 1988. Noah's last generation was 120 years, and the floods came and killed all the wicked people on earth. Before the flood in Gen. 6:3, God stated that a man's day will be 120 years. We have the 40 wicked years in the desert, plus 40 wicked years from 30 A.D. to 70 A.D. (Israel's last wicked generation), generation), and now we have the last wicked generation of the Gentiles from 1948 to 1988.

> Thus we have today's last 120-year wicked generation made up of three periods of 40 years each, totaling 120 years to wrap up this period of wickedness as the flood did. Then all the wicked people on earth will be killed again, but this time by the fire of thermonuclear weapons. (World War III starts sunset 3 Oct. 1988. World War IV is 1 May 1992 when Satan conquers all the people of the earth, and World War V is at Armageddon on 4 Oct. 1995.) So we have three last wicked generations of 40 years each, totaling the days of a man's years of 120 years (see Gen. 6:3).[iv]

Edgar Whisenant thought he had all the facts. But what he missed as he began this section is that when Jesus told the disciples in Matt. 24:32 about the fig tree, he was not making reference to some future generation.

He was telling them about events that would happen **to them**! All we have to do to verify this is to **look at the language Jesus used**. Notice his words again:

> Matt 24:32-34 "Now learn the parable from the fig tree: when its branch has already become tender and puts forth its leaves, you know that summer is near; so, **YOU** too, when **YOU** see all these things, recognize that He is near, right at the door. "Truly I say to YOU, THIS generation will not pass away until all these things take place." (NASB)

If Jesus had been referring to some future generation, wouldn't it have made ***much more sense*** for Him to have said it this way in verses 33 and 34?

> so, **THEY** too, when **THEY** see all these things, will need to recognize that He is near, right at the door. Truly I say to YOU, **THAT** generation will not pass away until all these things take place.

Although what Whisenant wrote years ago has now been discounted, the idea that we are looking for an event called *the rapture* remains to this day. For example Pastor David Jeremiah just recently completed his fifth version of his book, **Escape the Coming Night.** Just the fact that he has revised this book for **the fifth time**, and still touting that the time is near, should be enough to give us pause. Now I would like to say that even though I will show in the pages of this book a great deal of evidence of the error of this view of eschatology, I still **have a great deal of respect for Dr. Jeremiah** and I feel certain that he loves God with all of his heart. Having said that, I would like you to notice what Dr. Jeremiah has published in this book that defies logic:

> An angel told the Old Testament prophet Daniel that many prophecies would not be understood until the end times. "Go your way, Daniel, because the words are rolled up and sealed until the time of the end. . . . those who are wise will understand" (Daniel 12:9–10). In Revelation, prophecies are unsealed, and John is given opposite orders: "Then he told me, 'Do not seal up the words of the prophecy of this scroll, because the time is near'" (Revelation 22:10). John was told to get the word out! He was to use every method he could to relay this message to the world. Jesus told John not only to reveal prophecies, but also the order in which they would take place. "Write, therefore, what you have seen, what is now and what will take place later" (Revelation 1:19).[v]

Is it reasonable to think that we could have gone **nearly 2000 years** since these words were written, and yet this "time that is near" has not yet happened? **The notion of this is preposterous!** Especially is this true when we compare it to the words written by the prophet Daniel as Dr. Jeremiah quoted:

> Dan 12:4 But you, Daniel, shut up the words and seal the book, until the time of the end. (ESV)

From the time of Daniel's prophecy to the time of the destruction of Jerusalem, it is only a period of 530 years or so. **WOW!** Do you see the power of these words? Daniel was only **490** years away from the fulfillment of his prophecy about Jesus, and he was told to **SEAL UP the book until the time of the end**.

But John was told **NOT to seal up the book**, yet we are still waiting for the fulfillment **almost 2000 years later! This would make no sense!**

Additionally, the translation of Rev 1:19 above used by Dr. Jeremiah leaves out a very important word which is crucial to the meaning of the passage. Let's compare the New International Version of this passage with the Young's Literal Translation:

> Rev 1:19 Write, therefore, what you have seen, what is now and what will take place later. (NIV)
> Rev 1:19 Write the things that thou hast seen, and the things that are, and the things **that are about to come** after these things; (YLT)

Do you notice the profound difference here? Young's translation says that these things are **about to take place!** Why does he translate this in such a way?

It is because the NIV has left out a **crucial word** here. The Greek word μελλει is omitted here by the NIV. That word which is properly translated as "**about to**" is very clearly time based. John is saying that what is going to happen **is going to happen soon.**

In this book, I will show how these words of Jesus were indeed fulfilled **in the same generation** in which Jesus uttered them. I will also show that this was also prophesied by Jesus through the writings of the Apostle John in "The Revelation" a few decades later. I would like to introduce to you the term "eschatology." The term "eschatology" means "the part of theology concerned with death, judgment, and the final destiny of the soul and of humankind."

What I will show in this thesis is that the book of Revelation has been mostly or perhaps even completely fulfilled. Thus Jesus kept his promise made directly to his disciples in Mark 13:30 when he said: "Truly I say to you, this generation will not pass away until all these things take place." Thus we will analyze the thirteenth chapter of Mark, sometimes called "the Olivet Discourse" in fine detail in this book.

Why should any of this matter to you? What difference could this make in your life now? The fact is that our view of what the future may hold for us directly affects the way we live our lives right now! I know because when I believed what Hal Lindsey was teaching, I lived my life differently .... with no view to the future! I was sure that the rapture rescue was coming any day. It definitely affected my future life planning.

So what about you? **Do you want the facts** about this prophecy given to the Apostle John? Or do you just want to go on believing **with blinders on**? I challenge you to read this book! If after you read it, you still want to believe as you do now, then you have lost nothing, but gained insight.

It is with this background that I present to you my findings on the book of Revelation. Although you will find most, if not all of the book of Revelation quoted within these pages, this is not a long commentary on the book. I **do not** have, **nor does anyone** have all the answers to the writings of the Apostle John on this matter, but in this book, I am presenting an approach which follows a well-defined theme.

I firmly believe it **is logical** and **makes sense** during a period where those touting that we are living in the last days now are seeing one prophecy after another **constantly being proven wrong**. Such false predictions only serve to further **embarrass the Christian community**, and lead people away from the saving grace of our Lord Jesus.

Finally, before we begin looking at the evidence of the promises made and kept by the Lord Jesus, I would like to say that the purpose of this book is to give the reader overwhelming evidence that The Revelation given to John was the **culmination of the promises made by Jesus and then faithfully kept by him.** There has been enough said about the book of Revelation that has served to totally embarrass the Christian community. It is my sincere desire that this treatise will not do that. Additionally, I have not written this publication with the desire to impugn those who promulgate the eschatological systems of Dispensational theology, Amillennial theology, or Postmillennial theology. But I will say that it is my belief that these systems seem to me to make the keeping of Jesus promises suspect, especially with regard to the timing. It is my opinion that if an eschatology is to be valid, it must assure the fact that Jesus always keeps His promises, and on time!

As you read this book, you will find that I have repeated myself several times. This includes the repetition of Scripture passages which bear on the case. This is a deliberate act. It is a strategy called repetition for emphasis. You will see that these points bear repeating because they very powerfully help to make the points I am stressing.

It is my hope that upon the conclusion of this volume the reader will have more insight as to why Jesus gave this revelation to John, and it will give us more faith **that he kept His promises.**

This should help us have faith that **we can ALWAYS TRUST JESUS to deliver on every promise that he ever made!**

With this in mind let us proceed.

Section One
The Background

Chapter 1

First Things First

The book of Revelation was given to the Apostle John by Jesus to explain how He would fulfill His promise made to the Apostles. These promises are recorded in Matthew 24, Mark 13, and Luke 21. In order to understand this promise, we have to go back to these chapters. For the most part they say the same thing, but by different writers. Since Mark is the shortest and most succinct of the Gospels, we will use this one for most of our analysis.

But before we do this, let's look at a couple of preliminary things. So, as we begin a discussion of "The Revelation of Jesus Christ," we must first look at **the name of the book**. The word revelation in the Greek language is the word **αποκαλυψις**. The correct pronunciation of this word is *apocaloopsis.* The English translation for this Greek word is apocalypse. This is a noun, with the English meaning of "the revealing", or the "unveiling." This book was inspired in the mind of the Apostle John by the Lord Jesus Christ to **reveal something** very, very important and relevant to him. Just exactly **what** was being revealed to the Apostle John has been the subject of controversy to Christians for the past 2000 years. As a result of what we have heard about this book, when thinking about this book, we often think of horrific things stored up for the future. Yes, the prophecy pundits have been obsessed with their interpretation that this book is speaking of a coming disaster. Therefore, because of all of this talk of a coming disaster, when we hear anything about the Bible book of Revelation, also named the Apocalypse, we often think of horrific things stored up for the future. Why is this so? Is it because most of what we hear from America's pulpits concerning this book? Is it because of the portrayal in the media, including Hollywood, that this book contains messages of doom and gloom and the dreaded mark of the beast 666? In both cases, I would say a resounding YES!! From many of America's pulpits we hear about the coming great tribulation, and how the Christians are going to be rescued by an event called the rapture of the Church. But there is another reason why this is true.

Yes, even the word apocalypse, and apocalyptic have taken on definitions that are outside of their original meaning. The Merriam Webster dictionary defines **apocalypse** as: ***a great disaster: a sudden and very bad event that causes much fear, loss, or destruction.*** But is that **really** the original meaning of this name? Is that really indicative of why the Apostle John was given this book?

However, if we look at the root meaning of the word **revelation**, it is "reveal." The Merriam Webster dictionary defines revelation as: ***a usually secret or surprising fact that is made known.*** We often use that word ourselves don't we? For example when we learn a new concept, we might say something like; Wow, that was a huge revelation to me! You will notice that the book is named "The Revelation of Jesus Christ," or "The Revelation to John." That is because this book was inspired in the mind of the apostle John by the Lord Jesus Christ **for the purpose of revealing something to him.** But the most important thing is that Jesus wanted to reveal something **of great relevance and importance to him.** Many have told us that this book is a mystery. And to us who live in the twenty-first century, it could be construed as such. But such a view is not in line with the knowledge of the imagery and the events that were pending during the lifetime of the Apostle John. It is also in complete disharmony with the actual original meaning of the term "Apocalypse" or "Revelation." Now I have made the claim that book called "Revelation" is a fulfillment of a prophecy given by Jesus. But before we begin, we must understand that there are three things very important to the examination of any passage of Scripture.

These are:

1. When was it written?
2. To whom was it written?
3. What was the purpose for writing it?

These three questions highlight the problem that has existed with those trying to understand this throughout the centuries. But as you will see, these questions are answered by informational clues that are contained in pages of the book itself!

It's in there! But because of **preliminary biases**, most people miss it.

So now in this series, I would like for you to embark on a journey with me. This journey will involve a big picture analysis of this most misunderstood book, an analysis that **must make sense.** I would like to repeat that! **It must make sense!** After all, as we just said, the meaning of this book is "the revealing." **If what is being revealed makes no sense, then nothing is actually being revealed, correct?**

Among those attempting such an interpretation there are a vast diversity of opinions. Let's quickly look at the ones that seem to be the most prevalent. These views are categorized around the words of Revelation 20 which speaks of a 1000 year period of time called "the Millennium." Some believe this to be a figurative period of time, others a literal period of time. Here are the most prevalent views:

By far the most prevalent is that after the first three chapters, the remainder of the book is **entirely in our future.** The most prevalent of these is called **the dispensational view**, and through its various descriptions, all interpretations under this heading point to an event which will be a literal one thousand year reign of Jesus Christ on the earth after He returns in the flesh, followed at some point by a complete destruction of the entire cosmos, and a recreation of heaven and earth.

Those who interpret this book in this form spend a huge amount of time developing "the Antichrist." But a close examination of the book shows that there is not even a whisper of this enigmatic individual in the pages of this book.

Then there is the **partial fulfillment view**. Under this view, some believe the events of Revelation are partially fulfilled. The Millennium is said to be a figurative period of time that began in the first century and has continued through the centuries up to and including now. This view is called **Amillenialism**. Strangely, the meaning of the term Amillenialism is "no Millennium," but those adherents to this view believe that we are living in the Millennium now.

As explained in the next view, the Revelation contains a prophetical description of a past event, and that event is the most important event in the history of Israel, the destruction of Jerusalem. It includes the Jewish war, and the related civil wars between the Jews and the Romans. There are two camps of thought here. One is that the book is entirely in our past. The other camp in this view is that although **most** of it is in our distant past, **some** of it is yet in our future.

Though these are the primary views, there is another one that is somewhat popular. This view is called the **idealist** view, although it may have literal components. Using Webster's Dictionary view of the term apocalypse as previously stated, this view states that the book is predominately apocalyptic in nature, but it is also an epistle as is indicated by the opening and closing of the book. As such the book may have no actual connection with any particular events. Yet, it may have various fulfillments throughout the ages without exhausting its meaning.

But in consideration of these views, we must ask some primary questions. These are:

1. What was it that the Lord Jesus wanted to reveal to John?
2. Why did He want him to know it?
3. To whom was John to give this revelation?
    a. Was it to those in close association with him at the time?
    b. Was it to those Christians 500 or 1000 years into the future?
    c. Could it have even been to us today living 2000 years into the future?

Yes, without question, we need to know **who the intended audience was** for this important information **revealed** to John. It would not make any sense for the Lord Jesus to reveal this important information to John for him to keep to himself. **There had to be an intended audience for this**!

A quick look at the opening of this book reveals a lot of answers to these questions. So let's look at just what is said as the book opens:

> The Revelation of Jesus Christ, which God gave Him **to show to His bond-servants**, the things which must **SOON** take place; and He sent and communicated *it* by His angel to His bond-servant John, who testified to the word of God and to the testimony of Jesus Christ, *even* to all that he saw. (Rev 1:1,2)

John was a bond-servant to the Lord Jesus. That means that he willingly had committed to do whatever the Lord wanted him to do. And yes, just from these two opening verses we see some things that are very important and must not be overlooked.

The first thing is the fact that Jesus gave John information about the things which **must SOON take place.** Does this sound like something that would not happen for thousands of years into the future? If it was **NOT** to happen soon, wouldn't our Lord say something like: "to show His bondservants things which will take place **in the distant future**?"

Now some have said: When Jesus said that, He was talking about events that would happen soon in God's time. But I ask you in all sincerity, do you really think that our Lord would start off an important revelation to John ***by misleading him*** right from the very beginning? Does this seem like our Lord to you? I am sure that He wanted **no confusion** in the mind of the apostle John as to what time frame was being revealed.

In verse two we notice that this revelation was given by the angel to John. It appears to be implied that it was given because he "testified to the word of God and to the testimony of Jesus Christ, *even* to all that he saw." From this we get the first indication of who the audience was that would receive this revelation. But we get our final answer very quickly. Let us continue:

> Blessed is he who reads and those who hear the words of the prophecy, and heed the things which are written in it; **for the time is NEAR**. John to the seven churches that are in Asia: Grace to you and peace, from Him who is and who was and who is to come, and from the seven Spirits who are before His throne, and from Jesus Christ, the faithful witness, the firstborn of the dead, and the ruler of the kings of the earth. To Him who loves us and released us from our sins by His blood—(Rev 1:3-5)

In verse 3 we see that those who hear the words and heed the things which were written in this urgent message would be blessed. This is obviously a blessing to those who would obey the admonition in the revealed message and act on it. For as **verse three** clearly states, the time for its fulfillment was **NEAR.**

And then in **verse four** we see that the intended audience for this revelation was the seven churches in Asia. This revealing information was addressed to them! But just exactly why was the Apostle John compelled to send this message to the seven churches at the time he sent it? And if it is a reference to some future event that would not impact the earth for thousands of years, **why do we see so much urgency** stressed in these first three chapters?

It is because John was one of the Apostles who heard Jesus tell them an amazing prophecy during the time he was alive. And this prophecy was about to get its fulfillment. The prophecy is explained in Mark chapter thirteen. Later on we will explore that prophecy. But before we begin looking at that chapter, we must address the question of the time of writing of the book, and the message of the Old Testament prophecies leading up to it.

Chapter 2

Dating the Book of Revelation

Note: Much of the information in this chapter has been taken from my already published book, "**God's Promise of Redemption, a Story of Fulfilled Prophecy**" published in 2015, available at Amazon.com or your favorite book retailer.

The next most important thing to discuss, before any discussion of the contents of the Revelation, **has to be the time of the writing of the book**. Why is this so? The reason is because **if** the book is about **the destruction of Jerusalem** and the events surrounding it, then it **must have** been written prior to this event. If it was written after the year AD 70, when Jerusalem was destroyed, then it would have been written in a different style, one as a review of the events which had already occurred. If it was written prior to AD 70, then this by necessity would totally eliminate one of the aforementioned views.

So now, let's consider the evidence that the book was written prior to AD 70. This will not be by any means an exhaustive look at this evidence, but an overview of the evidence. For a detailed description of these events, I will be referring to a book written by **Kenneth L. Gentry Jr**. entitled **"Before Jerusalem Fell."** Dr.

Gentry has solidly documented this in fine detail, and I would like to show why I agree with his conclusions.[vi]

The External Evidence

Those who say the book of Revelation was written after the destruction of Jerusalem, primarily rest their evidence on comments made by Irenaeus, the Bishop of Lyons who was born in the first half of the second century, or somewhere around 100 years after Christ walked the earth. His life spans from perhaps AD 130, through AD 202. As one of the early Church Fathers, his writings are considered by many to be foundational to the early development of Christian theology. He also was acquainted with Polycarp who was a disciple of the Apostle John.

Some of the comments of Irenaeus seem to be directly applicable to the dating of the book of Revelation. Irenaeus wrote his most famous work entitled *Against Heresies* to dispute the teachings of the Gnostics, and it is in Book 5 that the question of the time of writing of The Revelation is taken up.

Originally composed in the Greek language, most of the copies did not survive in its original form. But the statement in question upon which the late date advocates rest their conclusion is preserved in Greek for us in Eusebius' *Ecclesiastical History*.

For those who profess belief in the later dating of the book of Revelation, the writings of Irenaeus seem to provide them with their most potent information to prove the late date, or a writing which is post-AD70.

The words translated in English below are what we find when we search for this statement now. It says:

> We will not, however, incur the risk of pronouncing positively as to the name of Antichrist; for if it were necessary that his name should be distinctly revealed in this present time, it would have been announced by him who beheld the apocalyptic vision. For that was seen no very long time since, but almost in our day, towards the end of Domitian's reign.[vii]

To say the least, this statement, even when translated in English as done so above is very vague in its contents. Is it saying that there was an antichrist revealed at the end of Domitian's reign, or is it saying that it was announced by John in the apocalyptic vision near the end of Domitian's reign? Or still another interpretation could be that the apostle John who saw the apocalyptic vision was seen during Domitian's reign.

Those who advocate a late date for the writing of the Apocalypse (Revelation) state that it means that John wrote the Apocalypse toward the end of Domitian's reign. Domitian is said to have reigned from AD 81 to AD 96. According to this interpretation of these words, this would mean that John wrote this in the early to mid-90's (AD). But several questions arise from this. First of all, this statement above is a translation of a translation. It was written in Greek, and then translated to Latin. From that Latin translation, it was translated into English. This multiplies the chance of error. Second of all, as we said before, the statement is vague. There is a lack of clarity to what is actually meant here. The statement here quoted by Irenaeus is completely lacking in specificity. Irenaeus is also known to have made errant statements throughout his volumes. For example he is specifically stated as saying that Jesus' ministry embraced a period of 10 and even up to 20 years as noted below in Book two of *Against Heresies*:

> He preached only one year reckoning from His baptism. On completing His thirtieth year He suffered, being in fact still a young man, and who had by no means attained to advanced age. Now, that the first stage of early life embraces thirty years,(1) *and that this extends onwards to the fortieth year, every one will admit; but from the fortieth and fiftieth year a man begins to decline towards old age, which our Lord possessed while He still fulfilled the office of a Teacher, even as the Gospel and all the elders testify; those who were conversant in Asia with John, the disciple of the Lord, [affirming] that John conveyed to them that information.*(2) And he remained among them up to the times of Trajan. (3) Some of them, moreover, saw not only John, but the other apostles also, and heard the very same account from them, and bear testimony as to the [validity of] the statement. Whom then should we rather believe? Whether such men as these, or Ptolemaeus, who never saw the apostles, and who never even in his dreams attained to the slightest trace of an apostle? [viii]

Yes, even this passage from *Against Heresies* is plagued with vague statements, making just exactly what Irenaeus is saying about Jesus, John, and the other apostles difficult to understand. But he certainly appears to be saying that Jesus lived to the age of forty or fifty.

Additional evidence concerning the Apostle John shows that he was **banished to Patmos by the Emperor Nero** during his reign. This is from the Syriac Writings; *The History of John, the son of Zebedee*, and also the *Syriac Peshitta* version from the sixth and seventh century which contains *The Apocalypse of St. John*. The title of this latter volume states: "written in Patmos, whither

John was sent by Nero Caesar." Nero ruled from AD 64-68, prior to the destruction of Jerusalem. Having said that, there are also statements which show John was exiled to Patmos during the reign of Domitian (AD 81-96). Of course John could have been exiled twice, which would solve this problem.[ix]

There is much more that could be considered. If this documentation is of interest to you, please explore Dr. Gentry's book as listed below.

The Internal Evidence

When we say that we need to look at the internal evidence of why the book of Revelation was written before AD 70, we mean that we need to show why we know that the city of Jerusalem and the temple were still in existence. And in this category, there appears to be **overwhelming evidence** that it was written prior to the demise of the Holy City. To begin with, the churches to which the book was written were warned of an impending crisis. What other crisis was there at hand during that entire time period that would affect the churches mentioned? As you read the passages below, the urgency of the warnings almost scream at you.

The First Vision

With the number seven prominent in the book, the Apostle John was given seven visions. In his first vision, which covers the first three chapters, we find that he wrote this letter specifically to seven churches. His message was very specific, and he wanted them to understand the words he was writing. Notice these instances:

To the loveless church at Ephesus he warns:

> 'Therefore remember from where you have fallen, and repent and do the deeds you did at first; or else I am coming to you and will remove your lampstand out of its place--unless you repent. (Rev 2:5)

To the persecuted church at Smyrna he writes:

> 'Do not fear what you are about to suffer. Behold, the devil is about to cast some of you into prison, so that you will be tested, and you will have tribulation for ten days. Be faithful until death, and I will give you the crown of life (Rev 2:10)

To the compromising church at Pergamum he writes:

> 'Therefore repent; or else I am coming to you quickly, and I will make war against them with the sword of My mouth. (Rev 2:16)

To the corrupt church at Thyatira, to those tolerating the woman Jezebel and acts of immorality and Idol worship, he writes:

> 'I gave her time to repent, and she does not want to repent of her immorality. 'Behold, I will throw her on a bed *of sickness,* and those who commit adultery with her into great tribulation, unless they repent of her deeds. 'And I will kill her children with pestilence, and all the churches will know that I am He who searches the minds and hearts; and I will give to each one of you according to your deeds. 'But I say to you, the rest who are in Thyatira, who do not hold this teaching, who have not known the deep things of Satan, as they call them--I place no other burden on you. (Rev 2:21-24)

To the dead church of Sardis he writes:

> 'So remember what you have received and heard; and keep *it,* and repent. Therefore if you do not wake up, I will come like a

> thief, and you will not know at what hour I will come to you. (Rev 3:3)

To the faithful church at Philadelphia he writes:

> 'Because you have kept the word of My perseverance, I also will keep you from the hour of testing, that *hour* which is about to come upon the whole world, to test those who dwell on the earth. 'I am coming quickly; hold fast what you have, so that no one will take your crown. (Rev 3:10-11)

To the lukewarm church at Laodicea he writes:

> 'So because you are lukewarm, and neither hot nor cold, I will spit you out of My mouth. (Rev 3:16)

And then in general he writes to all of these churches:

> 'Behold, I stand at the door and knock; if anyone hears My voice and opens the door, I will come in to him and will dine with him, and he with Me. 'He who overcomes, I will grant to him to sit down with Me on My throne, as I also overcame and sat down with My Father on His throne. 'He who has an ear, let him hear what the Spirit says to the churches.'" (Rev 3:20-22)

Now as we look at these warnings, we have to realize that **the only cataclysmic event** of that time period which involved those churches was the **destruction of Jerusalem and the temple,** which occurred in the year AD 70. Of course we know that these churches were not in Jerusalem, but the impact of this coming destruction was felt strongly by these churches. The persecution of that era was brought on primarily by the Jews, and also severely at the hands of the Emperor Nero. Thus, the second and third chapters without question were addressing these churches, **which were all real churches** present within the Roman Empire. And they would feel the effects of this judgment that was **soon to come**, spoken by the Lord Jesus through the pen of the Apostle John. As we look at more of the internal evidence, we see in looking at Rev 1:7 the words:

> Lo, he doth come with the clouds, and see him shall every eye, even those who did pierce him, and wail because of him shall all the tribes of the land. Yes! Amen! (Rev 1:7 Young's Literal Translation)

This unquestionably qualifies the time frame, and refers to the prophecy Jesus himself made to the members of the Jewish Sanhedrin, upon the occasion of His trial before His crucifixion. Although not literally driving the nails in His hands and feet, **they are the ones who pierced Him!** It is impossible that the time reference could be any other than this same generation! Notice how specific Jesus is on this occasion:

> But Jesus remained silent. And the high priest said to him, "I adjure you by the living God, tell us if you are the Christ, the Son of God." Jesus said to him, "You have said so. But I tell you, from now on **YOU** will see the Son of Man seated at the right hand of Power and coming on the clouds of heaven." (Matt 26:63-64)

Jesus was not speaking to some future group of people, but was speaking **directly** to this group of Scribes and Pharisees, and directly to the High Priest. And in Josephus' account of the destruction of Jerusalem, we have presented the evidence that this prophetic event **did** happen, and **was** fulfilled. Next, we see that the book of Revelation speaks of the temple as still in existence, followed by the trampling of the city for 42 months.

> Then I was given a measuring rod like a staff, and I was told, "Rise and <u>measure the temple of God</u> and the altar and those who worship there, but <u>do not measure the court</u> outside the temple; leave that out, for it is given over to the nations, and they will trample the holy city for forty-two months. And I will

> grant authority to my two witnesses, and they will prophesy for 1,260 days, clothed in sackcloth." (Rev 11:1-3)

First of all, from verse 1, we know that measuring the temple **would be impossible** if the temple was not present at the time of the writing. Some have said that this was not a literal measurement, but if this is so, why was he given a measuring rod? Unmistakably, the sources for this time statement are Luke 21:24: "and Jerusalem will be trampled underfoot by the Gentiles, until the times of the Gentiles are fulfilled," and Daniel's referent to "the time, times, and half time" in (Daniel 7:25).

Noted Author, Don K. Preston provides insight concerning verse two and three:

> This is confirmed when we remember, as noted above, that the sealed book that John has seen, that only the Lamb is worthy to open, is the sealed book of Daniel's prophecy of the time of the end (Daniel 8: 25-26; 12: 4) . . . . i.e. forty -two months, time, times and half times, 1260 days, etc. are used. However, note that there is a **common thread** in them that ties them all together: 1.) The persecution of the saints (Daniel 7: 25). 2.) The time of the Great Tribulation and the time of the end (Daniel 12: 7). 3.) The treading down of the holy city (Revelation 11: 2). 4.) The ministry of the two witnesses (Revelation 11: 3). 5.) The protection of the woman during the persecution (Revelation 12: 6). 6.) The blasphemy and persecution by the beast (13: 5). What emerges from these references is that there would be a period of intense persecution of God's people, during which time Jehovah would providentially–and even miraculously (Revelation 11: 5f)– prevent the church from being overwhelmed and defeated, although for all appearances sake, the outlook was bleak. Nonetheless, **at the end** of the foreordained time, the persecutor would be judged and **God's saints would be identified, vindicated, avenged, and glorified**.[x]

Eighteenth century British Methodist scholar and commentator Adam Clarke states concerning chapter eleven and verse one:

> This *must* refer to the temple of Jerusalem; and this is *another presumptive evidence* that it was yet standing. (emphasis mine)[xi]

The Beast of Revelation

When we consider the internal evidence for the dating of the book of Revelation, it is imperative that we consider the seven headed, ten horned beast. This beast is first identified in Rev. 13:1:

> And the dragon stood on the sand of the seashore. Then I saw a beast coming up out of the sea, having ten horns and seven heads, and on his horns *were* ten diadems, and on his heads *were* blasphemous names. (Rev 13:1)

There have been a great number of commentators who have identified this beast by proclaiming that it is a history lesson which spans several centuries. However, I reiterate that **we must keep in mind** that the Revelation given to John was given to him **for the purpose outlined** in the opening verse of the book:

> The Revelation of Jesus Christ, which God gave Him to show to His bond-servants, the things which must SOON take place; and He sent and communicated *it* by His angel to His bond-servant John, who testified to the word of God and to the testimony of Jesus Christ, *even* to all that he saw. Blessed is he who reads and those who hear the words of the prophecy, and heed the things which are written in it; for the time is NEAR. John to the SEVEN CHURCHES that are in Asia: Grace to you and peace, from Him who is and who was and who is to come, and from the seven Spirits who are before His throne, and from Jesus Christ, the faithful witness, the firstborn of the

> dead, and the ruler of the kings of the earth. To Him who loves us and released us from our sins by His blood-- and He has made us *to be* a kingdom, priests to His God and Father--to Him *be* the glory and the dominion forever and ever. Amen. (Rev 1:1-6)

In a way, this sort of reminds us of a last will and testament. Of course it is not, because it speaks of events which are about to take place. But it is the same **in that it very specifically outlined to whom it is written and for what purpose.** It is not to give the churches a history lesson, nor is it to outline thousands of years of events to take place in the future.

I mentioned earlier that there have been a great number of commentators who have identified this beast by proclaiming that it is a history lesson which spans several centuries. But if we stop and think about this for a minute, this makes no sense to the literary theme of the epistle. Specific to the beast outlined in Rev 13:1 above, there are commentators who would say that this is a reference to seven world monarchies; Egypt, Assyria, Babylon, Persia, Greece, Rome, and then to future dynasties hundreds of years into the future. But this cannot be when we consider the purpose as outlined in the very opening of the book!

The apostle to whom this Revelation was given clearly expects this prophecy to be fulfilled **during his lifetime.** Why would he imply to these persecuted Christians that they needed to think about the history of the world powers and then speculate on future powers? This would be of **absolutely no interest** to them. Consequently, we must conclude that this beast outlined in verse one of chapter thirteen is a first century figure.

When John writes this book, the Emperor Nero is ruling. In addition to the passage in chapter 13, we see a clue to the identity in chapter seventeen. In Revelation 17:1-6 John gives a vision of a seven headed beast. And then in verses 9-11 the interpreting angel gives the meaning of the seven headed beast.

> "Here is the mind which has wisdom. The seven heads are seven mountains on which the woman sits, and they are seven kings; five have fallen, one is, the other has not yet come; and when he comes, he must remain a little while. "The beast which was and is not, is himself also an eighth and is *one* of the seven, and he goes to destruction. (Rev 17:9-11)

This passage is properly explained by Jonathan Welton in his book, *The Art of Revelation*:

> **This passage, which speaks of the line of rulers in** Rome, tells us exactly how many rulers had already come, which one was currently in power, and that the next one would only last a short while. Take a look at how perfectly it fits with Nero and the Roman Empire of the first century. The rule of the first seven Roman Emperors is as follows: "Five have fallen... "Julius Caesar (49–44 BC) Augustus (27 BC–AD 14) Tiberius (AD 14–37) Caligula (AD 37–41) Claudius (AD 41–54) "One is... Nero (AD 54-68) "the other has not yet come; but when he does come, he must remain for only a little while." Galba (June AD 68–January AD 69, a six-month rulership) Of the first seven kings, five had come (Julius Caesar, Augustus, Tiberius, Gaius, and Claudius), one was currently in power (Nero), and one had not yet come (Galba), but would only remain a little time (six months). The current Caesar at the time of John's writing was the sixth Caesar, Nero.[xii]

Let me reiterate the **incredible specificity** of this! The angel is telling John that these kings represent the emperors in succession of the Roman Empire. If we look up these emperors according to secular history, we find that they are:

- **Julius Caesar (49 - 44 BC),**
- **Augustus Caesar (31BC – AD 14),**
- **Tiberius Caesar (14 - AD 37),**
- **Gaius Caesar (37 - AD 41),**
- **Claudius (41 - AD 54),**
- **Nero (54 - AD 68),**
- **Galba (June AD 68 – January AD 69)**

The five that have fallen:

Julius, Augustus, Tiberius, Gaius, and Claudius.

One is:

Nero

One is yet to come:

Galba (only a little while)

Notice **how precisely** the succession of emperors is described in the book! There is no way this could be a coincidence! All of them reigned over a period of years with the exception of Galba who only reigned for about 6+ months. The reason Galba reigned such a short period of time is because it was the beginning of a civil war in Rome, and amazingly, this exact scenario was described **precisely** in verse 10 of chapter 17.

With this established it appears very evident that the book of Revelation **had to be written prior to June 8, AD 68**, the day that Nero committed suicide.

Then finally we must consider the information found in the final chapter of the Revelation. It says:

> And he said to me, "DO NOT SEAL UP the words of the prophecy of this book, for the time is NEAR." (Rev 22:10)

As I stated in the Prologue of this book, is it reasonable to think that we could have gone nearly 2000 years since these words were written, and yet this "time that is near" has not yet happened? The notion of this is preposterous! Especially is this true when we compare it to the words written by the prophet Daniel:

> Dan 12:4 But you, Daniel, shut up the words and seal the book, until the time of the end .... (ESV)

From the time of Daniel's prophecy to the time of the destruction of Jerusalem, it is only a period of 530 years or so. Do you see the power of these words? Daniel was only **490** years away from the fulfillment of his prophecy, and he was told to **seal up the book**. But John was told **not to seal up the book**, yet we are still waiting for the fulfillment **almost 2000 years later! This would make no sense!**

The evidence in the context of the message

All of the evidence we have considered here leads us to believe that the book of Revelation was written **for** the seven churches to which it was addressed. But considering all of the hype that has been attached to this book, we must ask some important questions. Was it written to be understood? Or was it meant to be an enigma, and completely unintelligible to the readers?

The prophecy pundits have told us that it speaks of our future. Some have proposed that it has reference to tanks, helicopters, and modern nations, not even in existence during the time of its writing. Some have said that it has reference to the Catholic Church and medieval popes, as well as historical figures throughout the centuries, sometimes labeled as "the antichrist."

But if this were true, **of what possible value** would this information have been to those seven churches addressed in the first three chapters of the Revelation?

These Christians, as citizens of the nations of the Roman Empire, were undergoing persecution from two sources, Jerusalem, and Rome. They were suffering greatly. The apostle John was inspired to send them a message with a warning, **an urgent warning!** So then, how is it possible that John would send them all of this irrelevant information, especially considering that the message was urgently inspired by the Lord Jesus? Would this not be a form of mockery? Of course it would!

Therefore, we must conclude that the Apocalypse was without question meant to be understood by the **original** readers. It must be speaking of events relative to the time of those early Christians, and that period of time **had to be relatively short** in its span. This is not a matter of speculation. I know that I am repeating myself with some of these verses, but it is very clear. For in the very beginning of the book we read:

> The Revelation of Jesus Christ, which God gave Him to show to His bond-servants, the things which must SOON take place... (Rev 1:1)
> Blessed is he who reads and those who hear the words of the prophecy, and heed the things which are written in it; for the time is NEAR. (Rev 1:3)

With this information settled pertaining to the date of writing, lets look at the prophecies given in the Old Testament which led up to the time of Jesus giving the Revelation to John.

Chapter 3
Old Testament Prophecy

Part 1

The Old Testament book of Daniel contains the majority of the prophecies that relate to the Revelation our Lord Jesus gave to the Apostle John. In my book, ***God's Promise of Redemption, a story of Fulfilled Prophecy***, I cover this prophecy in great detail in chapters 2-4. In this chapter, I will look at it from the perspective of its relationship to ***The Revelation*** given to John.

When considering the book of Daniel it is important to remember that the first 6 chapters of Daniel's book are history, and the second 6 chapters are prophecy. We also must remember that the purpose of Daniel's prophecy was to encourage the Jews in exile. This would be done by revealing to them God's program for them, both in the short term, and in the long term. By the long term, I mean a period of roughly 600 years. This is the time when Daniel's prophecies would be fulfilled. A time when just as Jesus predicted, the city of Jerusalem would be destroyed along with the temple. Why would God sanction such an event? Because the Lamb of God came to the earth as noted by John the Baptist:

> The next day he saw Jesus coming to him and said, "Behold, the Lamb of God who takes away the sin of the world!" (John 1:29)

This would forever put an end to the need for animal sacrifices. Yes! The temple would no longer be necessary! Now, let's notice how this unfolds.

Daniel has been reputed to have descended from the royal family of David. After the Babylonian siege, he appears to have been carried into Babylon when very young. He and his three younger associates, who eventually were called by the names Shadrach, Meshach and Abednego, were chosen because of their abilities. These three would be trained to have an education which would suit them for what the king had determined. Thus, Daniel was instructed in all the wisdom of the Chaldeans, which was at that time considered to be greatly superior to the learning of the other cultures; but in reading the book of Daniel we find that he was singled out by the Kings for his ***divinely appointed*** wisdom and devotion to his God. This allowed him to tell these kings things which would happen in their future.

When he told Nebuchadnezzar exactly what his dream was, and then gave him the exact interpretation of the metallic image, he was given the title of Governor of the province of Babylon. Nebuchadnezzar made him chief of all the magicians, or wise men in that country.

Even in Babylon, Daniel was considered to be one of the wisest and most noble men of his time. God ranks him among the most holy and exemplary of men. Ezekiel 14 ranks him with Noah and Job (Ezekiel 14:14, 20). As we look at the prophetic side of the book of Daniel we see in chapter 7 the prophet's vision of the four beasts, which arose out of the sea. Daniel describes these, and then as we note in verse eight:

> "While I was contemplating the horns, behold, **another horn, a little one, came up among them,** and three of the first horns were pulled out by the roots before it; and behold, this horn possessed eyes like the eyes of a man and a mouth uttering great boasts. (Dan 7:8)

Notice that it said in this verse, that "*while I was contemplating the horns another horn, a little one, came up among them.*" Since it happened while he was contemplating, this indicates a little passage of time, not too long. Then it says that "three of the first horns were pulled out by the roots before it." If you search among the commentators, you will find many opinions as to the identity of this little horn. But nowhere in Scripture is this "little horn" specifically identified. But by looking at the timeline, we can get a clue. The next verse helps us with this timeline.

Notice the description of the Ancient of Days described in verse nine:

> "I kept looking Until thrones were set up, And the Ancient of Days took His seat; **His vesture was like white snow And the hair of His head like pure wool. His throne was ablaze with flames, Its wheels were a burning fire.** A river of fire was flowing And coming out from before Him; Thousands upon thousands were attending Him, And myriads upon myriads were standing before Him; The court sat, And the books were opened." (Dan 7:9-10)

Now notice how specific this timeline is. The events of verses 9 and 10 happened ***after*** the "little horn" appeared. This time frame ***is crucial to the determination*** of the identity of the "little horn." Verse 8 also says that "three of the first horns were pulled out before it." But notice that it **does not say** that the little horn did the pulling up, but was present for the pulling up of these kings by the roots. This is also helpful in determining the identity of this "little horn."

Later, Daniel's prophecy declares concerning this "little horn" the following:

> 'As for the ten horns, out of this kingdom ten kings will arise; and another will arise after them, and he will be different from the previous ones and will subdue three kings. 'He will speak out against the Most High and **wear down the saints of the Highest One,** and he will intend to make alterations in times and in law; and they will be given into his hand for a time, times, and half a time. (Dan 7:24-25)

This happened during the reign of Emperor Nero, but although he was indeed instrumental in the persecution of the Christians, the greatest persecutors of the Christians were the ruling class of the Jews, the religious leaders themselves! There is no question about the exceptional influence that the religious leaders of Old Covenant Israel had on the Roman Empire.

Within the bounds of the Roman Empire, no matter which city you visited, there were Jewish synagogues, and throngs of Jews to fill them. All of this history of the Roman Empire and its emperors unfolded in front of them.

Now compare the description which we saw in Daniel 7: 9-10 with the following verses in the book of Revelation:

> Then I turned to see the voice that was speaking with me. And having turned I saw seven golden lampstands; and in the

> middle of the lampstands I saw one like a son of man, clothed in a robe reaching to the feet, and girded across His chest with a golden sash. His head and **His hair were white like white wool, like snow; and His eyes were like a flame of fire.** His feet were like burnished bronze, when it has been made to glow in a furnace, and His voice was like the sound of many waters. In His right hand He held seven stars, and out of His mouth came a sharp two-edged sword; and His face was like the sun shining in its strength. (Rev 1:12-16)

These amazingly similar descriptions of our Lord are **not a coincidence!** The prophet Daniel gave a prophecy which would have its fulfillment a few hundred years later after Jesus took His rightful place in heaven.

As we continue with Daniel chapter seven we see the following prophecy:

> "I kept looking in the night visions, And behold, with the clouds of heaven One like a Son of Man was coming, And He came ***UP TO*** the Ancient of Days And was presented before Him. And to Him was given dominion, Glory and a kingdom, That all the peoples, nations and men of every language Might serve Him. His dominion is an everlasting dominion Which will not pass away; And His kingdom is one Which will not be destroyed. (Dan 7:13-14)

When Jesus was standing before Caiaphas as He was being condemned by the Sanhedrin, please carefully notice how Jesus responds as He is questioned:

> The high priest stood up and said to Him, "Do You not answer? What is it that these men are testifying against You?" But Jesus kept silent. And the high priest said to Him, "I adjure You by the living God, that You tell us whether You are the Christ, the Son of God." Jesus said to him, "You have said it yourself; nevertheless I tell you, hereafter *YOU* will see THE SON OF

> MAN SITTING AT THE RIGHT HAND OF POWER, and COMING ON THE CLOUDS OF HEAVEN." (Matt 26:62-64)

Yes! What Jesus was stating was that soon ***HE HIMSELF*** would fulfill this prophecy, and Caiaphas and the members of the Sanhedrin ***WOULD SEE IT!*** But it is important to notice that Jesus was not saying what many people have stated. He was **NOT** stating that He would come **TO THE EARTH** thousands of years later! The prophecy of Daniel above states that his destination was heaven.

Matthew's account above shows that He was speaking directly to Caiaphas! Notice how I have emphasized the ***YOU*** in Jesus' words above. And Jesus, speaking in fulfillment of the words of the prophet Daniel did ***NOT*** say He was returning to the earth! As the passage notes:

> "One like a Son of Man was coming, and He came ***UP TO*** the Ancient of Days and was presented before Him." (Dan 7:13)

This was the ***official presentation*** in heaven of what ***had already*** been given to Jesus upon His resurrection!

Jesus had already made it clear that judgment was coming to Israel as recorded in Matthew's Gospel account. Notice the words of Jesus:

> Therefore, behold, I am sending you prophets and wise men and scribes; some of them you will kill and crucify, and some of them you will scourge in your synagogues, and persecute from city to city, so that **UPON YOU** may fall *the guilt of* all the righteous blood shed on earth, from the blood of righteous Abel to the blood of Zechariah, the son of Berechiah, whom you murdered between the temple and the altar. "Truly I say

> to you, **all these things will come upon this generation.** "Jerusalem, Jerusalem, who kills the prophets and stones those who are sent to her! How often I wanted to gather your children together, the way a hen gathers her chicks under her wings, and you were unwilling. "Behold, **YOUR house is being left to you desolate!"** (Matt 23:34-38)

Yes! The ***generation in which Jesus lived*** would experience an overwhelming judgment which would include their house (the temple) being left desolate! In fact, it was also a self-proclaimed judgment when the crowd said before Pilate in Matt 27:25: "His blood shall be on ***us and our children***!" Sadly, they did not know how accurate that statement would be.

The eventual end of this would be just as Daniel recorded centuries earlier:

> But the court will sit *for judgment,* and his dominion will be taken away, annihilated and destroyed forever. 'Then the sovereignty, the dominion and the greatness of *all* the kingdoms under the whole heaven will be given to the people of the saints of the Highest One; His kingdom *will be* an everlasting kingdom, and all the dominions will serve and obey Him.' (Dan 7:26-27)

This directly ties with Daniel's prophecy in the ninth chapter. It also ties directly with Daniel's prophecy in chapter 12. In the first three verses we see a great tribulation as referred to in Daniel 9:26, we see a rescue, and a resurrection, in which certain ones would shine brightly forever. Reading from Daniel 12 we see:

> And at that time, Michael shall stand up, the great ruler who stands for the sons of your people. And there shall be **a time of distress, such as has not been from the being of a nation until that time.** And at that time, your people shall be delivered, everyone that shall be found written in the Book. And many of those sleeping in the earth's dust shall awake, some to

> everlasting life, and some to reproaches *and* to everlasting abhorrence. And those who act wisely shall shine as the brightness of the firmament, and those turning many to righteousness as the stars forever and ever. (Dan 12:1-3)

This was fulfilled in the years following the death of Jesus on the cross. The Apostle John himself was a part of this time of great distress. Notice the words from the Revelation given to John:

> I, John, your brother and **fellow partaker in the tribulation** and kingdom and perseverance which are in Jesus, was on the island called Patmos because of the word of God and the testimony of Jesus. (Rev 1:9)
>
> 'I know **your tribulation** and your poverty (but you are rich), and the blasphemy by those who say they are Jews and are not, but are a synagogue of Satan. Do not fear what you are about to suffer. Behold, the devil is about to cast some of you into prison, so that you will be tested, and **YOU will have tribulation** for ten days. Be faithful until death, and I will give you the crown of life. (Rev 2:9-10)
>
> I said to him, "My lord, you know." And he said to me, "These are the ones who **come out of the great tribulation,** and they have washed their robes and made them white in the blood of the Lamb. (Rev 7:14)

Comparing Daniel 12:1-3 with these verses in the book of Revelation, we notice how in verse one Daniel makes it clear that this time of distress is specifically pointed to the nation of Israel, that it would be the greatest time of distress ever for that nation. But it also pointed out that there would be deliverance for the true people of God. This is a reference to the true believers of the Lord Jesus! This same sentiment is expressed in the midst of the tribulation by the Apostle John. Continuing on in Daniel, verse 4 we find that God told Daniel to seal up the book until the **time of the end.**

In verse four he writes:

> "But you, Daniel, shut up the words, and seal the book until the **time of the end;** many shall run to and fro, and knowledge shall increase." (Dan 12:4 NKJV)

Although some versions such as the NASB translate this "end of time," this is inaccurate. The Bible **never speaks** of the end of time. God has determined that this earth will stand forever:

> A generation goes and a generation comes, **But the earth remains forever.** (Ecc 1:4, See also Psalm 78:69; 104:5)

The "time of the end" in Daniel 12:4 is a reference to the generation alive when Jesus was crucified. How do we know this? In the next chapter, we find out in the remainder of Daniel's prophecy.

Chapter 4
Old Testament Prophecy Part 2

In the eighth chapter of Daniel, he is given a vision of events that would happen during the period of five centuries between the Babylonian exile and the time of Christ. He is given the specifics of the dream first and then the interpretation of the vision. But it is in the ninth chapter of Daniel's prophecy that we see the timing.

As the ninth chapter of Daniel opens, we find Daniel contemplating the fact that the end of the period of exile of the Jews was to happen very soon in accordance with the prophecy of the prophet Jeremiah.

> "For thus says the LORD, 'When seventy years have been completed for Babylon, I will visit you and fulfill My good word to you, to bring you back to this place." (Jer 29:10)

Knowing this seventy year period was nearing completion, Daniel approaches God in prayer. Here, Daniel prays that God would turn his anger away from them. His plea with God was to act without delay for His own sake, and so that the people called by His name could be restored. His prayer was a desperate plea because he realized that by their repeated disobedience, Israel broke the covenant given through Moses. Notice Daniel's humility as he prays:

> So I gave my attention to the Lord God to seek Him by prayer and supplications, with fasting, sackcloth and ashes. I prayed to the LORD my God and confessed and said, "Alas, O Lord, the great and awesome God, who keeps His covenant and lovingkindness for those who love Him and keep His commandments, we have sinned, committed iniquity, acted wickedly and rebelled, even turning aside from Your commandments and ordinances." (Dan 9:3-5)

Yes, Daniel was deeply concerned. As he looked around, even though he could see the words of Jeremiah before him, there seemed to be no indication that this was about to happen. Therefore, as was typical in times of public mourning, he prayed, fasted, dressed in sackcloth, and put ashes upon his head. His prayer was a corporate prayer on behalf of all of those in exile and is recorded for us in verses 9-14 of the ninth chapter.

In this deeply sincere prayer Daniel correctly declared the sins of the people as he made supplication in their behalf. The history of this people is replete with total rebellion against God. The prophet Jeremiah, tabbed as the weeping prophet, preached to this stubborn people for over 39 years ***without a single sign of repentance*** on their part, and ***Daniel saw nothing that would indicate a change of heart*** in them. Notice how he prays:

> "As it is written in the law of Moses, all this calamity has come on us; yet we have not sought the favor of the LORD our God by turning from our iniquity and giving attention to Your truth. Therefore the LORD has kept the calamity in store and

> brought it on us; for the LORD our God is righteous with respect to all His deeds which He has done, **but we have not obeyed His voice."** (Dan 9:13-14)

But in verse 16, we see the real focus of this prayer.

> "O Lord, in accordance with all ***Your righteous acts***, let now Your anger and Your wrath turn away from Your city Jerusalem, Your holy mountain; for because of our sins and the iniquities of our fathers, Jerusalem and Your people have become a reproach to all those around us." (Dan 9:16)

Daniel's pleading was **not** due to the repentance of the people, but his prayer was fixed on **the character of God!** For it was based on **God's** justice, **God's** mercy, and **God's** goodness. It was based on the **faithfulness of God** to His people. **So in view of all of these character traits**, he pleaded and begged that God would intervene and turn away His anger from His people now. In the following verses we can see the deep sincerity of Daniel. His words sound as though they are bathed in tears:

> "So now, our God, listen to the prayer of Your servant and to his supplications, and for Your sake, O Lord, let Your face shine on Your desolate sanctuary. O my God, incline Your ear and hear! Open Your eyes and see our desolations and the city **which is called by Your name;** for we are not presenting our supplications before You on account of any merits of our own, **but on account of Your great compassion. O Lord, hear! O Lord, forgive**! O Lord, listen and take action! **For Your own sake, O my God, do not delay**, because Your city and Your people are called by Your name." (Dan 9:17-19)

But Daniel did not even get to complete his prayer before God provided a response. The God who searches hearts saw the heart of this faithful loyal servant, and immediately sent the Angel

Gabriel. Yes! And Gabriel even interrupted Daniel as he was praying:

> "**while I was still speaking** in prayer, then the man **Gabriel**, whom I had seen in the vision previously, **came to me** in my extreme weariness about the time of the evening offering. He gave me instruction and talked with me and said, "O Daniel, I have now come forth **to give you insight with understanding**. At the beginning of your supplications the command was issued, and I have come to tell you, for **you are highly esteemed**; so give heed to the message and gain understanding of the vision." (Dan 9:21-23)

Then he begins to enlighten Daniel about what would happen ***over the next 490 years***. But this prophecy is not just some average prophecy about some small event in the Middle East. This prophecy is **absolutely monumental**! This is **one of the most important prophecies in the Bible.** Therefore it demands our detailed attention.

I have selected this passage to be read from J.P. Green's Literal Translation **(LITV)**. This is because it appears to be the closest to the original text, and appears to have no translator bias. However, since I am making reference to much of what Albert Barnes wrote in his commentary on this passage, the details written by him and others of the 19th century will reflect the writings of the King James Version.

Here is what the angel told Daniel:

> Seventy weeks are decreed as to your people, and as to your holy city, to finish the transgression, and to make an end of sins, and to make atonement for iniquity, and to bring in everlasting righteousness, and to seal up the vision and prophecy, and to anoint the Most Holy. (Dan 9:24 LITV)

Nineteenth century American theologian Albert Barnes did a thorough job in analyzing this phrase. Note his words:

> . . . a portion of time - to wit, **four hundred and ninety years** - was designated or appointed with reference to the city, to accomplish the great and important object which is immediately specified.
>
> A certain, definite period was fixed on, and when this was past, the promised Messiah would come. . . . .The true meaning seems to be, that the seventy weeks are spoken of "collectively," as denoting a period of time; that is, a period of seventy weeks is determined. The prophet, in the use of ***the singular verb***, seems to have contemplated the time, ***not as separate weeks, or as particular portions, but as one period***. [xiii]

The Angel Gabriel continued speaking to Daniel:

> Know, then, and understand *that* from the going out of a word to restore and to rebuild Jerusalem, to Messiah *the* Prince, *shall be* seven weeks and sixty two weeks. The street shall be built again, and the wall, even in times of affliction. And after sixty two weeks, Messiah shall be cut off, but not *for* Himself. And the people of a coming ruler shall destroy the city and the sanctuary. And its end *shall be* with the flood, and ruins are determined, and war *shall be* until *the* end. And he shall confirm a covenant with the many *for* one week. And in the middle of the week he shall cause the sacrifice and the offering to cease. And on a corner *of the altar will be* abominations *that* desolate, even until *the* end. And that which was decreed shall pour out on the desolator. (Dan 9:25-27 LITV)

In my book, "***God's Promise of Redemption, a story of fulfilled prophecy***" I go through the remaining verses in the ninth chapter in detail. Here I offer a summary of my findings:

The Angel Gabriel brought him a message that the coming of the Messiah was to accomplish 6 things. These were as follows:

1. **To finish the transgression** - The coming of the Messiah was to restrain or cover up the sin of the world. His work, **through the sacrifice made on the cross,** is such that it covered up the sin of the elect, and would **eventually** succeed in atoning for sin altogether! This did not refer to the particular transgressions for which the Jewish people had suffered in their long captivity, but sin (הפשע *hapesha'*) in general - the sin of the world.
2. **To make an end of sins** – This is normally understood as חתם *châthēm* - from חתם *châtham* - "to seal, to seal up." The idea to be conveyed here is that sin was to be sealed up, or closed, or hidden, so that they will not be seen. It can be compared to a sealed book, or a lock box, the contents of which cannot be seen. And although Daniel had no idea of the meaning of this at the time, we can. Since we have Christ revealed, *we can* understand how this was to be accomplished. It was **accomplished by the blood of the atonement**, by which sin is now forgiven. It is as if it were hidden from the view, sealed with a seal that cannot be broken.
3. **To make reconciliation for iniquity** – This He did by the once offering up of himself. This is different from the second purpose in that reconciliation is the word which is commonly used with reference to atonement. As Luther understood it, it meant "to reconcile for transgression." Its

bearing would be on human iniquity; on the way **by which it might be pardoned and removed**.

4. **To bring in everlasting righteousness – The word** "everlasting" used here denotes that the righteousness would be permanent and perpetual. In reference to the method of becoming righteous, it would become the ***only method*** by which men would become holy. In this way, it would be a righteousness which would continue forever.
5. **To Seal up Vision and Prophecy** - The idea seems to be sealed in the sense that they would be closed or shut up - no longer open matters. Also, sealing up can carry the meaning of ***authentication.*** Thus, we could rightly interpret this to mean "To authenticate or close up vision and prophecy." Once a scroll was sealed, it would be marked with a seal mark. The purpose was that it would be authentic until it was opened. If opened, it would need to be sealed and authenticated again by the mark. Christ would settle this matter **once and for all.** Only Christ could authenticate this prophecy, for only Christ could provide the answers to the other parts of this prophecy.
6. **To anoint the Most Holy** – This is **the most important point**. The entire ninth chapter of Daniel follows the pattern set forth in Leviticus 26. Although the term "most holy" does not appear in Leviticus 26, it is important to point out that it appears in Leviticus **only** in reference to a sacrifice. In **every instance** in which this term is found in the book of Leviticus, it is in reference to **a sacrifice.** And we find a reference to the lamb in Leviticus 14:13. Here the slain lamb is referred to as **most holy.**

(Those Bible versions which have added the word "place" after Most Holy **have therefore mistranslated this verse**. The reference is to Christ, not the Most Holy place in the temple.)

This ties this time frame together as one unit of time in which the coming of the Messiah will accomplish these 6 things! As the Scripture says: "He is the Lamb of God who takes away the sin of the world" (John 1:29). The Angel Gabriel was giving Daniel a message showing that within the 490 years, these 6 items would lead to and be fulfilled in the promised Messiah.

Next the Angel Gabriel gives the time frame. He gives it in 3 periods of time. The three periods are:

1. Seven weeks, that is, forty-nine years.
2. Sixty-two weeks, that is, four hundred and thirty-four years.
3. One week, that is, seven years.

The first period of time refers to the rebuilding of Jerusalem. As previously mentioned, this was from the 2nd decree given by king Artaxerxes. It had to be this decree because it was the first of the four decrees that included rebuilding the wall of Jerusalem. There is considerable debate among historians regarding this date, and this is tied into the calendar corrections made by historians. However, Sir Isaac Newton established the Julian date of 4257 which corresponds to 457 BC.[xiv]

> *Seventy weeks are cut out upon thy people, and upon thy holy city, to finish transgression*, &c. Here, by putting a week for seven years, are reckoned 490 years from the time that the dispersed *Jews* should be re-incorporated into [7] a people and a holy city, until the death and resurrection of *Christ*; whereby

> *transgression should be finished, and sins ended, iniquity be expiated, and everlasting righteousness brought in, and this Vision be accomplished, and the Prophet consummated,* that Prophet whom the *Jews* expected; and whereby *the most Holy* should be *anointed,* he who is therefore in the next words called the *Anointed*, that is, the *Messiah*, or the *Christ*.
>
> For by joining the accomplishment of the vision with the expiation of sins, the 490 years are ended with the death of *Christ*. Now the dispersed *Jews* became a people and city when they first returned into a polity or body politick; and this was in the seventh year of *Artaxerxes Longimanus*, when *Ezra* returned with a body of *Jews* from captivity, and revived the *Jewish* worship; and by the King's commission created Magistrates in all the land, to judge and govern the people according to the laws of God and the King, *Ezra* vii. 25.
>
> There were but two returns from captivity, *Zerubbabel*'s and *Ezra*'s; in *Zerubbabel*'s they had only commission to build the Temple, in *Ezra*'s they first became a polity or city by a government of their own. Now the years of this *Artaxerxes* began about two or three months after the summer solstice, and his seventh year fell in with the third year of the eightieth *Olympiad*; and the latter part thereof, wherein *Ezra* went up to *Jerusalem*, was in the year of the *Julian Period* 4257. Count the time from thence to the death of *Christ*, and you will find it just 490 years.
>
> If you count in *Judaic* years commencing in autumn, and date the reckoning from the first autumn after *Ezra*'s coming to *Jerusalem*, when he put the King's decree in execution; the death of *Christ* will fall on the year of the *Julian Period* 4747, *Anno Domini* 34; and the weeks will be *Judaic* weeks, ending with sabbatical years; and this I take to be the truth: but if you had rather place the death of *Christ* in the year before, as is commonly done, you may take the year of *Ezra*'s journey into the reckoning.[xv]

Thus, Newton's timeline is similar, but not exact. Since the Jews used a lunar calendar, determining with exact precision these dates is a challenge. But using this beginning date, and subtracting the first 7 weeks of years or 49 years, we come to 408 BC. Now if we add another 62 weeks of years (434years), this would bring us to somewhere around AD 27. This was the beginning of Christ's ministry. After approximately 3 ½ years He was crucified or "cut off" (Dan 9:26, See Barnes explanation as previously noted). Adding another 3 ½ years we come to AD 34 for the end of Daniel's 70 weeks of years. This was very likely at the stoning of Stephen. It was absolutely apparent that the Jews present **DETESTED even the mention of the name of the Lord Jesus.** Acts 7:57 tells that they hated this name so much that **they cried out with a loud voice and covered their ears** as they **rushed to murder** that precious saint in cold blood. It only served to reinforce what Jesus told them in Matt 23:

> Because of this, behold, I send to you prophets and wise ones and scribes. **And *some* of them you will kill and crucify**, and some of them you will flog in your synagogues and will persecute from city to city; so that should come on **YOU** all *the* righteous blood poured out on the earth, from the blood of righteous Abel to the blood of Zechariah the son of Berechiah **whom you murdered** between the Holy Place and the altar. Truly I say to you, All these things will come on this generation. (Matt 23:34-36 LITV)

These Jews were pronounced guilty! And their future actions **included more murdering** of the Lord's sheep. Their sentence was given, and now the Lord's prophecy of Matt. 24:34 was left to be fulfilled when He said:

> Truly I say to you, **this generation will not pass away** until all these things take place. (Matt 24:34)

That is also when the disciples **started their ministry outside of the Jewish community**. From this point forward, the message started going to the Gentiles in the Roman world.

Of course these calculations may vary slightly, but it gives us valid assurance that this prophecy is a reference to Messiah the Prince spoken of in Daniel 9:25.[4] The Scripture tells us that it would be in troublous times. If you study the book of Nehemiah, you see a similar pattern that they also had a lot of trouble building the city, due to the opposing efforts of Sanballat the Horonite, and Tobiah the Ammonite.

Next we see that ***after*** the 62 weeks there would appear a prince who would destroy the city and the sanctuary (although nothing in this text says it would happen immediately). The Roman prince Titus did appear soon after this, and he did destroy the city, thus fulfilling the prophecy given by Jesus concerning the temple in Matt 24:2: "And Jesus said unto them, See ye not all these things? Verily I say unto you, there shall not be left here one stone upon another that shall not be thrown down." This prophecy would have been thought impossible 40 years prior. The temple was an amazing architectural structure. It was the pride of the Jewish nation. *Under the command of Titus, in AD 70 there was complete destruction.* ***As Jesus said, not one stone was left upon another!***

Daniel's prophecy was a promise to the nation of Israel. There would be a Messiah who would come, in whom all these things **would be fulfilled**. The writer of Hebrews notes in chapter 9 that Christ came as high priest with a greater and more perfect tabernacle, not made with hands, **to offer the perfect sacrifice** and mediate **a New Covenant** (Heb 9:11-16). Later we read of God's final answer for sin in Hebrews 9:24-28. This time quoting from the English Standard Version:

> "For Christ has entered, not into holy places made with hands, which are copies of the true things, but into heaven itself, now to appear in the presence of God on our behalf. Nor was it to offer himself repeatedly, as the high priest enters the holy places every year with blood not his own, for then he would have had to suffer repeatedly since the foundation of the world. But as it is, he has appeared **once for all** ***at the end of the ages*** to put away sin by the sacrifice of himself. And just as it is appointed for man to die once, and after that comes judgment, so Christ, having been offered once to bear the sins of many, will appear a second time, not to deal with sin ***but to save those who are eagerly waiting for him."***

Now as we look closely, we see the timeline as follows:

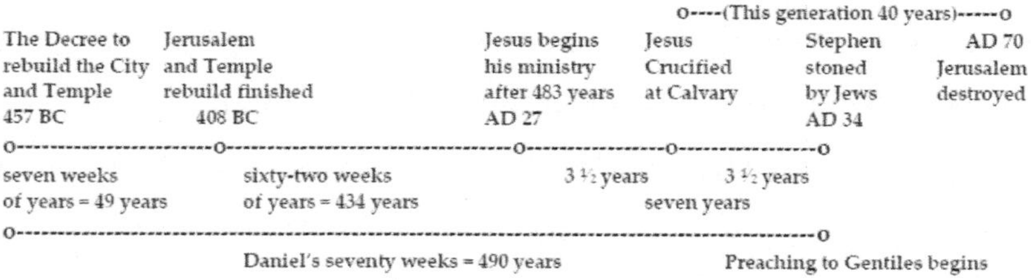

```
                                                                  o----(This generation 40 years)-----o
The Decree to       Jerusalem                            Jesus begins     Jesus          Stephen        AD 70
rebuild the City    and Temple                           his ministry     Crucified      stoned         Jerusalem
and Temple          rebuild finished                     after 483 years  at Calvary     by Jews        destroyed
457 BC                   408 BC                          AD 27                           AD 34
o-----------------------o----------------------------------o----------------o----------------o
seven weeks                sixty-two weeks                        3 ½ years        3 ½ years
of years = 49 years        of years = 434 years                           seven years
o----------------------------------------------------------------------------------------------o
                           Daniel's seventy weeks = 490 years                Preaching to Gentiles begins
```

Thus, Daniel was instructed to seal up the words of this prophecy for the next 490+ years until the judgment of those spoken of by our Lord would come to pass. **It all ties together to come to a conclusion on the timeline above!** Notice this as we look at the corresponding verses:

> 'He will speak out against the Most High and wear down the saints of the Highest One, and he will intend to make alterations in times and in law; and they will be given into his

> hand for a time, times, and half a time." (Dan 7:25)
>
> I heard the man dressed in linen, who was above the waters of the river, as he raised his right hand and his left toward heaven, and swore by Him who lives forever that it would be for a time, times, and half a time; and as soon as they finish shattering the power of the holy people, all these events will be completed. (Dan 12:7)
>
> But the two wings of the great eagle were given to the woman, so that she could fly into the wilderness to her place, where she was nourished for a time and times and half a times, from the presence of the serpent. (Rev 12:14)

Yes! When was the power of the holy people shattered? There is only one period of time that matches this criterion, namely:

- The seventy weeks - consisting of three periods: sixty two weeks, seven weeks, and one week (Dan 9:24-27)
- The 490 years (70 x 7)
- The time, times, and half a times (Rev 12:14)
- The shattering of the power of the holy people (The destruction of the temple in AD 70)

This ties together the prophecy of the seventy weeks of years, and the judgment that our Lord spoke of when he pronounced judgment on Israel in Matthew 23 as mentioned above. The nation of Israel was found guilty. The sentence was pronounced by Jesus and the execution was performed by Titus and the Roman armies in the year AD 70.

The power of the holy people was **so completely shattered** and destroyed that it **brought an end to the entire system of sacrificial worship**. **The temple was gone**! It was no longer necessary! The Lamb of God as described by John the Baptist has been sacrificed! (John 1:29)

Chapter 5

Jesus' Greatest Prophecy

We all know of the beloved Christian Apologist C.S. Lewis. He is often quoted famously for his description of Jesus in his book Mere Christianity. The statement is absolutely profound. Why? Because it so perfectly describes how we must view Jesus! Here is what he says:

> I am trying here to prevent anyone saying the really foolish thing that people often say about Him: I'm ready to accept Jesus as a great moral teacher, but I don't accept his claim to be God. That is the one thing we must not say. A man who was merely a man and said the sort of things Jesus said would not be a great moral teacher. He would either be a lunatic — on the level with the man who says he is a poached egg — or else he would be the Devil of Hell. You must make your choice. **Either this man was, and is, the Son of God, or else a madman or something worse.** You can shut him up for a fool, you can spit at him and kill him as a demon or you can fall at his feet and call him Lord and God, but let us not come with any patronizing nonsense about his being a great human teacher. He has not left that open to us. He did not intend to.[xvi]

But our beloved C.S. Lewis also said the following which has bothered Christians for decades. In this quote he calls into question the knowledge Jesus had of what he prophesied in Mark 13. Notice what Lewis said:

> Say what you like, we shall be told, the apocalyptic beliefs of the first Christians proved to be false. It is clear from the New Testament that they all expected the Second coming *in their lifetime*. And worse still, they had a reason, and one which you will find very embarrassing, *Their Master told them so*. He shared, and indeed created their delusion. He said in so many words 'this generation will not pass until all these things are done.' And he was wrong. He clearly knew no more about the end of the world than anyone else. It is certainly the most embarrassing verse in the Bible.[xvii]

Yes, as much as we all love C.S. Lewis and all he has done for the Christian Faith, **he was wrong** about this. Jesus **DID return** in **THAT VERY SAME** generation, and I will show the evidence here. And even though Lewis **was wrong**, it is clear from his statement, that he **knew** that when Jesus spoke those words in Mark 13, it clearly **meant the generation in which he was living.** Now let's examine the evidence.

As we open the book of Mark, we see something in the very first chapter which is very noteworthy in this discussion. Just after Mark records the Baptism of Jesus, it states that he went into the wilderness to be tempted by Satan. But immediately following this forty day event, we find Mark records the following:

> Now after John was arrested, Jesus came into Galilee, proclaiming the gospel of God, (Mark 1:14)

Now ***notice very carefully*** what Jesus said:

> and saying, "The time ***IS*** **FULFILLED**, and the kingdom of God ***IS*** **AT HAND**; repent and believe in the gospel." (Mark 1:15)

I am sure that when C.S. Lewis read these words he was expecting Jesus to show His disciples that the words he just spoke **were TRUE** and were **about to be fulfilled**! And how could it mean anything else? Jesus was proclaiming that His presence on this earth would bring about the fulfillment of **ALL Bible prophecy**. Gospel writer Luke records the words which confirm this; words that Jesus himself spoke. Notice the fine detail which Jesus himself gives:

> "But when you see Jerusalem surrounded by armies, then recognize that her desolation is near. "Then those who are in Judea must flee to the mountains, and those who are in the midst of the city must leave, and those who are in the country must not enter the city; because these are days of vengeance, so that **ALL THINGS WHICH ARE WRITTEN** will be fulfilled." (Luke 21:20-22)

Can there be any mistake in what Jesus himself proclaimed!? How is it possible that Jesus could make himself ***any clearer*** in the matter?

So from these readings we can see why the beloved C.S. Lewis expected Jesus to keep His promise. But our beloved brother in Christ did not see what was right before his very eyes. As I will state again: **LEWIS WAS WRONG** about this! And now let's begin to look at the proof:

The Olivet Discourse

As we begin exploring Jesus' prophecy in Mark 13, which is often referred to as "The Olivet Discourse," I want to encourage you to listen closely for these specific items. And as we begin going through them, I will be asking you questions to make you think about what is being said here in these verses, and to find out if you think it makes sense for the fulfillment to be in some future generation. Beginning in Mark 13:1 we read:

> And as he came out of the temple, one of his disciples said to him, "Look, Teacher, what wonderful stones and what wonderful buildings!" And Jesus said to him, "Do you see these great buildings? There will NOT BE LEFT HERE one stone upon another that will not be thrown down." (Mark 13:1,2)

Here in the second verse is the prophecy which sets the timeline for the entire chapter. Because just exactly as Jesus predicted, history records that the temple complex was completely reduced to rubble in the year AD 70. We will discuss more on this later.

> And as he sat on the Mount of Olives opposite the temple, Peter and James and John and Andrew asked him privately, "Tell us, when will these things be, and what will be the sign when all these things are about to be accomplished?" (Mark 13:3,4)

So here we find the four apostles closest to Jesus getting very specific with Jesus and asking him 2 questions:

- When will this happen?
- And what will be the sign that will let us know it is about to take place?

Jesus elaborates on the second question first, as we continue. Now keep in mind that we now know the time frame He is talking about here, because as I said previously, history has recorded it for us. The temple complex was completely destroyed and reduced to rubble in the year AD 70. I would also like you to notice as we read through verse 23 how many times He specifically tells these four disciples that **this would happen to THEM**....not some future generation...

> And Jesus began to say to them, "See that no one leads **YOU** astray." (Mark 13:5)

Even reading this very first sentence, I have to ask, why would He say this **to them** if the meaning of what He was saying was for some future generation? Wouldn't He say something like "pray that **THEY** will not be led astray?"

> Many will come in my name, saying, 'I am he!' and they will lead many astray. And when YOU hear of wars and rumors of wars, do not be alarmed. This must take place, but the end is not yet. For nation will rise against nation, and kingdom against kingdom. There will be earthquakes in various places; there will be famines. These are but the beginning of the birth pains. (Mark 13:6-8)

Now notice in the next verse, Jesus uses the word **YOUR** and **YOU** nine times.

> "But be on YOUR guard. For they will deliver YOU over to councils, and YOU will be beaten in synagogues, and YOU will stand before governors and kings for my sake, to bear witness before them. And the gospel must first be proclaimed to all nations. And when they bring YOU to trial and deliver YOU over, do not be anxious beforehand what YOU are to say, but say whatever is given YOU in that hour, for it is not YOU who speak, but the Holy Spirit." (Mark 13:9-11)

It is abundantly clear here that Jesus was speaking **to THESE four disciples**, and what **THEY** would experience, not some future generation!

> And brother will deliver brother over to death, and the father his child, and children will rise against parents and have them put to death. And YOU will be hated by all for my name's sake. But the one who endures to the end will be saved. But when

> YOU see the abomination of desolation standing where he ought not to be (let the reader understand), then let those who are in Judea flee to the mountains. (Mark 13:12-14)

Clearly, this would not apply to anyone else. The context would not fit. If this is a futurist passage, would that future generation be required to come back to Judea, so they could flee to the mountains? If not, then what about those who do not live in Judea? What should they do? Is there any indication of any instructions for them? This makes it clear that **Jesus' words were only for this specific audience**. Next we read:

> Let the one who is on the housetop not go down, nor enter his house, to take anything out, (Mark 13:15)

How many of us have flat roofs with an outside stairway? But this was a typical house in Jesus' day. If Jesus was speaking to our generation, would He have stated such a thing in this way?

> and let the one who is in the field not turn back to take his cloak. And alas for women who are pregnant and for those who are nursing infants in those days! (Mark 13:16-17)

Jesus gave them this information for a good reason. For Jewish Historian Josephus documents in detail the fact that when Jerusalem was under siege from the Roman armies, that mothers of infants trapped inside of Jerusalem **were so desperate** that they had nothing with which to feed their children, and some of them committed **unspeakable atrocities**, such as cooking and eating their own children!

> Pray that it may not happen in winter. For in those days there will be such tribulation as has not been from the beginning of the creation that God created until now, and never will be. And if the Lord had not cut short the days, no human being

> would be saved. But for the sake of the elect, whom he chose, he shortened the days. (Mark 13:18-20)

Yes, it is true. Jesus used some very strong language here. He said that this would be the greatest tribulation that would ever be. But did He mean that literally? One could argue that it was the worst when you read the account of Josephus in Wars of the Jews. But this type of expression is commonly referred to as hyperbolic language. I will expound on this in a few more verses. Continuing on . . .

> And then if anyone says to YOU, 'Look, here is the Christ!' or 'Look, there he is!' do not believe it. For false Christs and false prophets will arise and perform signs and wonders, to lead astray, if possible, the elect. But be on guard; I have told YOU all things beforehand. (Mark 13:21-23)

Were there false Christs and false prophets in the days following this? Yes! This is documented by Jewish Historian Josephus in “The Wars of the Jews.” Now notice the extreme emphasis Jesus puts on the following verses:

> But in those days, after that tribulation, the sun will be darkened, and the moon will not give its light, and the stars will be falling from heaven, and the powers in the heavens will be shaken. (Mark 13:24-25)

Is what Jesus saying to be taken literally? Was the sun to be **literally darkened**? Was the moon **literally said not to give its light?** Were there **literally stars falling** from the heavens, and were the powers of heaven **literally shaken?** My answer to these questions are a resounding **NO.**

This is **NOT** literal. So now you ask, “How can you say this with so much certainty? What makes you so sure? After all, this is one of the reasons that everyone is saying this still has not happened. Most people are waiting for such a sign to occur to know that the end is near!

I can tell you that I am so sure of this **because we have precedent in the Old Testament** for such a thing. Listen to what commentator Albert Barnes says about this in his commentary written over a hundred and fifty years ago. Commenting on Matthew's exact account of this, Barnes notes about this extreme verbiage:

> The images used here are *not to be taken literally*. They are often employed by the sacred writers to denote "any great calamities." As the darkening of the sun and moon, and the falling of the stars, would be an inexpressible calamity, so any great catastrophe - any overturning of kingdoms or cities, or dethroning of kings and princes is represented by the darkening of the sun and moon, and by some terrible convulsion in the elements. Thus the destruction of Babylon is foretold in similar terms Isa 13:10, and of Tyre Isa 24:23. The slaughter in Bozrah and Idumea is predicted in the same language, Isa 34:4. See also Isa 50:3; Isa 60:19-20; Ezek 32:7; Joel 3:15.

So then considering what Barnes said, let's look for ourselves. Let's read what the prophet Isaiah says in Isaiah 13:10:

> "For the stars of the heavens and their constellations will not give their light; the sun will be dark at its rising, and the moon will not shed its light."

Continuing on in verse 13 we read:

> "Therefore I will make the heavens tremble, and the earth will be shaken out of its place, at the wrath of the LORD of hosts in the day of his fierce anger."

Was this a prediction of some future event? NO!! For in verse one of this chapter we read:

> "The oracle concerning Babylon which Isaiah the son of Amoz saw. "

That's right! This was a prophecy concerning the **destruction of Babylon**. A prophecy which came about **exactly** as foretold. The language which was used here is commonly referred to as apocalyptic language. It contains verbiage which is extreme in order to make a point. We do this all the time, don't we by saying such things as: "It's colder than blue ice out there," or "I'm so hungry I could eat an elephant!"

Now as we look at this prophecy in Isaiah 13 concerning Babylon, we have to ask: Did the sun, moon, and stars actually go dark? Did the heavens actually tremble, and was the earth actually shaken out of its place. Of course not!! This was merely a common way of expressing judgment upon a nation or nations, and is frequently used in the Old Testament.

And in Mark 13: verses 24, and 25 we have Jesus using the same type of language to describe the destruction of Jerusalem as it occurred in AD70. The apostles understood this and were used to hearing this type of verbiage.

As we move on to Mark 13:26 and 27, we note the wording:

> "And then THEY will see the Son of Man coming in clouds with great power and glory. And then he will send out the angels and gather his elect from the four winds, from the ends of the earth to the ends of heaven."

Now, for the first time in this account, we hear the word **THEY.** This solidifies the point I have been making! Previously, everything was directed to the four disciples. And now Jesus is saying "**THEY** will see the Son of Man coming in clouds with great power and glory." So now who is Jesus referring to?

For a clue, we can look at the parallel account of Matthew from Green's Literal Translation

> And then the sign of the Son of Man will appear in the heavens. And then all the tribes of the LAND will wail. And they will see the Son of Man coming on the clouds of heaven with power and much glory. (Matt 24:30 LITV)

Yes, the word translated as **earth** in most translations is more accurately translated as **land** by Green. So Jesus is referring to the Jewish nation who rejected and crucified him. For the first time in this chapter, we see a reference to someone outside of the circle of the apostles who would see these things. We will have much more to say on the translation of this word later.

Once again, this is not a reference to some far distant future event, but a reference to something which would happen during the lifetime of the disciples to whom He was speaking. Did this occur? Was there a sign? Was there a presence of power and great glory seen in the heavens? Listen to what Josephus records in his account in the "Wars of the Jews."

> "Thus there was a star resembling a sword, which stood over the city, and a comet, that continued a whole year. Thus also, before the Jews rebellion, and before those commotions which preceded the war, when the people were come in great crowds on the feast of unleavened bread....so great a light shone that it appeared to be bright daytime; which light lasted

> for half and hour. This light seemed to be a good sign to the unskillful, but was so interpreted by the sacred scribes, as to portend those events that followed immediately upon it. At that same festival also, a heifer, as she was led by the high priest to be sacrificed, *brought forth a lamb* in the midst of the temple." [xviii]

Wow! Can there be any question, that this was a sign from heaven? It is completely impossible that these events were some natural occurring thing. You talk about a sign? **Wow!** A star resembling a sword that stood over the city, and a comet **lasting a whole year!** A bright light **shining on the holy house** in the dark of night. **A heifer giving birth to a lamb** at the very time that it was brought into the temple to be sacrificed. **Yes, the Jews always wanted a sign and Jesus delivered it to them in a mighty way**. But there is more. Listen as Josephus continues:

> Moreover, the eastern gate of the inner court of the temple, which was brass, and vastly heavy, and had been with difficulty shut by twenty men, and rested upon a basis armed with Iron, and had bolts fastened very deep into the firm floor which was made of entire stone, **was seen to be opened of its own accord** about the sixth hour of the night...But the men of learning understood it, that the security of their holy house was dissolved of its own accord, and that the gate was opened for the advantage of their enemies. So these publicly declared that this signal foreshadowed the desolation that was coming upon them.[xix]

Yes, no question, that gate was opened by the Lord Jesus as part of the sign He promised, and those religious leaders knew it! But there is still more. Listen to this as recorded by Josephus!

> Besides these, a few days after the feast, on the twenty-first day of the month Artemisius [Jyar], a certain prodigious and

> incredible phenomenon appeared; I suppose the account of it would seem to be a fable, were it not related by those who saw it, and were not the events that followed it of so considerable a nature as to deserve such signals; for, before the sunsetting, chariots and troops of soldiers were seen **RUNNING ABOUT AMONG THE CLOUDS**, and surrounding cities. Moreover at that feast which we call Pentecost, as the priests going by night into the inner [court of the] temple, as their custom was, to perform their sacred ministrations, they said that, in the first place, they felt a quaking, and heard a great noise, and after that they heard a sound of a great multitude saying, "Let us remove hence." [xx]

Now I have to ask you, have you ever heard of anything like this being documented by a notable historian, one whose credibility is undeniable? Isn't it extremely noteworthy to see that Almighty God would use a credible historian to record such events? By using a notable historian to record this, there is no space here to ridicule the Scriptures as many liberal college professors tend to do. This is recorded by one whose credibility ranks very high in the educational ranks. Regarding the credibility of Flavius Josephus, look at this quotation.

> "Our knowledge of the last two centuries of the Second Commonwealth depends very substantially on the writings of Josephus. Matters such as his credibility, accuracy and sources are therefore foremost among the topics which should occupy scholarship. The most obvious data for examination, it would seem to us, is *archaeological* material. In many instances, numerous details provided by Josephus can be checked, including architectural data and their accuracy confirmed. Such precision, where it can be established, is surprising, especially since the information was set down in writing years after Josephus had left Palestine."[xxi] -

Having established this now, let's return to the subject at hand. But now you ask the question, but what about Jesus coming in the clouds? Are you saying that this judgment described in detail in the writings of Josephus is what Jesus was speaking of here?

Well let's determine this from the **scriptural evidence!**

Once again, the term coming in the clouds was not something new to the disciples to whom Jesus was speaking. Having an understanding of the Old Testament, as taught by Jesus, they knew what this meant. Let's look at some examples:

> And the LORD said to Moses, "Behold, I am coming to you in a **THICK CLOUD**, that the people may hear when I speak with you, and may also believe you forever." (Exodus 19:9)

> The LORD descended in the CLOUD and stood with him there, and proclaimed the name of the LORD. (Exodus 34:5)

Now let's look at how Isaiah worded it in this prophecy against Egypt.

> An oracle concerning Egypt. Behold, the LORD is riding on a **SWIFT CLOUD** and comes to Egypt; and the idols of Egypt will tremble at his presence, and the heart of the Egyptians will melt within them. (Isaiah 19:1)

Again, I have to ask: In this judgment of Egypt, did the Lord ride on a **literal cloud**? Did the idols **literally** tremble? Did the hearts of the Egyptians **literally** melt in their chests? NO! It was just the way the prophet described it, using extreme language to make his point. And the cloud reference is quite common in the Old Testament.

In fact, in Exodus alone we find over 15 examples of the Lord appearing to Israel in the clouds, and over 70 such references throughout the Old Testament.

But now, once again, let's go back to Mark 13:26 because we still have to finish one item in this verse. Who is the **THEY** that is spoken of in this verse where it says: **THEY** will see the Son of Man coming in clouds with great power and glory?

We touched on this earlier, but let's look at it closer. We find it documented in Matthew chapters 26 and 27. Yes, it is those who, instead of embracing Jesus as Lord and Savior, actually decided to murder him.... And not only to put Him to death, but to torture Him, and lead Him to a disgraceful death as a criminal, nailing Him to the cross. This included two groups of people. First we have the religious leaders that Jesus spoke to directly in Matt. 26. Let's listen to this account of Jesus standing before the High Priest, and the scribes, and Pharisees of the Jewish Sanhedrin:

> But Jesus remained silent. And the high priest said to him, "I adjure you by the living God, tell us if you are the Christ, the Son of God." Jesus said to him, "You have said so. But I tell YOU, from now on YOU will see the Son of Man seated at the right hand of Power and coming on the clouds of heaven." (Matt 26:63-64)

Then we see:

> Then the high priest tore his robes and said, "He has uttered blasphemy. What further witnesses do we need? You have now heard his blasphemy. What is your judgment?" They answered, "He deserves death." Then they spit in his face and struck him. And some slapped him, (Matt 26:65-67)

Also included in this judgment were those whom Pilate addressed in Matthew 27:

> Pilate said to them, "Then what shall I do with Jesus who is called Christ?" They all said, "Let him be crucified!" And he said, "Why, what evil has he done?" But they shouted all the more, "Let him be crucified!" So when Pilate saw that he was gaining nothing, but rather that a riot was beginning, he took water and washed his hands before the crowd, saying, "I am innocent of this man's blood; see to it yourselves." And all the people answered, "His blood be on us and on our children!" (Matt 27:22-25)

Yes, these people created their own indictment! They did have the innocent blood of Jesus on their hands! And all of them were pronounced guilty by Jesus, and were to be judged **SHORTLY.**

It is important for us to understand that the Wars of the Jews which lasted from AD 66 through about AD 73 was not just some small skirmish in the Middle East. Let's look at some statistics on this war. During the final siege of Jerusalem in AD 70, Josephus reports that there were 1.1 million Jews killed. But from Book 2 through Book 7 of the Wars of the Jews, Josephus reports that the total killed in all of this was over 1.3 million Jews which includes over 200,000 that were killed in over 20 cities and regions throughout all of Judea. He reports that in Jerusalem the bodies were piled so high all over what was left of the city that the soldiers had to walk over them as they lay in big heaps everywhere. Additionally, Josephus reports that 97,000 were taken captive.

And in fulfillment of verse 27 of Mark chapter 13, the Christians did flee the city as instructed by Jesus. In his commentary on the Bible, noted Theologian Albert Barnes stated:

> It is said that there is reason to believe that not one Christian perished in the destruction of that city, God having in various

> ways secured their escape, so that they fled to Pella, where they lived when the city was destroyed.[xxii]

So from all of this we see that this evil that those Jews did on that occasion by rejecting the Savior, and nailing Him to that cross came back on them in one of the most powerful ways ever recorded in the annals of history. For in doing this, our Lord Jesus fulfilled the prophecy of John the Baptist in John 1:29: "Behold, the Lamb of God, who takes away the sin of the world!"

And aren't we thankful that our Lord Jesus became that Lamb, shedding His precious blood for us, and thus giving us the promise of life eternal for those of faith! Aren't we so appreciative of this that we will always be deeply indebted to Him for this wonderful selfless act? These disciples poured out their lives for Jesus because of this. Each of us needs to dig down deep and ask ourselves if we would be willing to do the same.

As we continue with Mark thirteen we need to take note as we stated above that Jesus said in Mark 13:26 that there would be certain ones of people who would see Jesus coming in the clouds of glory. In Matthew 26 and 27 we were able to identify who these were.

It is very important that you notice that when Jesus spoke to these disciples, He changed from saying "**you will see**" to "**they will see**." This is consistent in all three Gospel accounts. We also looked at the testimony of Josephus, and how he said that there were many who had reported to him that they had seen chariots of troops and soldiers running about in the sky. This does not directly say that they saw Jesus, but Josephus was not a part of the audience Jesus mentioned, and was merely recording what was told to him. Also, keep in mind that the book of Acts records that Stephen looked into heaven and saw Jesus standing at the right hand of God. In the book of Acts we find:

> But he, full of the Holy Spirit, gazed into heaven and saw the glory of God, and Jesus standing at the right hand of God. And he said, "Behold, I see the heavens opened, and the Son of Man standing at the right hand of God." (Acts 7:55)

Why did this enrage the council so much that they wanted to kill him? It was because he was **confirming** the very words that they heard our Lord tell them. And believe me, **they never** forgot those words, especially when at the moment that He died on the cross, there was a great earthquake and the veil of the temple was torn in two. They were probably scared to death at these events happening.

Thus, we actually see that there is precedence in this account for someone seeing Jesus in the heavens during that generation. Therefore I ask you in all sincerity, is it so hard to believe that these ones spoken to by Jesus when He was on trial actually saw Jesus just as Stephen had done?

Now we turn back to the Gospel of Mark to continue reading:

> From the fig tree learn its lesson: as soon as its branch becomes tender and puts out its leaves, you know that summer is near. So also, when you see these things taking place, you know that he is near, at the very gates. Truly, I say to you, **THIS GENERATION will not pass away** until all these things take place. (Mark 13:28-30)

Notice here that Jesus did not say “that generation” in reference to some different generation. No, Jesus makes it plain here that this would happen within the generation in which the apostles were living. But there has been considerable controversy regarding this passage. Some notable atheists have said Jesus was a false prophet. Some Christians have **even said** that Jesus was wrong, **because He didn't return at all.** Notable among these is the beloved C.S. Lewis as we quoted in the beginning of this chapter. Jesus did return (on the clouds) in that **very same generation.** And even though Lewis was wrong, it is clear from his statement, that Lewis himself **knew** that Jesus meant the generation in which He himself was living!

Some have said that Jesus did not return in that generation, but what this really means is that "the generation that would see all these signs would also see the end of the ages." But I ask you, is that really what Jesus said? Why do people make this so complicated? It was a simple statement by our Lord, and requires no further interpretation. Others have said that the term "this generation" actually meant "This race will not pass away." Why would they try to put such a meaning on this, when it seems so clear? It's because they too, want to say that Jesus didn't really mean the generation He was living in. He meant it for a future time, most likely ours. Therefore, they want it to have a meaning that would make this verse fit our time. But the word generation comes from the Greek word **γενεα** (English – genea).

As to trying to force this word to mean "race," notice what Thayer's Greek Lexicon notes concerning this:

> A begetting, birth, nativity, 2. That which has been begotten, men of the same stock, a family.

In continuing, note how it is further clarified by item three:

> The whole multitude of men living *at the same time*: Matt xx1v. 34; Mk xxi. 30; . . . . used especially of the Jewish race living at one and the same period.[xxiii]

I would also like to point out that **there is** a Greek word for "race" which is not used here. That word is **γενος** (genos) of which Thayer's Lexicon states:

> Race, offspring, nation, (i.e. nationality or decent from a particular people) [xxiv]

This is the word that Jesus would have used if He had intended for this to mean "race." But we find that there is so much futurist bias in some of these translations, that although they will not actually translate the word genea as race, they will attempt to convince the reader that this is its meaning by adding it in the footnote.

In his book "Unraveling the End" John Noe makes this important point concerning the use of this word:

> "Please notice that after Jesus' "this generation" time statement in Matt 24:34 some Bibles place a footnote clarifying its meaning or possible meaning as being "race." However, no footnote is added to the identical usage of this phrase in Matthew 23:36. If, however, Jesus' "this generation" meant "race," then Jesus did not answer his disciples time question in Matthew 24:3, which preceded this entire discourse: "Tell us," they said, "when will this happen, and what will be the sign of your coming and the end of the age?"[xxv]

Yes, my friend John Noe is precisely correct. Jesus excoriated the scribes and Pharisees in Matthew 23:34-36 when He told them:

> Therefore I send YOU prophets and wise men and scribes, some of whom YOU will kill and crucify, and some YOU will flog in your synagogues and persecute from town to town, so

> that on YOU may come all the righteous blood shed on earth, from the blood of righteous Abel to the blood of Zechariah the son of Barachiah, whom YOU murdered between the sanctuary and the altar. Truly, I say to YOU, all these things will come upon THIS generation.

And this passage further confirms the judgment that Jesus was pronouncing upon THIS group, not some future group. Nowhere is there any attempt to say that in this verse the word "genea" means race. Without a doubt, the attempt to say genea means "race" in Matt. 24:34 is not exegesis, but eisegesis (adding to a passage to make it mean what one wants it to mean).

Next, Jesus tells these four disciples how much they can depend upon what He said with these words in Mark 13:31.

> Heaven and earth will pass away, but my words will not pass away.

As Matthew Henry words it in his commentary:

> "The word of Christ is more sure and lasting than heaven and earth."

Albert Barnes says:

> "You may sooner expect to see the heaven and earth pass away and return to nothing, than my words to fail."

But the Old Testament gives evidence that the term "heaven and earth" was a reference to the temple in Jerusalem, the central point of the entire Jewish system, and along with it, the entire system of sacrificial worship. Commentator John Lightfoot adds that Jesus' words had a deeper meaning when he noted concerning this verse. After surveying how this language is used throughout the Bible and in Jewish literature, he believes the "passing away of heaven and earth" refers to the "destruction of

Jerusalem and the whole Jewish state ... as if the whole frame of this world were to be dissolved."

But whether or not Jesus' meaning was this deep, one thing is certain: We can depend on Jesus' words. They did come to pass, and we can depend on all of His precious promises. And now as we conclude this chapter, Jesus tells them that he cannot tell them *exactly when* within this generation this will happen, and at the same time gives them a warning. Notice here that Jesus is still addressing them, and not some other group of people.

> "But concerning that day or that hour, no one knows, not even the angels in heaven, nor the Son, but only the Father. Be on guard, keep awake. For you do not know when the time will come. It is like a man going on a journey, when he leaves home and puts his servants in charge, each with his work, and commands the doorkeeper to stay awake. Therefore stay awake—for you do not know when the master of the house will come, in the evening, or at midnight, or when the rooster crows, or in the morning — lest he come suddenly and find you asleep. And what I say to you I say to all: Stay awake." (Mar 13:32-37)

Jesus gave them the final words here in this chapter, and wanted them to pass it on to all of the disciples, because He did not want them to be asleep on the watch. Although three of the four mentioned here in this chapter died as martyrs, He knew that this would be a horrible and terrifying event, and that if the others were not watchful, they could be trapped inside the city when these things occurred.

So now we have **concluded** the exposition of what Jesus said concerning the last days in Mark 13, and we have seen from recorded history that what Jesus said **WOULD** happen, **DID** happen. From this we have seen that Jesus was pronouncing **judgment** upon the Jewish nation in general, and more specifically the city of Jerusalem and its temple. The Jewish Historian Josephus wrote an extensive history called "The Wars of the Jews" which outlines precisely how that judgment was carried out. But as for the Christians, He gave them instructions as to what to do and when. For it says in Luke's account:

> "But when you see Jerusalem surrounded by armies, then know that its desolation has come near. Then let those who are in Judea flee to the mountains, and let those who are inside the city depart, and let not those who are out in the country enter it, for these are days of vengeance, to fulfill all that is written." (Luke 20:20-22)

The apostles themselves were the subject of much persecution and gave their lives for the message of Christ as they did what they were told and preached the message throughout all of Judea and the surrounding nations. But the remaining Christians that were in Judea **DID** flee to the mountains as they were told, and they **were spared**.

I would like to add that there are many who would tell us that this was but a shadow of what is coming in our future...that the events of the Olivet Discourse given here in Mark chapter 13 are going to play out all over again as we are staring down the last days in our time. But to those who would say this, I issue a challenge:

Where is there even the slightest hint in Jesus words that this was going to happen twice? Yes, you can search all three accounts of this, and you will find that there is **not a single word** conveying anything that would **hint** of a dual fulfillment.

This completes the exposition of the thirteenth chapter of Mark. But now that we have finished this, the question arises, how should this affect us? How should we proceed now that we know this?

Well, for starters, we should bask in the realization that we can have **complete confidence** in what our Lord and Savior told us when He was alive on this earth. We can absolutely know that our Lord Jesus **KEEPS HIS PROMISES**. Here is what He said: (All in the book of John)

> John 6:48 "I AM the bread of life."
> John 8:12 "I AM the light of the world."
> John 8:58 "Truly, truly, I say to you, before Abraham was, I AM."
> John 10:9 "I AM the door."
> John 10:11 "I AM the good shepherd"
> John 11:25 "I AM the resurrection and the life".
> John 14:6 "I AM the way, and the truth, and the life. No one comes to the Father except through me."
> John 15:5 "I AM the vine; you are the branches. Whoever abides in me and I in him, he it is that bears much fruit, for apart from me you can do nothing.

There is not another person in history that offered more proof of these claims than Jesus did. He backed up His word with the miracles He performed while He was here.

Chapter 6

A Comparison of the Olivet Discourse and the Revelation Given to John

As we begin this chapter, I would like to highlight that which was spoken by Jesus from Mark 13:30 in the last chapter:

> "Truly, I say to you, THIS GENERATION will not pass away until all these things take place."

As we examined, from the way this is worded, we know that Jesus was speaking specifically to His disciples and the generation in which He was living.

Had He been referring to some future generation He would have said "**that** generation will not pass away..." Now we will examine how this matches up with what the Apostle John wrote in the book of Revelation.

In his book, *Who is this Babylon?* Don K. Preston, D. Div. notes the following comparison:

> Very few deny that Matthew 24 predicts the fall of Jerusalem. However, many have failed to realize that Revelation recreates the Olivet Discourse in form and outline. R. H. Charles was one of the first to recognize that the seals of

Revelation 6 follow exactly the pattern predicted by Jesus in Matthew 24:7.[xxvi]

In *Who is this Babylon?* Dr. Preston does an excellent job of showing the pattern in relationship to Matthew 24. Since we have just completed an analysis of the prophecy outlined in Mark 13, in this chapter I will use Preston's format here to show how this pattern is in relationship to Mark 13. Using the NASB (New American Standard Bible), we will list the passage in Mark 13 and show the corresponding passages in the book of Revelation. So now let us proceed with the pattern we find there.

The Prophecy

1. Wars and Rumors of Wars

Mark 13: 7 When you hear of **wars and rumors of wars**, do not be frightened; those things must take place; but that is not yet the end.

First we know there was war in heaven:

- (Rev 2:16) Therefore repent; or else I am coming to you quickly, and I will make war against them with the sword of My mouth.
- (Rev 11:7) When they have finished their testimony, the beast that comes up out of the abyss will make war with them, and overcome them and kill them.
- (Rev 12:7) And there was war in heaven, Michael and his angels waging war with the dragon. The dragon and his angels waged war,

Next we find John showing that this affects the nation of Israel:

- (Rev 12:17) So the dragon was enraged with the woman, and went off to make war with the rest of her children, who keep the commandments of God and hold to the testimony of Jesus.

It also affects the beast and his subjects (more on this later):

- (Rev 13:4) they worshiped the dragon because he gave his authority to the beast; and they worshiped the beast, saying, "Who is like the beast, and who is able to **wage war** with him?"(Rev 13:7) It was also given to him to **make war** with the saints and to overcome them, and authority over every tribe and people and tongue and nation was given to him.
- (Rev 16:14) for they are spirits of demons, performing signs, which go out to the kings of the whole world (oikoumenes – the Roman world), to gather them together **for the war** of the great day of God, the Almighty. (parenthesis mine, more on oikoumenes later)
- (Rev 17:14) "These will **wage war** against the Lamb, and the Lamb will overcome them, because He is Lord of lords and King of kings, and those who are with Him are the called and chosen and faithful."
- (Rev 19:11) And I saw heaven opened, and behold, a white horse, and He who sat on it is called Faithful and True, and in righteousness He judges and **wages war**.
- (Rev 19:19) And I saw the beast and the kings of the earth and their armies assembled **to make war** against Him who sat on the horse and against His army.
- (Rev 20:8) and will come out to deceive the nations which are in the four corners of the earth, Gog and Magog, **to gather them together for the war**; the number of them is like the sand of the seashore.

International Conflict

Mark 13: 8 For **nation will rise up against nation**, and kingdom against kingdom;

- Rev 6:3-4 When He broke the second seal, I heard the second living creature saying, "Come." And another, a red horse, went out; and to him who sat on it, it was granted **to take peace from the earth**, and that men would **slay one another**; and a great sword was given to him.
- Rev 16:19 The great city was split into three parts, and the cities of the nations fell. Babylon the great was remembered before God, to give her the cup of the wine of His fierce wrath.
- Also note Rev 20:8 as quoted above.

Earthquakes

Mark 13:8b . . . there will be earthquakes in various places

- Rev 6:12 I looked when He broke the sixth seal, and there was a great **earthquake**; and the sun became black as sackcloth made of hair, and the whole moon became like blood;
- Rev 8:5 Then the angel took the censer and filled it with the fire of the altar, and threw it to the earth; and there followed peals of thunder and sounds and flashes of lightning and an **earthquake.**
- Rev 11:13 And in that hour there was a great **earthquake**, and a tenth of the city fell; seven thousand people were killed in the **earthquake**, and the rest were terrified and gave glory to the God of heaven.
- Rev 11:19 And the temple of God which is in heaven was opened; and the ark of His covenant appeared in His temple, and there were flashes of lightning and sounds and peals of thunder and an **earthquake** and a great hailstorm.
- Rev 16:18 And there were flashes of lightning and sounds and peals of thunder; and there was a great **earthquake**, such as there had not been since man came to be upon the earth, so great an **earthquake** was it, and so mighty.

Famine

Mark 13:8c . . . there will be famines.

- Rev 6:8 I looked, and behold, an ashen horse; and he who sat on it had the name Death; and Hades was following with him. Authority was given to them over a fourth of the earth, to kill with sword and with **famine** and with pestilence and by the wild beasts of the earth.
- Rev 18:8 For this reason in one day her plagues will come, pestilence and mourning and **famine**, and she will be burned up with fire; for the Lord God who judges her is strong.

Persecutions

Mark 13:9 "But be on your guard; for they will deliver you to the courts, and you will be flogged in the synagogues, and you will stand before governors and kings for My sake, as a testimony to them."

Mark 13:12-13 "Brother will betray brother to death, and a father his child; and children will rise up against parents and have them put to death. You will be hated by all because of My name, but the one who endures to the end, he will be saved."

- Rev 6:9 When the Lamb broke the fifth seal, I saw underneath the altar the souls of those who had been slain because of the word of God, and because of the testimony which they had maintained;
- Rev 6:10 and they cried out with a loud voice, saying, "How long, O Lord, holy and true, will You refrain from judging and avenging our blood on those who dwell on the earth?"

- Rev 6:11 And there was given to each of them a white robe; and they were told that they should rest for a little while longer, until the number of their fellow servants and their brethren who were to be killed even as they had been, would be completed also.
- Rev 18:24 "And in her was found the blood of prophets and of saints and of all who have been slain on the earth."

Tribulation

Mar 13:19 "For those days will be a time of tribulation such as has not occurred since the beginning of the creation which God created until now, and never will."

- (Rev 1:9) I, John, your brother and fellow partaker in the tribulation and kingdom and perseverance which are in Jesus, was on the island called Patmos because of the word of God and the testimony of Jesus.
- (Rev 2:9) 'I know your tribulation and your poverty (but you are rich), and the blasphemy by those who say they are Jews and are not, but are a synagogue of Satan.'
- (Rev 2:10) 'Do not fear what you are about to suffer. Behold, the devil is about to cast some of you into prison, so that you will be tested, and you will have tribulation for ten days. Be faithful until death, and I will give you the crown of life.'
- (Rev 2:22) 'Behold, I will throw her on a bed of sickness, and those who commit adultery with her into great tribulation, unless they repent of her deeds.'
- (Rev 7:14) I said to him, "My lord, you know." And he said to me, "These are the ones who come out of the great tribulation, and they have washed their robes and made them white in the blood of the Lamb."

Unfathomable Events

But in those days, after that tribulation, THE SUN WILL BE DARKENED AND THE MOON WILL NOT GIVE ITS LIGHT,

AND THE STARS WILL BE FALLING from heaven, and the powers that are in the heavens will be shaken. "Then they will see THE SON OF MAN COMING IN CLOUDS with great power and glory. And then He will send forth the angels, and will gather together His elect from the four winds, from the farthest end of the earth to the farthest end of heaven." (Mark 13:24-27 NASB)

- Rev 6:12 I looked when He broke the sixth seal, and there was a great earthquake; and the sun became black as sackcloth made of hair, and the whole moon became like blood;
- Rev 6:13 and the stars of the sky fell to the earth, as a fig tree casts its unripe figs when shaken by a great wind.
- Rev 6:14 The sky was split apart like a scroll when it is rolled up, and every mountain and island were moved out of their places.

Note: The language used above is considered hyperbolic language and is not to be taken literally. Here are some examples of such language used in the Old Testament:

> Isaiah 13:10 For the stars of heaven and their constellations Will not flash forth their light; **The sun will be dark** when it rises And the **moon will not shed its light.**

Listen to what Albert Barnes says about this in his commentary written over a hundred and fifty years ago. Commenting on Matthew's exact account of this, Barnes notes about this extreme verbiage:

> This verse **cannot be understood literally**, but is a metaphorical representation of the calamities that were coming upon Babylon. The meaning of the figure evidently is, that those calamities would be such as would be appropriately denoted by the sudden extinguishment of the stars, the sun, and the moon. As nothing would tend more to anarchy,

distress, and ruin, than thus to have all the lights of heaven suddenly and forever quenched, this was an apt and forcible representation of the awful calamities that were coming upon the people.

Darkness and night, in the Scriptures, are often the emblem of calamity and distress (see the note at Mat_24:29). The revolutions and destructions of kingdoms and nations are often represented in the Scriptures under this image. So respecting the destruction of Idumea Isa_34:4 :

> And all the hosts of heaven shall be dissolved,
> And the heavens shall be rolled together as a scroll;
> And all their host shall fall down,
> As the leaf falleth from off the vine,
> And as a falling fig from the fig-tree.[xxvii]

Continuing on in verse 13 we read:

> Therefore I will make the **heavens tremble**, and the **earth will be shaken out of its place**, at the wrath of the LORD of hosts in the day of his fierce anger.

Was this a prediction **of some event in the distant future? NO!!** For in verse one of this chapter we read:

> Isaiah 13:1 The oracle **concerning Babylon** which Isaiah the son of Amoz saw.

This was a prophecy concerning **the destruction of Babylon.** A prophecy which came about exactly as foretold. The language which was used here is commonly referred to as hyperbole. It is a statement which contains verbiage which is extreme in order to make a point. So, now as we look at this prophecy in Isaiah 13 concerning Babylon, we have to ask: Did the sun, moon, and stars **actually go dark?** Did the heavens **actually tremble**, and was the earth **actually shaken** out of its place? Of course not!! This was merely a common way of expressing judgment upon a nation or nations, and is frequently used in the Old Testament.

And in Mark 13:24-25, we have Jesus using the same type of language to describe the destruction of Jerusalem as it occurred in AD 70. The apostles understood this and were used to hearing this type of verbiage. As I pointed out earlier, Jesus told the four disciples He was closest to that they would have to suffer many things, and that this instruction was **specifically given to them**.

For more proof of the similarities of Mark's version of the Olivet Discourse in chapter 13 to the Revelation given to the Apostle John, we must also compare the following:

Mark 13:10 "The gospel must first be preached to all the nations."

> Rev 14:6 And I saw another angel flying in mid-heaven, having an eternal gospel to preach to those who live on the earth, and to every nation and tribe and tongue and people;

Notice how both are showing the work of the gospel being preached to the nations. Now compare:

Mark 13:14 "But when you see the ABOMINATION OF DESOLATION standing where it should not be (let the reader understand), then those who are in Judea must flee to the mountains."

> Rev 18:3-5 "For all the nations have drunk of the wine of the passion of her immorality, and the kings of the earth have committed acts of immorality with her, and the merchants of the earth have become rich by the wealth of her sensuality." I heard another voice from heaven, saying, "Come out of her, my people, so that you will not participate in her sins and receive of her plagues; for her sins have piled up as high as heaven, and God has remembered her iniquities."

Notice above how **both show the directive to flee** the wicked city due to the coming judgment.

Now compare:

Mark 13:21-22 "And then if anyone says to you, 'Behold, here is the Christ'; or, 'Behold, He is there'; do not believe him; for false Christs and **false prophets** will arise, and will show signs and wonders, in order to lead astray, if possible, the elect."

> Rev 2:2 I know your deeds and your toil and perseverance, and that you cannot tolerate evil men, and you put to the test those who call themselves apostles, and they are not, and you found them to be false;
>
> Rev 16:13 And I saw coming out of the mouth of the dragon and out of the mouth of the beast and out of the mouth of **the false prophet**, three unclean spirits like frogs;
>
> Rev 19:20 And the beast was seized, and with him **the false prophet** who performed the signs in his presence, by which he deceived those who had received the mark of the beast and those who worshiped his image; these two were thrown alive into the lake of fire which burns with brimstone.
>
> Rev 20:10 And the devil who deceived them was thrown into the lake of fire and brimstone, where the beast and **the false prophet** are also; and they will be tormented day and night forever and ever.

Notice how both show the existence of false prophets.

In this comparison I have shown the relationship between Mark's version of the Olivet Discourse and the Revelation. If we consider the versions written by Matthew and Luke, we find that there are more comparisons. For example:

In Matthew's version we find:

Matt 24:31 "And He will send forth His angels with A GREAT

TRUMPET and THEY WILL GATHER TOGETHER His elect from the four winds, from one end of the sky to the other."

Notice from the Revelation:

> Rev 11:15 Then the seventh angel sounded; and there were loud voices in heaven, saying, "The kingdom of the world has become the kingdom of our Lord and of His Christ; and He will reign forever and ever."
>
> Rev 14:15 And another angel came out of the temple, crying out with a loud voice to Him who sat on the cloud, "Put in your sickle and reap, for the hour to reap has come, because the harvest of the earth is ripe."
>
> Rev 14:16 Then He who sat on the cloud swung His sickle over the earth, and the earth was reaped.

In this verse written by Matthew we see that the elect were gathered together as a shepherd gathers his sheep. In the Revelation to John, chapter 14 shows two reapings. The one recorded here was the Lord Jesus sitting on the cloud reaping His elect. In the remainder to the chapter he records the reaping of the lost by an angel.

In Luke's version we find:

> Luke 21:20 "But when you see Jerusalem surrounded by armies, then recognize that her desolation is near."

Notice from the Revelation:

> Rev 19:19 And I saw the beast and the kings of the earth and their armies assembled to make war against Him who sat on the horse and against His army.

Yes, and as a result of this prophecy, in AD 70 the great city and the temple (which now had become totally unnecessary because of the sacrifice of the Lamb of God) were destroyed by the Roman armies.

These Roman armies and the Roman General Vespasian thought they had wiped out the "theocracy" of the Jews, but this was all part of God's plan!

Both Matthew and Luke recorded that Jesus said:

> Matt 24:28 "Wherever the corpse is, there the vultures will gather."
>
> Luke 17:37 And answering they said to Him, "Where, Lord?" And He said to them, "Where the body is, there also the vultures will be gathered."

The Apostle John recorded:

> Rev 19:17 Then I saw an angel standing in the sun, and he cried out with a loud voice, saying to all the birds which fly in midheaven, "Come, assemble for the great supper of God,"
>
> Rev 19:21 And the rest were killed with the sword which came from the mouth of Him who sat on the horse, and all the birds were filled with their flesh.

So what do we have here with all of this evidence? We have the Bible writers of the Gospels of Matthew, Mark and Luke showing Jesus' greatest prophecy. This prophecy was to have its fulfillment in the year AD 70 when the city of Jerusalem and its temple were destroyed. Yes, this great city was spoken of in all of its corruption in the Revelation where it said:

> Rev 18:2 And he cried out with a mighty voice, saying, "Fallen, fallen is Babylon the great! She has become a dwelling place of demons and a prison of every unclean spirit, and a prison of every unclean and hateful bird.

Yes! To the "disciple whom Jesus loved," namely, the Apostle John, Jesus gave a more detailed prophecy of the same event. This same chapter warned the Christians to get out of the wicked city before its destruction.

Rev 18:4,5 I heard another voice from heaven, saying, "Come out of her, my people, so that you will not participate in her sins and receive of her plagues; for her sins have piled up as high as heaven, and God has remembered her iniquities."
Rev 18:9 "And the kings of the earth, who committed acts of immorality and lived sensuously with her, will weep and lament over her when they see the smoke of her burning,"
Rev 18:10 standing at a distance because of the fear of her torment, saying, 'Woe, woe, the great city, Babylon, the strong city! For in one hour your judgment has come.'

Jewish Historian Josephus recorded the tragic end to the great city in language which showed the exact fulfillment of the prophecy given to John. Even though the merchants would weep over her destruction, the Roman soldiers did not:

It is therefore impossible to go distinctly over every instance of these men's iniquity. I shall therefore speak my mind here at once briefly: -

That neither did any other city ever suffer such miseries, **nor did any age ever breed a generation more fruitful in wickedness than this was, from the beginning of the world**. Finally, they brought the Hebrew nation into contempt, that they might themselves appear comparatively less impious with regard to strangers.

They confessed what was true, that they were the slaves, the scum, and the spurious and abortive offspring of our nation, while they overthrew the city themselves, and forced the Romans, whether they would or no, to gain a melancholy reputation, by acting gloriously against them, and did almost draw that fire upon the temple, which they seemed to think came too slowly; **and indeed when they saw that temple burning from the upper city, they were neither troubled at it, nor did they shed any tears on that account**, while yet these passions were discovered among the Romans themselves; which circumstances we shall speak of hereafter in their proper place, when we come to treat of such matters.[xxviii]

God could no longer tolerate the mountain of sin that was in the city. The Lamb of God was now securely in heaven and the temple was no longer necessary. This was an event which would completely put an end to the Old Covenant with its animal sacrifices. It would put an end to the wicked use of the temple for commercial purposes. It would put an end to every aspect of the Old Covenant law forever.

Although both prophecies were to be fulfilled in that same generation, in the prophecy of Revelation given to John, the timeline was much shorter, most likely five years or less. It was a prophecy of the triumph of the King of Kings and the Lord of Lords!

Chapter 7

Misleading Translations of Important Words

In the book of Revelation we find three Greek words that **are translated** as earth and world that have ***greatly misled people*** with regards to the meaning of this book. In order to properly understand the book of Revelation, we must get a handle on these Greek words. They are as follows:

- κοσμος – In English, it is pronounced *kosmos.* This word is found **three times** in the book of Revelation.
    - This word means "the world as the sum total of everything here and now."[xxix]
    - It is correctly used in most translations to mean the entire world, sometimes even the entire universe.
    - This is used in Rev 11:15; Rev 13:8; Rev 17:8
- γη – In English, ge (pronounced ghay). This word is found **64 times** in the book of Revelation.
    - This word means soil, ground, land or earth.[xxx]
    - If you pick up some dirt and put it in your hand you can say that you hold some earth in your hand.
- 3. οικουμενης – In English it is pronounced oikoumenes. This word is pronounced oikoomaynays. This word is found **twice** in the book of Revelation.
    - This word means 1. the inhabited earth, world. 2. The Roman Empire[xxxi]

- In the time of the Apostle John this was a reference to the portion of the earth "inhabited by the Greeks" or "the Roman empire" (From Thayer's Greek English Lexicon)
- This is used in Rev 3:10; Rev 16:14

By far the most common of these words used is the word γη (**ge'**). Among the five definitions given by Thayer's Greek Lexicon, we see one that reads as follows: "a country, land enclosed within fixed boundaries, a tract of land, territory, and region; simply, when it is plain from the context what land is meant, as that of the Jews." The other four are: arable land; the ground; the main land; and the earth as a whole as opposed to the heavens.

But as we look at the opening chapter of the book of Revelation, we find that it is very clear that this book has been written to the seven churches in that region. John even specifically calls them out by name, giving each of them a warning.

Therefore it is only reasonable that when we see the Greek term **ge'** that we realize that this is not speaking of the earth as a whole, but is speaking about the localized region and the people to whom this book was written. When John wanted to use a word which described the whole world, he used the Greek word **kosmos** which encompasses the entire globe, as we shall see. Let's look at how the Apostle John uses these terms in the writing of this book, and we will see how this problem is cleared up. We will also see how our translators have done us no favors in this matter when they could have been very helpful. First, let's look at Revelation 11:15:

"Then the seventh angel blew his trumpet, and there were

loud voices in heaven, saying, 'The kingdom of the world (κοσμος) has become the kingdom of our Lord and of his Christ, and he shall reign forever and ever.'"

It is obvious here that John wanted the readers to know that when he was referring to the Kingdom of our Lord Jesus Christ, he was making reference to the entire planet, earth as a whole. We know this because he used the Greek word "kosmos" This word is all encompassing in nature. It could even mean the entire universe. This makes sense when we consider the Universal nature of our God. We know that the Bible tells us in Philippians 2:9-11:

"Therefore God has highly exalted him and bestowed on him the name that is above every name, so that at the name of Jesus every knee should bow, in heaven **and on earth and under the earth,** and every tongue confess that Jesus Christ is Lord, to the glory of God the Father."

Clearly then we can see that this is a fitting use of the term "world" in Revelation 11:15, because the whole world **truly does now** belong to our Lord Jesus. Interestingly, the two Greek words translated as "earth" in the above passage are two different Greek words, neither of which is used in the book of Revelation, but that is another discussion.

Now let's look very closely at this next passage of Scripture, because it is very revealing about the way that these terms are used in the book of Revelation. The thirteenth chapter of Revelation speaks of the "seven headed, ten horned beast that comes out of the sea." The Apostle John states the following in Revelation 13:7-8:

"Also it was allowed to make war on the saints and to conquer them. And authority was given it over every tribe and people

> and language and nation, and all who dwell on earth will worship it, everyone whose name has not been written before the foundation of the world in the book of life of the Lamb who was slain"(ESV)

What is so important about this passage is that the Apostle John uses **a different Greek word** for "earth" and "world." Now if the terms "earth" and "world" mean the planet earth, then why would John use two different words in the same sentence to describe them?

Let's notice how Rev 13:7-8 is translated by "Young's Literal Translation," a translation that stems from the late 1890's:

> "and there was given to it to make war with the saints, and to overcome them, and there was given to it authority over every tribe, and tongue, and nation. And bow before it shall all who are dwelling upon **the land,** whose names have not been written in the scroll of the life of the Lamb slain from the foundation of the world;"

Do you see the difference? The first passage is from the English Standard version. It has translated the Greek word "ge" as earth, whereas Young's Literal Translation has translated the Greek word "ge" as land!

Do you see the profound effect of this translation?

In the ESV it appears that John is talking about the entire globe, whereas in the YLT we see that John is speaking of a localized region. **WOW! Do you see the bias here? ... But the ESV is not alone in this rendering.**

We find the same scenario in this passage (Revelation 13:7,8) using the NASB translation. Notice the wording here:

> It was also given to him to make war with the saints and to overcome them, and authority over every tribe and people and tongue and nation was given to him. All who dwell **on the earth** will worship him, everyone whose name has not been written from the foundation of the world in the book of life of the Lamb who has been slain.

Now notice once again (Rev 13:7-8) the wording in the YLT:

> "and there was given to it to make war with the saints, and to overcome them, and there was given to it authority over every tribe, and tongue, and nation. And bow before it shall all who are dwelling upon **the land**, whose names have not been written in the scroll of the life of the Lamb slain from the foundation of the world;"

Before we move on to the next Greek word, we must make a consideration of the final time we find the Greek word kosmos in the book of Revelation. This is found in Revelation 17:8, which we will be reading from the NIV:

> "The beast, which you saw, once was, now is not, and yet will come up out of the Abyss and go to its destruction. The inhabitants of the **earth** (γε) whose names have not been written in the book of life from the creation of the **world** (κοσμος) will be astonished when they see the beast, because it once was, now is not, and yet will come."

What we must notice here is that once again, two different Greek words are used in the same sentence. First we find the word the NIV has chosen to translate as "earth." The use of the Greek word **γε** (ge) in this sentence by the Apostle John is indicative of the fact that this was a local event. A better translation would have been "The inhabitants of the land (**γε**) whose names have not been written in the book of life from the creation of the world (**κοσμος**) will be astonished . . ."

By using the Greek word "ge" in the first incidence, we know that because the Greek language is so specific, the meaning should not be global in nature, but local in nature. Conversely, the second Greek word "kosmos" was indicative of something which was global in nature! Once again we see that our translators have failed us.

Now let's look at the next Greek word which has significance here and that is the Greek word **οικουμενης,** pronounced as oikoumenes. As stated previously, Thayer's Lexicon notes that this term is a reference to the "inhabited earth, or, in this case, "the Roman empire." When speaking of the registration which was required of all in the days of Herod, we find in 2nd chapter of the book of Luke:

> "In those days Caesar Augustus issued a decree that a census should be taken of **the entire Roman world**." (Luke 2:1 NIV)

Yes, in this passage we find the Greek word oikoumenes used in reference to the entire Roman world.

This makes much more sense than the way in is translated in the ESV. Notice the following translation of this verse:

> "In those days a decree went out from Caesar Augustus that **all the world** should be registered."

It is fairly obvious that the meaning of this word could not possibly mean the entire planet. Therefore we see that the ESV translation is not specific enough, even though in the introduction of this translation it claims "the ESV Bible text, which as an 'essentially literal' translation is especially suited for Bible Study. Here we see that this translation violates its own charter. If used like this in the book of Revelation, it could be very misleading.

So let's look at the two times we find this in the book of Revelation. First we will look at it in the English Standard Version of Revelation 3:10:

> Because you have kept my word about patient endurance, I will keep you from the hour of trial that is coming on the **whole world**_(κοσμος), to try those who dwell on the earth (γε).

This most certainly sounds like a disaster which affects the entire planet doesn't it? But as in the case of Luke 2:1, this is very misleading. Notice the same passage in the Lexham English Bible:

> Because you have kept the word of my patient endurance, I also will keep you from the hour of testing that is about to come upon the whole **inhabited world**, to put to the test those who live **on the earth**.

Here we see that the first term, "inhabited world" defines the term earth which is used later. A less confusing rendering of the test that was about to occur would be "to test those living in the land." Even the NIV has rendered this verse in a similar manner, even though it is the same word as used in Luke 2:1!

Do you see the profound effect of this mistranslation? It completely changes the meaning of this verse in the mind of the reader!

Now we come to another verse which truly is very misleading in most of our translations. Let's look first at the English Standard rendering of Revelation 16:14:

> For they are demonic spirits, performing signs, who go abroad

> to the kings of the whole world (oikoumenes), to assemble them for battle on the great day of God the Almighty.

Looking at the NIV, we see a similarly misleading translation. This certainly sounds like a global event doesn't it? But when you look at the Greek word for world here, you find that it is actually a localized event. Notice the rendering of the Lexham English Bible:

> For they are the spirits of demons performing signs that go out to the kings of the whole **inhabited world** (oikoumenes), to gather them for the battle of the great day of God the All-Powerful.

The Greek word used here is a reference once again to the *inhabited world* at that time which encompassed the **Roman Empire!** Once again, we are misled!

It is **not the word kosmos** as used when speaking of the realm of authority of Jesus as it did in Revelation 11:15. Here we noticed earlier that this realm of authority was the entire planet as explained by the Greek word that was used, and **that word was "kosmos" which means in that passage "the entire orderly arrangement, or the entire planet.** Notice once again the words of this verse:

> "The kingdom of the world (**kosmos**) has become the kingdom of our Lord and of his Christ, and he shall reign forever and ever."

No, Rev. 16:14 was NOT a global event! It was a local event (The Roman Empire) as the Greek word ***oikumenes*** shows. We should also note that the expression Day of the Lord is also not uncommon. There have been other such events recorded in the Old Testament when speaking of localized events.

Now let's look at some of the 64 times the Greek word 'ge' (γε) is used. It will once again become apparent how our translations have misled us.

In the English Standard Version we find that the Greek word 'ge' is **only translated as land 3 times**. But in Young's Literal Translation **we find it used 32 times.** Let's look at a few of these.

First of all let's compare Revelation 1:7 in these two translations:

> Rev 1:7 Behold, he is coming with the clouds, and every eye will see him, even those who pierced him, and all tribes **of the earth** will wail on account of him. Even so. Amen. (ESV)
>
> Rev 1:7 Lo, he doth come with the clouds, and see him shall every eye, even those who did pierce him, and wail because of him shall all the tribes **of the land.** Yes! Amen! (YLT)

If you closely examine the ESV translation of this verse, it **does not** make sense. How can every eye in the entire planet see him, even those who pierced him? If this truly means 'those who pierced him,' it would still have had to have happened in the first century, but we know that it is impossible that every eye could have seen him.

But the YLT **does** make sense because it shows it to be a local event that happened during the time that it would have been possible that "every eye" could see Him "even those who did pierce him."

A Comparison of ESV and the YLT translations of the Greek word ge (γε).

By reading these few comparisons, it is easy to see that there is definitely translator bias in the ESV. By doing what they are doing in this "literal translation" the ESV is deliberately promulgating a futurist perspective. Please note the following comparisons:

> (Rev 1:7 YLT) Lo, he doth come with the clouds, and see him shall every eye, even those who did pierce him, and wail because of him shall all the tribes of **the land**. Yes! Amen!
>
> (Rev 1:7 ESV) Behold, he is coming with the clouds, and every eye will see him, even those who pierced him, and all tribes of **the earth** will wail on account of him. Even so. Amen.
>
> (Rev 6:4 YLT) and there went forth another horse—red, and to him who is sitting upon it, there was given to him to take the peace from **the land**, and that one another they may slay, and there was given to him a great sword.
>
> (Rev 6:4 ESV) And out came another horse, bright red. Its rider was permitted to take peace from **the earth**, so that people should slay one another, and he was given a great sword.
>
> (Rev 6:8 YLT) and I saw, and lo, a pale horse, and he who is sitting upon him—his name is Death, and Hades doth follow with him, and there was given to them authority to kill, (over **the fourth part of the land**,) with sword, and with hunger, and with death, and by the beasts of the land.
>
> (Rev 6:8 ESV) And I looked, and behold, a pale horse! And its rider's name was Death, and Hades followed him. And they were given authority over a fourth **of the earth**, to kill with sword and with famine and with pestilence and by wild beasts of the earth.

(Rev 6:10 YLT) and they were crying with a great voice, saying, 'Till when, O Master, the Holy and the True, dost Thou not judge and take vengeance of our blood from those dwelling **upon the land?**'

(Rev 6:10 ESV) They cried out with a loud voice, "O Sovereign Lord, holy and true, how long before you will judge and avenge our blood on those who dwell **on the earth?**"

Yes, the use of the word earth as translated in the ESV portrays a global perspective, whereas the use of the word land in the YLT correctly portrays a local perspective. This is only a small portion of verses that could be compared. If you would like to do further research, please note the following verses as translated in ***Young's Literal Translation,*** and compare them to the more popular modern translations. You will see that this is a common trait of almost all of them.

(Rev 7:1) And after these things I saw four messengers, standing upon the four corners of the land, holding the four winds of the **land**, that the wind may not blow upon the land, nor upon the sea, nor upon any tree;

(Rev 7:2) and I saw another messenger going up from the rising of the sun, having a seal of the living God, and he did cry with a great voice to the four messengers, to whom it was given to injure the **land** and the sea, saying,

(Rev 7:3) 'Do not injure the **land,** nor the sea, nor the trees, till we may seal the servants of our God upon their foreheads.'

(Rev 8:7) and the first messenger did sound, and there came hail and fire, mingled with blood, and it was cast to the **land**, and the third of the trees was burnt up, and all the green grass was burnt up.

(Rev 8:13) And I saw, and I heard one messenger, flying in the

> mid-heaven, saying with a great voice, 'Woe, woe, woe, to those dwelling upon the **land** from the rest of the voices of the trumpet of the three messengers who are about to sound.'
>
> (Rev 10:2) and he had in his hand a little scroll opened, and he did place his right foot upon the sea, and the left upon the **land**,
>
> (Rev 10:5) And the messenger whom I saw standing upon the sea, and upon the **land**, did lift up his hand to the heaven,
>
> (Rev 10:6) and did swear in Him who doth live to the ages of the ages, who did create the heaven and the things in it, and the **land** and the things in it, and the sea and the things in it—that time shall not be yet,
>
> (Rev 10:8) And the voice that I heard out of the heaven is again speaking with me, and saying, 'Go, take the little scroll that is open in the hand of the messenger who hath been standing upon the sea, and upon the **land**:'
>
> (Rev 11:6) These have authority to shut the heaven, that it may not rain rain in the days of their prophecy, and authority they have over the waters to turn them to blood, and to smite the **land** with every plague, as often as they may will.
>
> (Rev 11:10) and those dwelling upon the land shall rejoice over them, and shall make merry, and gifts they shall send to one another, because these—the two prophets—did torment those dwelling upon the **land**.'

I have quoted 10 verses here, but there are many more. See for yourself by looking up Rev 11:18; Rev 12:12; Rev 12:16; Rev 13:8; Rev 13:11; Rev 13:12; Rev 13:14; Rev 14:7; Rev 16:2; Rev 17:18; and Rev 20:9.

Interestingly, the NIV, ESV, NASB, and NKJV **all translate** the Greek word *ge'* as land in Revelation 10:2-5. Note the following:

> Rev 10:2 and he had in his hand a little book which was open. He placed his right foot on the sea and his left **on the land**;
>
> Rev 10:3 and he cried out with a loud voice, as when a lion

> roars; and when he had cried out, the seven peals of thunder uttered their voices.
>
> Rev 10:4 When the seven peals of thunder had spoken, I was about to write; and I heard a voice from heaven saying, "Seal up the things which the seven peals of thunder have spoken and do not write them."
>
> Rev 10:5 Then the angel whom I saw standing on the sea and on **the land** lifted up his right hand to heaven,

It is my contention that "land" is the best translation for the Greek word "ge" in most cases. So why have these modern translations chosen to render this word as "land" in the above verses, but "earth" in the previous verses? I believe that it is **because the translators had a bias toward futurism**, and using "earth" in the previous verses protects that bias. This passage, however, could be translated in this manner, using the word "land" without endangering such a bias.

I hope this chapter has been helpful in pointing out this perspective.

Chapter 8

An Outline of the Book of Revelation

When considering the Bible's pattern with regard to prophecy, we see that a prophecy is given, and later on we see that the fulfillment is revealed. The Revelation given to John shows both the prophecy and the fulfillment as it was about to be played out. Thus from the information above, we can form an outline for the first nineteen chapters, and then delve into the fulfillment. It is **not** an outline that is unfamiliar to the first readers of the words penned by the Apostle John, because **it is similar** to other sections of the Bible. The first of such sections is from the Torah, specifically, Leviticus 26 and Deuteronomy 28. God's relationship with Israel was always defined **in terms of the covenant.** That covenant in Leviticus 26 was a simple one. If Israel would **obey God**, she would be **blessed.** If Israel **disobeyed God**, she would be subject to the **horrible curses** outlined in these two chapters (Leviticus 26:14-39; Deut. 28:15-68). Just listen to what is said in Leviticus 26. It is so exact in the precision with which God acted upon the nation of Israel, and it is **such a close match** for what happened during the destruction of Jerusalem, that it **literally**

will raise the hair up on the back of your neck! Notice the words:

> Lev 26:29-33 You shall **eat the flesh of your sons**, and you shall eat the flesh of your daughters. And I will destroy your high places and cut down your incense altars and cast your dead bodies upon the dead bodies of your idols, and my soul will abhor you. And I will **lay your cities waste** and will **make your sanctuaries desolate**, and I will not smell your pleasing aromas. And I myself will **devastate the land**, so that your enemies who settle in it shall be appalled at it. And I will **scatter you among the nations**, and I will unsheathe the sword after you, and your land shall be a desolation, and your cities shall be a waste.

And from Deuteronomy 28 we also read the shockingly accurate words:

> Deut 28:25-26 "The LORD will cause you to be defeated before your enemies. You shall go out one way against them and flee seven ways before them. And you shall be a horror to all the kingdoms of the earth. And **your dead body shall be food for all birds of the air** and for the beasts of the earth, and there shall be no one to frighten them away.
> Deut 28:49-51 The LORD will bring **a nation against you from far away, from the end of the earth, swooping down like the eagle**, a nation whose language you do not understand, a hard-faced nation who shall not respect the old or show mercy to the young. It shall eat the offspring of your cattle and the fruit of your ground, until you are destroyed; it also shall not leave you grain, wine, or oil, the increase of your herds or the young of your flock, until they have caused you to perish.
> Deut 28:56-57 **The most tender and refined woman among you**, who would not venture to set the sole of her foot on the ground because she is so delicate and tender, will begrudge to the husband she embraces, to her son and to her daughter, **her afterbirth that comes out** from between her feet and her children whom she bears, because lacking everything **she will**

> **eat them secretly**, in the siege and in the distress with which your enemy shall distress you in your towns.
> Deut 28:64-65 "And the LORD will **scatter you among all peoples**, from one end of the earth to the other, and there you shall serve other gods of wood and stone, which neither you nor your fathers have known. And among these nations you shall find no respite, and there shall be no resting place for the sole of your foot, but the LORD will give you there a trembling heart and failing eyes and a languishing soul.

Now as shockingly accurate as this is, I want you to notice something else. Notice what it says in Leviticus 26:18, 21, 24, and 28:

> Lev 26:18 And if in spite of this you will not listen to me, then I will discipline you again **sevenfold for your sins,**
> Lev 26:21 "Then if you walk contrary to me and will not listen to me, I will continue striking you, **sevenfold for your sins**.
> Lev 26:24 then I also will walk contrary to you, and I myself will strike you **sevenfold for your sins.**
> Lev 26:28 then I will walk contrary to you in fury, and I myself will discipline you **sevenfold for your sins.**

Not just once does he say this in the chapter, but **four times**! And yes, there is significance even in this. It is **not** just happenstance that he would mention this four times in Leviticus. Notice the words of the prophets in other judgments that would happen in Israel's future:

> Jer 15:3 I will appoint over them four kinds of destroyers, declares the LORD: **the sword to kill**, the **dogs to tear**, and the **birds of the air and the beasts of the earth to devour and destroy.**
> Ezek 14:21 For thus says the Lord GOD: How much more when I send upon Jerusalem my four disastrous acts of judgment, **sword, famine, wild beasts, and pestilence,** to cut off from it man and beast!

So as we can see from this, the numbers **four** and **seven** have **profound significance** when looking through the Bible's prophetic history and it is no different in looking at the last book of the Bible. In fact, we find this scenario fully developed in the book of Revelation, for there are **four sets of seven** present in its pages.

These are:

1. The letters to the **Seven** Churches;
2. The book containing the opening of the **Seven** Seals;
3. The sounding of the **Seven** Trumpets;
4. The judgment of the **Seven** Bowls of Wrath.

Thus we see that the structure is the same. The use of the numbers four and seven are once again used in the final prophecy of the Bible. These match the prophecy given to the Apostle John.

Thus, we can make an outline for the book of Revelation as follows:

1) Introduction
    a) An opening statement of the Revelation of Jesus Christ (1:1-3)
        i) A definitive time statement that this would happen **soon**.
        ii) A blessing for those who read and hear, for the time is **near.**
    b) Introduction to the message John was to send to the **seven** churches (1:4-7)
        i) Jesus now in a position of power and glory.
        ii) Soon to be coming in the clouds of Glory.
        iii) He is the Alpha and the Omega, Lord and God of all!
    c) The Island of Patmos Vision
        i) A command to write that which he is about to see, including the fact that this **is written for** the seven churches.

   ii) An astounding vision of the glorified Jesus, profoundly testifying that he is now the glorious King of Kings and Lord of Lords.
   iii) He is no longer a man. He has now returned to his glory as God the Son.

2) The Letters to the churches (2:1-3:22)
   a) Ephesus (2:1-7)
   b) Smyrna (2:8-11)
   c) Pergamum (2:12-17)
   d) Thyatira (2:18-29)
   e) Sardis (3:1-6)
   f) Philadelphia (3:7-13)
   g) Laodicea (3:14-22)
3) The Throne Room in Heaven (4:1-5:14)
   a) The scene in heaven
   b) A vision of the throne
   c) The book of the seven seals
   d) The appearance of the Lion who was also the Lamb who is worthy
   e) The worship of the Lamb of God
4) Judgment (6:1-14:19)
   a) The seven seals (6:1-8:5)
   b) The seven trumpet judgments (8:6-11:19)
   c) The ouster of Satan (12:1-17
   d) The beasts (13:1-18)
   e) The lamb and the 144,000 (14:1-5)
   f) The gospel and the wine of wrath (14:6-13)
   g) The harvest for wrath (14:14-19)
5) Victory in Heaven (15:1-19:21)
   a) The bowls
   b) Babylon's doom
   c) The Lambs victory
   d) The marriage of the Lamb
   e) The doom of the false prophets
6) Satan bound, freed, and judged (20:1-15)
7) New heaven and new earth (21:1-27)
8) The river of the water of life, The tree of life (22:1-9)
9) The final message (22:10-21)
   a) Do not seal up – **The time is near**
   b) Plagues given for adding to or taking away from the book

c) Jesus coming quickly – repeated twice

The Letters to the Churches

The two chapters that are the letters to the seven churches were **very specific**. The specific names of the Churches are given. If you have a red letter Bible, you can see that these are Jesus' words. The warnings given were specific to each individual church!

There is **no appendix**! There is **no footnote for a distant future fulfillment.** With this incredible amount of detail specified, it gives rise to ask the following question: Where is it that the Bible Commentators have gotten the idea that these Churches which are so specifically addressed herein represent certain stages of the Church of Jesus Christ in the distant future? Do you find a single verse in those passages which indicate anything of this sort? NO! You can search the words **carefully** and you will find **no such indication**.

But here is what we do see:

To the Church in Ephesus:

> . . . I am coming to **YOU** and will remove **YOUR** lampstand out of its place--unless **YOU** repent. (Rev 2:5)

To the Church in Smyrna:

> Do not fear what **YOU** are about to suffer. Behold, the devil is about to cast some of **YOU** into prison, so that **YOU** will be tested, and **YOU** will have tribulation for ten days. Be faithful until death, and I will give **YOU** the crown of life. (Rev 2:10)

To the Church in Pergamum:

> Therefore repent; or else I am coming to **YOU** quickly. . . (Rev 2:16)

To the Church in Thyatira:

> Nevertheless what **YOU** have, hold fast until I come. (Rev 2:25)

To the Church in Sardis:

> Therefore if **YOU** do not wake up, I will come like a thief, and **YOU** will not know at what hour I will come to **YOU**. (Rev3:3)

To the Church in Philadelphia:

> I am coming quickly; hold fast what **YOU** have, so that no one will take **YOUR** crown. (Rev 3:11)

To the Church in Laodicea:

> So because you are lukewarm, and neither hot nor cold, I will spit you out of My mouth. (Rev 3:16) Behold, I stand at the door and knock; (Rev 3:20)

Once again, please notice not a single word which indicates anything relating to the distant future. To the contrary, each of these Churches are addressed with the word YOU as I have highlighted in these passages. With this settled in our logical minds that **must mean** that the judgments that are given which follow this are also given as information which is relevant for **THESE SPECIFIC CHURCHES.** Of course we can learn from this just as we learn from all passages of Scripture.

> All Scripture is breathed out by God and profitable for teaching, for reproof, for correction, and for training in righteousness, (2 Tim 3:16)

But there is a huge difference between drawing application to our lives from what we read and fulfillment of prophecy. As to the timing of the judgments to follow, we are reminded of what the Apostle Peter wrote:

> The end of all things is **AT HAND**; (1 Pet 4:7)

The judgment was **AT HAND**, not thousands of years later! And then just ten verses later he tells where it would begin:

> For it is time for judgment to begin **AT THE HOUSEHOLD OF GOD;** (1 Pet 4:17)

Yes! Unquestionably, this is to fulfill the prophecy given by our Lord as He said:

> O Jerusalem, Jerusalem, the city that **kills the prophets and stones those who are sent** to it! How often would I have gathered your children together as a hen gathers her brood under her wings, and you were not willing! **Behold, your house is forsaken.** (Luke 13:34,35)

There can be no doubt. This was a judgment upon that wicked city. This directly addresses this same generation and no other one! So now, let us look at the judgments which follow to whom the Revelation was addressed.

Section Two

The Judgment Visions Given to John

(Visions 2-6)

In his book, “The Parousia” J. Stuart Russell shows that the book of Revelation can be divided up into seven visions given to the Apostle John. This seems to be appropriate, even though they are not labeled as such in the book itself.

Having looked at the first vision in chapter two, we found that the first vision was the Vision of the Seven Churches. Visions two through six deal with the judgments given to John. In this section, we will look at the Judgment Visions. We will deal with the seventh vision in section three.

Chapter 9

The Second Vision – The Seal Judgments

The Throne Room in Heaven

As previously stated, it is not a coincidence that the number 7 is used frequently in the Revelation. Among the Jews, this number was the symbol of completeness. So when we look at the message sent to the seven churches, we must realize that the number was symbolic, and it was very likely sent to many more than seven churches. It highlighted the main problems Jesus saw in the churches. Depicted in the Revelation we also find the seven spirits, the seven golden lampstands, the seven stars, seven lamps of fire before the throne, seven seals, seven horns, seven eyes, seven angels, seven trumpets, seven peals of thunder, seven thousand killed in the great earthquake, seven heads, seven diadems, seven blasphemous names, seven plagues, seven mountains and seven kings. Besides these things, we observe that there are seven visions depicted in the Revelation. In this section we will look at the judgment visions, which are visions 2 through 6. Since this is a pattern in the Revelation, it is impossible for us to think, even preposterous for us to think that in each of these cases, an exact number is represented. These numbers are in many cases symbolic of completeness.

One of the things which have caused a lot of problems in the understanding of this book is the nature of the judgments (or visions) outlined in it. What I have come to realize through various studies I have undertaken is that these judgments are actually different depictions of the same event. All of these judgments depict the judgment upon Babylon the Great, the city of Jerusalem. Notice what eighteenth century Bible Commentator John Lightfoot said about this:

> "The composure of the Book is much like **Daniel's in this, that it repeats one story over and over again,** in varied and inlarged expressions: and exceeding like Ezekiel's in method and things spoken. The style is very Prophetical, as to the things spoken; and very Hebraizing, as to the speaking of them. Exceeding much of the old Prophets language, and matter adduced to intimate new stories: and exceeding much of the Jews language, and allusion to their customs and opinions, thereby to speak the things more familiarly to be understood. And as Ezekiel wrote concerning the ruin of Jerusalem, when the ruining of it was now begun, so I suppose doth John of the final destruction of it, when the Wars and miseries were now begun, when bred its destructions."[xxxii]

So with this in mind, let's look closely at the seal judgments, and then I will show how the other judgments relate to them. As John begins to show his vision we see that the fourth chapter of Revelation takes him to the throne room in heaven. In fact, what he saw was so awesome that he had to describe it in detail. This included a detailed description of the magnificent beauty and awe of the One seated on the throne and the creatures seated around the throne praising God and giving Him glory and honor. Notice how the fourth chapter ends:

> And when the living creatures give glory and honor and thanks to Him who sits on the throne, to Him who lives forever and ever, the twenty-four elders will fall down before Him who sits on the throne, and will worship Him who lives forever and ever, and will cast their crowns before the throne, saying, "Worthy are You, our Lord and our God, to receive glory and honor and power; for You created all things, and because of Your will they existed, and were created." (Rev 4:9-11)

In chapter five we see the mention of the seven seals which would open up the judgments. No one was worthy to open these except the Lion of the tribe of Judah which is of course Jesus, and He stepped forward to open them. What we see with clarity upon reading this chapter is that God loves His saints so much that their prayers are kept in golden bowls before the throne. We also see that the words are crafted in such a way as to bring maximum honor to the Lamb of God, and that He was the only one worthy of opening the seals. Notice how this is shown in the vision:

> Then I looked, and I heard the voice of many angels around the throne and the living creatures and the elders; and the number of them was myriads of myriads, and thousands of thousands, saying with a loud voice, "Worthy is the Lamb that was slain to receive power and riches and wisdom and might and honor and glory and blessing." And every created thing which is in heaven and on the earth and under the earth and on the sea, and all things in them, I heard saying, "To Him who sits on the throne, and to the Lamb, be blessing and honor and glory and dominion forever and ever." And the four living creatures kept saying, "Amen." And the elders fell down and worshiped. (Rev 5:11-14)

The Seal Judgments

Before we look at the seal judgments, we must remember that we are at the point of fulfillment of the prophecy of the words given to Daniel. In Daniel chapter 12 we are told:

> "At that time shall arise Michael, the great prince who has charge of your people. And there shall be a time of trouble, such as never has been since there was a nation till that time. But at that time your people shall be delivered, everyone whose name shall be found written in the book. And many of those who sleep in the dust of the earth shall awake, some to everlasting life, and some to shame and everlasting contempt. And those who are wise shall shine like the brightness of the sky above; and those who turn many to righteousness, like the stars forever and ever. But you, Daniel, shut up the words and **seal the book, until the time of the end**. Many shall run to and fro, and knowledge shall increase." (Dan 12:1-4 ESV))

And now **the time of the end spoken of here has finally arrived. It is the end of the generation** that would see all these things as Jesus foretold in Matt 24:34. Let the unsealing begin!

In chapter 6 Jesus opens the first seal. Upon its opening, the first of the famous "four horsemen of the Apocalypse" is revealed. Judgment is about to be executed upon the Israelite people. Considering all of the background information we have given concerning this book, we know that the time frame for this is prior to the destruction of Jerusalem. With this in mind, here is what I consider to be the most comprehensive explanation of the meaning of the four horsemen mentioned in this chapter.

The White Horse – Our Lord has a history of using the governing authorities to do His work of judgment, and as we shall see this is no exception. The Apostle Paul confirmed this:

> Every person is to be in subjection to the governing authorities. For there is no authority except from God, and those which exist are established by God. (Rom 13:1)

God used Nebuchadnezzar in the year 587 to bring a siege upon the city of Jerusalem in judgment upon that city. One year later, the city was completely destroyed by the Babylonian armies, and the remaining people of Jerusalem were taken captive in Babylon. Now we notice:

The First Seal – A Rider on a White Horse

> Then I saw when the Lamb **broke one of the seven seals**, and I heard one of the four living creatures saying as with a voice of thunder, "Come." I looked, and behold, a white horse, and he who sat on it had a bow; and a crown was given to him, and he went out conquering and to conquer. (Rev 6:1,2)

This time, under the rule of Nero, General Vespasian would be commissioned by the Lord to execute judgment. In the year AD 66 the city came under siege. No one was allowed in or out of the city, but the war on the city would not occur yet. Thus, the rider of **the white horse** would hold in His hand a bow, which is indicative of a weapon of warfare used at a distance. As we continue:

The Second Seal - War

> When He broke the **second seal**, I heard the second living creature saying, "Come." And another, a red horse, went out; and to him who sat on it, it was granted to take peace from the earth, and that men would slay one another; and a great

> sword was given to him. (Rev 6:3,4)

The **red horse** represents the color of blood, and in this depiction, a sword is used. Beginning in Galilee, Vespasian began his destruction, **and blood flowed upon the land.** Gradually, as the people in Jerusalem began starving to death, the general worked his way to the "great city," a city doomed for complete destruction. As they arrived at the city, a wave of crucifixions began. Josephus records:

> This miserable procedure made Titus greatly to pity them, **while they caught every day five hundred Jews**; nay, some days they caught more: yet it did not appear to be safe for him to let those that were taken by force go their way, and to set a guard over so many he saw would be to make such as great deal them useless to him. The main reason why he did not forbid that cruelty was this, that he hoped the Jews might perhaps yield at that sight, out of fear lest they might themselves afterwards be liable to the same cruel treatment. **So the soldiers, out of the wrath and hatred they bore the Jews, nailed those they caught, one after one way, and another after another, to the crosses, by way of jest, when their multitude was so great, that room was wanting for the crosses, and crosses wanting for the bodies.**[xxxiii]

What a horrific event! There were continual crucifixions just outside of the walls of Jerusalem. Yes, the blood was flowing in waves!

The Third Seal - Famine:

> When He broke the third seal, I heard the third living creature saying, "Come." I looked, and behold, a black horse; and he who sat on it had a pair of scales in his hand. And I heard something like a voice in the center of the four living creatures saying, "A quart of wheat for a denarius, and three quarts of barley for a denarius; and do not damage the oil and the

wine." (Rev 6:5,6)

As this passage depicts, the third horse represents famine. This is exactly the purpose of a siege, to create havoc within the city, by means of isolation. One of the horrific effects of this siege was famine. **Can you imagine a mother eating her own child?** As appalling as this sounds, it is true! The historian Josephus notes:

> But the famine was too hard for all other passions, and it is destructive to nothing so much as to modesty; for what was otherwise worthy of reverence was in this case despised; insomuch that **children pulled the very morsels that their fathers were eating out of their very mouths**, and what was still more to be pitied, so did the mothers do as to their infants; and when those that were most dear were perishing under their hands, they were not ashamed to take from them the very last drops that might preserve their lives: and while they ate after this manner, yet were they not concealed in so doing; but the seditious every where came upon them immediately, and snatched away from them what they had gotten from others; for when they saw any house shut up, this was to them a signal that the people within had gotten some food; whereupon they broke open the doors, and ran in, **and took pieces of what they were eating almost up out of their very throats**, and this by force: the old men, who held their food fast, were beaten; and if the women hid what they had within their hands, their hair was torn for so doing; nor was there any commiseration shown either to the aged or to the infants, but they lifted up children from the ground as they hung upon the morsels they had gotten, and shook them down upon the floor.[xxxiv]

In an endnote to Josephus writings in *The Wars of the Jews*, Book 6, chapter 3, we find recorded:

> What Josephus observes here, that no parallel examples had been recorded before this time of such sieges, wherein **mothers were forced by extremity of famine to eat their own children**, as had been threatened to the Jews in the law of Moses, upon obstinate disobedience, and more than once fulfilled, (see my Boyle's Lectures, p. 210214,) is by Dr. Hudson supposed to have had two or three parallel examples in later ages.[xxxv]

How could any famine be more horrible than this?

The Fourth Seal - Death

> When the Lamb broke the fourth seal, I heard the voice of the fourth living creature saying, "Come." I looked, and behold, an ashen horse; and **he who sat on it had the name Death;** and Hades was following with him. Authority was given to them over a fourth of the earth, to kill with sword and with famine and with pestilence and by the wild beasts of the earth. (Rev 6:7,8)

There is no exaggeration about this concerning the amount of death that would occur during the Wars of the Jews. **Over 1.1 million Jews perished,** whereas only **ninety-seven thousand were taken captive. That is a ratio of only about** ***one out of eleven surviving!*** Once again we see proof positive of this from recorded history:

> 3. Now the number of those that were carried captive during this whole war was collected to be ninety-seven thousand; ***as was the number of those that perished during the whole siege eleven hundred thousand,*** the greater part of whom were indeed of the same nation [with the citizens of Jerusalem], but not belonging to the city itself; for they were come up from all the country to the feast of unleavened bread, ***and were on a sudden shut up by an army,*** which, at the very first, occasioned so great a straitness among them, that there came a pestilential destruction upon them, and

> soon afterward such a famine, as destroyed them more suddenly.[xxxvi]

The Fifth Seal – The Cry of the Martyrs

> When the Lamb broke the fifth seal, I saw underneath the altar **the souls of those who had been slain because of the word of God**, and because of the testimony which they had maintained; and they cried out with a loud voice, saying, "**How long, O Lord, holy and true, will You refrain from judging and avenging our blood on those who dwell on the earth?"** And there was given to each of them a white robe; and they were told that they should rest for a little while longer, until the number of their fellow servants and their brethren who were to be killed even as they had been, would be completed also. (Rev 6:9-11)

In order to get the proper understanding of this passage we have to remember what Jesus told the Jews before His crucifixion. He warned them in no uncertain terms:

> Therefore, behold, I am sending **YOU** prophets and wise men and scribes; some of them YOU will kill and crucify, and some of them **YOU will scourge in your synagogues, and persecute from city to city, so that upon YOU may fall the guilt of all the righteous blood shed on earth**, from the blood of righteous Abel to the blood of Zechariah, the son of Berechiah, whom you murdered between the temple and the altar. Truly I say to you, all these things will come upon this generation. (Matt 23:34-36)

This was not some prophecy for a future generation. Jesus made it very clear that **this was for the very ones to whom He was speaking!** And we will observe throughout the Gospels and the writings of the Apostles that this short range prophecy which was also tied to their past was flawlessly fulfilled. The record of the apostles and of history showed that **they were mercilessly**

persecuted. In fact, history has shown that all of the apostles except the Apostle John were killed, or crucified. As for the apostles, Fox's Book of Martyrs records that:

- The apostle James was beheaded in AD 44. Philip was scourged, thrown into prison and crucified.
- Matthew was slain with a halberd, a sort of a sword and ax combination.
- James, the overseer of the Church in Jerusalem and half-brother of Jesus had his brains dashed out with a fullers club.
- The apostle Andrew was crucified on an x shaped cross which later became known as St. Andrew's cross.
- Mark, who wrote the book of Mark, was dragged to pieces by the people of Alexandria. Peter was crucified upside down on a cross in Rome.
- Paul was led out of Rome by the soldiers and gave his neck to the sword.
- Jude was crucified.
- Thomas was thrust through by a spear. Simon was crucified.
- The only apostle who survived was John, who was said to be boiled in oil, although reportedly he miraculously escaped without injury.[xxxvii]

This speaks nothing of all of the blood of the prophets shed over the course of history by these wicked Jews. Yes, without question it is obvious that the blood of the Martyrs was on the hands of those Jews who opposed the Christian faith. It was now time for judgment!

The Sixth Seal – Unfathomable Events

As we examine the prophecy of the sixth seal we find almost an exact word for word likeness to the words spoken by Jesus before

His crucifixion. This was pointed out over a century ago by J. Stuart Russell in his book ***The Parousia***. Here is what we find in chapter 6 about the opening of this seal:

> I looked when He broke the sixth seal, and there was a great earthquake; and **the sun became black** as sackcloth made of hair, and the **whole moon became like blood**; and the **stars of the sky fell to the earth**, as a fig tree casts its unripe figs when shaken by a great wind. The sky was split apart like a scroll when it is rolled up, and every mountain and island were moved out of their places. Then the kings of the earth and the great men and the commanders and the rich and the strong and every slave and free man **hid themselves in the caves and among the rocks of the mountains**; and they said to the mountains and to the rocks, "**Fall on us and hide us** from the presence of Him who sits on the throne, and from the wrath of the Lamb; for the great day of their wrath has come, and who is able to stand?" Rev 6:12-17

Now notice the words spoken earlier by Jesus:

> ... and there will be great earthquakes, (Luke 21:11)
>
> But immediately after the tribulation of those days THE SUN WILL BE DARKENED, AND THE MOON WILL NOT GIVE ITS LIGHT, AND THE STARS WILL FALL from the sky, and the powers of the heavens will be shaken. (Matt 24: 29)
>
> Then they will begin TO SAY TO THE MOUNTAINS, 'FALL ON US,' AND TO THE HILLS, 'COVER US.' (Luke 23:30)

Using metaphoric language, Jesus spoke the same as the prophets. Listen to what Albert Barnes says about this in his commentary written over a hundred and fifty years ago. Commenting on Matthew's exact account of this, Barnes notes about this extreme verbiage:

> The images used here are ***not to be taken literally***. They are ***often employed*** by the sacred writers to denote "any great calamities." As the darkening of the sun and moon, and the falling of the stars, would be an inexpressible calamity, so any

> great catastrophe - **any overturning of kingdoms or cities, or dethroning of kings and princes is represented by the darkening of the sun and moon**, and by some terrible convulsion in the elements. Thus the destruction of Babylon is foretold in similar terms Isa_13:10, and of Tyre Isa_24:23. The slaughter in Bozrah and Idumea is predicted in the same language, Isa_34:4. See also Isa_50:3; Isa_60:19-20; Eze_32:7; Joe_3:15. [xxxviii]

So then, considering what Barnes said, let's look for ourselves. Let's read what the prophet Isaiah says in Isaiah 13:10:

> For the stars of the heavens and their constellations will not give their light; the sun will be dark at its rising, and the moon will not shed its light.

Continuing on in verse 13 we read:

> Therefore I will make the heavens tremble, and the earth will be shaken out of its place, at the wrath of the LORD of hosts in the day of his fierce anger.

Was this a prediction **of some future event by the prophet? NO!!** For in verse one of this chapter we read:

> The oracle **concerning Babylon** which Isaiah the son of Amoz saw.

That's right! This was a prophecy concerning **the destruction of Babylon.** A prophecy which came about exactly as foretold. And now we see this same language employed by our Lord in prophesying about **the destruction of Babylon the Great!**

Once again, when we look at the fulfillment, the Jewish Historian Josephus records the fact that they were hiding in the caves. Notice what is recorded:

> So now the last hope which supported the tyrants, and **that crew of robbers who were with them, was in the caves and**

> **caverns under ground;** whither, if they could once fly, they did not expect to be searched for; but endeavored, that after the whole city should be destroyed, and the Romans gone away, they might come out again, and escape from them. This was no better than a dream of theirs; for **they were not able to lie hid either from God or from the Romans.**[xxxix]

A Notable Pause – Revelation Chapter 7

Here we notice that the vision given to John has another pause. This time it is to **acknowledge the chosen ones** and see to it that these ones are secured from the judgments. This is the message of the entire seventh chapter of the Revelation. First we notice the sealing of the one hundred and forty four thousand Jews. (Rev 7:1-8) This number is **most certainly symbolic**, as it does **NOT specify a very specific number of saints**. It would be **preposterous for us to think that this is an exact number.** Is it even thinkable that God would only save precisely twelve thousand from each of the tribes? Not 12,001, not 11,999, but exactly 12,000? Of course not! As nineteenth century commentator Albert Barnes points out a very relevant fact to this discussion. Notice what he says:

> **Ten of their tribes had been long before carried away,** and the distinction of the tribes was lost, no more to be recovered, and the Hebrew people never have been, since the time of John, in circumstances to which the description here could be applicable. **These considerations make it CLEAR that the description here is SYMBOLICAL.**[xl]

Following this, we see that the saints of the Gentiles are secured. (Rev 7:9-17) We must remember that Jesus preached first to the Jews. It was only in the book of Acts that we begin to see Gentiles converted. But Jesus **DID PROMISE** that His servants would be protected.

> "But when these things begin to take place, straighten up and lift up your heads, because your redemption is drawing near." (Luke 21: 28)

Jesus did indeed promise that ***ALL*** **of His elect** would be gathered together during this time of tribulation. Notice the words:

> "And then He will send forth the angels, and will gather together His elect from the four winds, from the farthest end of the earth to the farthest end of heaven. (Mark 13:27)
>
> And the Lord said, "Hear what the unrighteous judge said; now, will not God bring about justice for His elect who cry to Him day and night, and will He delay long over them? "I tell you that He will bring about justice for them quickly. . ." (Luke 18:6-8)

Historian Eusebius confirms this protection upon his servants!

> But the people of the church in Jerusalem had been commanded by a revelation, vouchsafed to approved men there before the war, **to leave the city and to dwell in a certain town of Perea called Pella.** And when those that believed in Christ had come there from Jerusalem, then, as if the royal city of the Jews and the whole land of Judea were entirely destitute of holy men, **the judgment of God at length overtook those who had committed such outrages against Christ and his apostles, and totally destroyed that generation of impious men.**[xli]

Now that **the servants of God are protected**, it is time to move on.

The Seventh Seal – A Transition

Now as we open the seventh seal, we find an appalling silence:

> When the Lamb broke the seventh seal, there was silence in heaven for about half an hour. And I saw the seven angels who stand before God, and seven trumpets were given to them. Another angel came and stood at the altar, holding a golden censer; and much incense was given to him, so that he might add it to the prayers of all the saints on the golden altar which was before the throne. And the smoke of the incense, with the prayers of the saints, went up before God out of the angel's hand. Then the angel took the censer and filled it with the fire of the altar, and threw it to the earth; and there followed peals of thunder and sounds and flashes of lightning and an earthquake. (Rev 8:1-5)

The silence in heaven was no doubt because of the fact that the devastation of seal judgments were so appalling. Now we will see that with the introduction of the seventh seal, another view from a different perspective of these devastating judgments is about to be shown. The seven angels are about to blow the trumpets.

Chapter 10

The Third Vision

The Trumpet Judgments

With the introduction of the trumpet judgments, it was time for the prayers of the saints to be answered. As mentioned earlier it was:

> "How long, O Lord, holy and true, will You refrain from judging and avenging our blood on those who dwell on the earth?" (Rev 6:10)

Now we will see from a different perspective the judgment that came upon those who persecuted and killed those servants of the living God!

> And the seven angels who had the seven trumpets prepared themselves to sound them. The first sounded, and there came hail and fire, mixed with blood, and they were thrown to the **EARTH**; and a third of the earth was burned up, and a third of the trees were burned up, and all the green grass was burned up. The second angel sounded, and something like **a great mountain burning with fire** was thrown into the sea; and a third of the sea became blood, and a third of the creatures which were in the sea and had life, died; and a third of the ships were destroyed. The third angel sounded, and a great star fell from heaven, burning like a torch, and it fell on a third of the rivers and on the springs of waters. The name of the

> star is called Wormwood; and a third of the waters became wormwood, and many men died from the waters, because they were made bitter. The fourth angel sounded, and a third of the sun and a third of the moon and a third of the stars were struck, so that a third of them would be darkened and the day would not shine for a third of it, and the night in the same way. Then I looked, and I heard an **EAGLE** flying in midheaven, saying with a loud voice, "Woe, woe, woe to those who dwell on the earth, because of the remaining blasts of the trumpet of the three angels who are about to sound!" (Rev 8:6-13)

Before we take this apart, I would like to point up what appears to be an error, or perhaps an instance of translator bias by the translators of the NASB. Here is Young's literal translation of these two verses:

> And the seven messengers who are having the seven trumpets did prepare themselves that they may sound; and the first messenger did sound, and there came hail and fire, mingled with blood, and it was cast to the **LAND**, and the third of the trees was burnt up, and all the green grass was burnt up. (Rev 8:6,7 YLT)

By the translation of the Greek word **γε** (ge) as EARTH (in the NASB) instead of LAND as is done in Young's literal Translation, it is falsely assumed that this judgment has global implications. As we have already shown in an earlier chapter, this misleads the reader. The judgments spoken of here are **NOT global** but **LOCAL** to the area of Judea. Once again I will reiterate, this is crucial to the understanding of the book of Revelation.

Now as we go back to verse 7, we find that as Adam Clarke points out in his commentary regarding the "hail and fire, mixed with blood" that was thrown to the earth:

> This was something like the ninth plague of Egypt. See Exo 9:18-24 : "The Lord sent thunder and hail - and fire mingled with the hail - and the fire ran along upon the ground." In the hail and fire mingled with blood, some fruitful imaginations might find gunpowder and cannon balls, and canister shot and bombs.[xlii]

The fire of God's judgment was prevalent throughout the land. The nation of Israel was symbolic of a mountain. Why, because they were the nation which was prophesied to bring the Savior to the earth. Now after rejecting that Savior, they set themselves up for a disaster of magnanimous proportions! Remember that Jesus himself prophesied this when He said:

> When He approached Jerusalem, He saw the city and wept over it, saying, "If you had known in this day, even you, the things which make for peace! But now they have been hidden from your eyes. "For the days will come upon you when your enemies will throw up a barricade against you, and surround you and hem you in on every side, and they will level you to the ground and your children within you, and they will not leave in you one stone upon another, because you did not recognize the time of your visitation." (Luke 19:41-43)

This was fulfilled in a mighty way. Not only did the Roman soldiers under the reign of Vespasian and through General Titus burn, pillage, and destroy trees, grass, people and villages. Notice what Josephus records:

> And now the Romans, although they were greatly distressed in getting together their materials, raised their banks in one and twenty days, **after they had cut down all the trees that were in the country that adjoined to the city,** and that for ninety furlongs round about, as I have already related. And truly the very view itself of the country was a melancholy thing; for those places which were before adorned with trees and pleasant gardens were now become a desolate country every

> way, **and its trees were all cut down: nor could any foreigner that had formerly seen Judea and the most beautiful suburbs of the city, and now saw it as a desert**, but lament and mourn sadly at so great a change: for the war had laid all the signs of beauty quite waste: nor if any one that had known the place before, had come on a sudden to it now, would he have known it again; but though he were at the city itself, yet would he have inquired for it notwithstanding.[xliii]

Even the zealots were objects of destruction themselves. They were intent on ruining everything as described by Josephus in the following manner:

> To say all in a word, no other gentle passion was so entirely lost among them as mercy; for what were the greatest objects of pity did most of all irritate these wretches, and they transferred their rage from the living to those that had been slain, and from the dead to the living. Nay, the terror was so very great, that he who survived called them that were first dead happy, as being at rest already; as did those that were under torture in the prisons, declare, that, upon this comparison, those that lay unburied were the happiest.
>
> **These men, therefore, trampled upon all the laws of men, and laughed at the laws of God; and for the oracles of the prophets**, they ridiculed them as the tricks of jugglers; yet did these prophets foretell many things concerning [the rewards of] virtue, and [punishments of] vice, which when these zealots violated, they occasioned the fulfilling of those very prophecies belonging to their own country; for there was a certain ancient
>
> oracle of those men, **that the city should then be taken and the sanctuary burnt, by right of war**, when a sedition should invade the Jews, and their own hand should pollute the temple of God. Now while these zealots did not [quite] disbelieve these predictions, **they made THEMSELVES the instruments of their accomplishment.**[xliv]

It was as if this land which was so much like a mountain of

strength because of God's favor was now being thrown into the sea, never to rise again as a nation under that protection. Meanwhile General Titus and his soldiers were burning and pillaging the land of Israel from Galilee to Masada and from the Mediterranean Sea to Jericho with great abandon. Notice the following:

> And when **he had laid waste all the places** about the toparchy of Thamnas, he passed on to Lydda and Jamnia; and when both these cities had come over to him, he placed a great many of those that had come over to him [from other places] as inhabitants therein, and then came to Emmaus, where he seized upon the passage which led thence to their metropolis, and fortified his camp, and leaving the fifth legion therein, he came to the toparchy of Bethletephon. **He then destroyed that place, and the neighboring places, by fire,** and fortified, at proper places, the strong holds all about Idumea; and when he had seized upon two villages, which were in the very midst of Idumea, Betaris and Caphartobas, **he slew above ten thousand of the people, and carried into captivity above a thousand, and drove away the rest** of the multitude, and placed no small part of his own forces in them, **who overran and laid waste THE WHOLE MOUNTAINOUS COUNTRY;** while he, with the rest of his forces, returned to Emmaus, **whence he came down through the country of Samaria,** and hard by the city, by others called Neapoils, (or Sichem,) but by the people of that country Mabortha, to Corea, where he pitched his camp, on the second day of the month Desius [Sivan]; and on the day following he came to Jericho; on which day Trajan, one of his commanders, joined him with the forces he brought out of Perea, all the places beyond Jordan being subdued already.[xlv]

These are horrendous events that took place, and show the profound nature of the effect of what is spoken of in the eighth chapter. The **WHOLE MOUNTAINOUS COUNTRY** was laid waste! There was mass destruction by fire and pillage of the nation of Israel.

In verses 9-13, we see a great symbolism shown with hyperbolic language. As it pronounces the judgment in the precise measurement of "one third" on many things relating to the environment of the land of Israel, it would be impossible to think that this should be historically verified as a literal quantity. As we have pointed out previously this type of language is commonly used by the prophets to show the devastating effects of the disastrous judgment. However, verse thirteen is very much noteworthy. Notice what is said:

> Then I looked, and I heard an **EAGLE** flying in midheaven, saying with a loud voice, "Woe, woe, woe to those who dwell on the earth, because of the remaining blasts of the trumpet of the three angels who are about to sound!"

There is great significance in the mention of the eagle in this verse. The eagle was the symbol of the Roman army. Yes the judgment at the hand of God using the Roman army would continue! However, once again we see futurist translator bias in the NASB and many other translations. The best translation of the Greek word ***ge*** is land as shown by Young's Literal Translation:

> 'Woe, woe, woe, to those dwelling upon **THE LAND** from the rest of the voices of the trumpet of the three messengers who are about to sound.'

The trumpet judgments were being brought on by **Almighty God** who is using the **Roman army** to accomplish this judgment upon the **land of Israel**, not the whole earth.

Next we see the blowing of the fifth trumpet.

> Then the fifth angel sounded, and I saw a star from heaven which had fallen to the earth; and the key of the bottomless pit was given to him. He opened the bottomless pit, and smoke went up out of the pit, like the smoke of a great furnace; and the sun **and the air were darkened** by the smoke of the pit. Then out of the smoke came locusts upon the earth, and power was given them, as the scorpions of the earth have power. They were told not to hurt the grass of the earth, nor any green thing, nor any tree, but only the men who do not have the seal of God on their foreheads. And they were not permitted to kill anyone, but to torment for five months; and their torment was like the torment of a scorpion when it stings a man. And in those days men will seek death and will not find it; they will long to die, and death flees from them**. The appearance of the locusts was like horses prepared for battle;** and on their heads appeared to be crowns like gold, and their faces were like the faces of men. They had hair like the hair of women, and their teeth were like the teeth of lions. They had breastplates like breastplates of iron; and the sound of their wings was like the sound of chariots, of many horses rushing to battle. (Rev 9:1-10)

This judgment is very similar to what is spoken of by the prophet Joel as the Babylonian army marched towards Jerusalem the first time to destroy it. Notice the words of Joel the prophet:

> Blow a trumpet in Zion, And sound an alarm on My holy mountain! Let all the inhabitants of the land tremble, For the day of the LORD is coming; Surely it is near, A day of darkness and gloom, A day of clouds and thick darkness. As the dawn is spread over the mountains, So there is a great and mighty people; There has never been anything like it, Nor will there be again after it To the years of many generations. **A fire consumes before them And behind them a flame burns.** The land is like the garden of Eden before them But a desolate wilderness behind them, And nothing at all escapes them. **Their appearance is like the appearance of horses; And like war horses, so they run.** With a noise as of chariots They leap on the tops of the mountains, Like the crackling of a flame of

> fire consuming the stubble, Like a mighty people arranged for battle. **Before them the people are in anguish; All faces turn pale.** They run like mighty men, They climb the wall like soldiers; And they each march in line, Nor do they deviate from their paths. They do not crowd each other, They march everyone in his path; When they burst through the defenses, They do not break ranks. They rush on the city, They run on the wall; They climb into the houses, They enter through the windows like a thief. **Before them the earth quakes, The heavens tremble, The sun and the moon grow dark And the stars lose their brightness.** The LORD utters His voice before His army; Surely His camp is very great, For strong is he who carries out His word. The day of the LORD is indeed great and very awesome, And who can endure it? (Joel 2:1-11)

Yes, the language is very much similar as now we see the Roman armies doing the desolation instead of the Babylonians. In both cases through much symbolic language we see the awesome effect of God's judgment upon the land! Even the zealots joined in on the pillage of the land as Josephus records:

> And now a fourth misfortune arose, in order to bring our nation to destruction. There was a fortress of very great strength not far from Jerusalem, which had been built by our ancient kings, both as a repository for their effects in the hazards of war, and for the preservation of their bodies at the same time. It was called Masada. . . . And indeed **these men laid all the villages that were about the fortress waste, and made the whole country desolate;** while there came to them every day, from all parts, not a few men as corrupt as themselves. At that time all the other regions of Judea that had hitherto been at rest were in motion, by means of the robbers. Now as it is in a human body, if the principal part be inflamed, all the members are subject to the same distemper; so, by means of the sedition and disorder that was in the metropolis,. had the wicked men that were in the country opportunity to ravage the same. Accordingly, **when every one of them had plundered their own villages, they then retired**

> **into the desert;** [xlvi]

As prophesied by our Lord, destruction was upon them, and it was coming from every direction.

Next we see the blowing of the sixth trumpet.

> And the sixth messenger did sound, and I heard a voice out of the four horns of the altar of gold that is before God, saying to the sixth messenger who had the trumpet, 'Loose the four messengers who are bound at the great river Euphrates;' and loosed were the four messengers, who have been made ready for the hour, and day, and month, and year, that they may kill the third of men; and the number of the forces of the horsemen *is* two myriads of myriads, and I heard the number of them. And thus I saw the horses in the vision, and those sitting upon them, having breastplates of fire, and jacinth, and brimstone; and the heads of the horses *are* as heads of lions, **and out of their mouths proceedeth fire, and smoke, and brimstone; by these three were the third of men killed, from the fire, and from the smoke, and from the brimstone, that is proceeding out of their mouth,** for their authorities are in their mouth, and in their tails, for their tails *are* like serpents, having heads, and with them they do injure; and the rest of men, who were not killed in these plagues, neither did reform from the works of their hands, that they may not bow before the demons, and idols, those of gold, and those of silver, and those of brass, and those of stone, and those of wood, that are neither able to see, nor to hear, nor to walk, yea they did not reform from their murders, nor from their sorceries, nor from their whoredoms, nor from their thefts. (Rev 9:13-21 YLT)

The sounding of this trumpet brings to mind the temple arrangement. The temple altar was set up like the heavenly altar before God. However, this trumpet is sounded in heaven from the very presence of the Most Holy one. Much symbolic imagery is used in these verses, but the collaboration of the armies was real. Now these forces which were in the vicinity of the Euphrates River would come together as a united force to cause the destruction of the land. Josephus describes the support armies in the following manner:

> Whether, therefore, we estimate the capacity of governing from the skill of a person in years, we ought to have Vespasian, - or whether from the strength of a young man, we ought to have Titus; for by this means we shall have the advantage of both their ages, for that they will afford strength to those that shall be made emperors, **they having already three legions, besides other auxiliaries from the neighboring kings, and will have further all the armies in the east to support them, as also those in Europe, so they as they are out of the distance and dread of Vitellius**, besides such auxiliaries as they may have in Italy itself; that is, Vespasian's brother, (21) and his other son [Domitian]; the one of whom will bring in a great many of those young men that are of dignity, while the other is intrusted with the government of the city, which office of his will be no small means of Vespasian's obtaining the government.[xlvii]

Despite the horrible events which history has outlined that occurred on that nation of Israel and the city of Jerusalem, there was no repentance. The destruction would be complete!

As for the seventh trumpet, we will wait until we see a couple of more things happen for this to occur.

The Little Book

The tenth chapter of the book reveals some **very important information regarding this prophecy.** Notice the words given to the apostle:

> I saw another strong angel coming down out of heaven, clothed with a cloud; and the rainbow was upon his head, and his face was like the sun, and his feet like pillars of fire; and he had in his hand **a little book** which was open. He placed his

> right foot on the sea and his left on the land; and he cried out with a loud voice, as when a lion roars; and when he had cried out, the seven peals of thunder uttered their voices. When the seven peals of thunder had spoken, I was about to write; and I heard a voice from heaven saying, "Seal up the things which the seven peals of thunder have spoken and do not write them." Then the angel whom I saw standing on the sea and on the land lifted up his right hand to heaven, and swore by Him who lives forever and ever, who created heaven and the things in it, and the earth and the things in it, and the sea and the things in it, **that there will be DELAY NO LONGER**, but in the days of the voice of the seventh angel, when he is about to sound, **then the mystery of God is FINISHED**, as He preached to His servants the prophets. Then the voice which I heard from heaven, I heard again speaking with me, and saying, "Go, take the book which is open in the hand of the angel who stands on the sea and on the land." So I went to the angel, telling him to give me the little book. And he said to me, "Take it and eat it; it will make your stomach bitter, but in your mouth it will be sweet as honey." I took the little book out of the angel's hand and ate it, and in my mouth it was sweet as honey; and when I had eaten it, my stomach was made bitter. And they said to me, "You must prophesy again concerning many peoples and nations and tongues and kings." (Rev 10:1-11)

This chapter contains a verbal representation of a glorious angel. The angel is described by his strength, by his attire, and by the attributes which make up his appearance. His face is as the sun, and his feet with pillars of fire. As to the identity of this angel, we are uncertain. One foot is on the sea, and the other is on the land. He has a little book in his hand by which he **SWORE BY HIM WHO LIVES FOREVER** that there would be **NO MORE** delay.

Do you realize the **profound implication of this statement**? Why would anyone think that this prophecy would take place hundreds or thousands of years later? If that were true, **then the**

angel LIED or was in ERROR! This is absolutely IMPOSSIBLE! God was about to bring about the judgment that he promised in order to answer the **beleaguered cries of the saints** who pleaded:

> **HOW LONG O LORD**, holy and true, will You refrain from judging and avenging our blood on those who dwell on the earth?" (Rev 6:10)

He follows this up in this tenth chapter and verse seven by declaring that the mystery of God is **FINISHED**. He does **NOT SAY** that it was **delayed, held off, to happen in the future,** or a prophecy to simulate the ages of man! He very specifically declares that the judgment about to be spoken **would happen WITHOUT DELAY, and would bring a COMPLETE AND FINAL END to the mysteries of God!**

This is also a direct indication that the judgments received by the apostle **were indeed just different depictions of the same event.** How do we know this? Because there are still more judgments described in this book. If indeed they were separate judgments, the angel would not make the statement that after this vision **the mystery of God is FINISHED, for it would be a false statement.**

Following this we see that he was told that the eating of this book would be sweet in his mouth, but bitter in his stomach. Oh yes, it would be **SWEET** for God to bring about the avenging of the blood of the saints and the prophets, but it would bring about a **BITTER END** to the prominence of the nation of Israel, the Old Law covenant, and the sacrificial form of worship, and the beloved and magnificent temple of God. The judgment was complete and final! Because of the loving sacrifice of the true Lamb of God, these things were no longer necessary!

Finally the chapter states that John would prophesy again before people, nations, tongues, and kings. The exact meaning of this is unknown. But here are the possibilities:

1. John would write another book that would contain prophecies seen by those groups
2. There are more prophecies following the trumpet judgments in this revelation which would be put before these groups
3. The visions following this would be relevant for other groups later on in history.

I believe that the last two statements do not make sense because the audience for the Revelation is very clearly stated as being written to the seven churches listed in Revelation chapter 1 verse eleven:

> "What you see, write in a book and send *it* to the seven churches which are in Asia: to Ephesus, to Smyrna, to Pergamos, to Thyatira, to Sardis, to Philadelphia, and to Laodicea." (Rev 1:11 NKJV)

Therefore, it is my conclusion that this was not the last book written by John. The last book would have been either the Epistles, or the Gospel of John. If John was indeed an old man living in exile on the island of Patmos in the AD 90's, then he would have plenty of time for such writings under the inspiration of Holy Spirit. I am sure that John was busy during the time he had left in exile on that island.

The Measuring of the Temple of God

As we mentioned in chapter two of this book, now we have come to a passage which confirms beyond any doubt that the Revelation given to John was written before the destruction of Jerusalem. For now we see that the temple is still in existence.

> Then I was given a measuring rod like a staff, and I was told, "Rise and **measure the temple of God** and the altar and those who worship there, but do not measure the court outside the temple; leave that out, for it is given over to the nations, and they will trample the holy city for forty-two months. And I will grant authority to my two witnesses, and they will prophesy for 1,260 days, clothed in sackcloth." (Rev 11:1-3 ESV)

As previously stated, measuring the temple **would be impossible** if the temple was not present at the time of the writing. This is reminiscent of the command given to the prophet Ezekiel:

> When he brought me there, behold, there was a man whose appearance was like bronze, with a linen cord and a measuring reed in his hand. And he was standing in the gateway. (Ezekiel 40:3 ESV)

Adam Clarke notes this in his commentary on Rev 11:1:

> This must refer to the temple of Jerusalem; and this is another presumptive evidence that it was yet standing.

The Two Witnesses

After this command is given, we find the mention of the two witnesses of Christ. There has been much speculation as to the identity of these two witnesses, and quite frankly, since there has been nothing found which documents their identity, we will say that we do not know who they were. After searching the historical documents, we find no mention of them or their identity. We do not even know if they are literal or symbolic.

They were given the assignment to prophesy for 1260 days in sackcloth. This would be the same time as was spoken of by Daniel in his reference to the "time, times, and a half a time" (Daniel 7:25)

Unmistakably, the sources for this time statement are Luke 21:24: "and Jerusalem will be trampled underfoot by the Gentiles, until the times of the Gentiles are fulfilled," and Daniel's referent to "the time, times, and half time" in (Daniel 7:25 and 12:12).

As for the documented evidence of the two witnesses, the closest thing I could find about this is taken from a highly suspicious document known as **the Gospel of Nicodemus.** This document is purported to have been derived from the original Hebrew document called **The Acts of Pontius Pilate** however some sources say it was compiled sometime in the fourth century from fragments pieced together from this original document. Nonetheless I have decided to show it here for the record.

> and when we were deliberating among one another about the miracles which Jesus had wrought, we found many witnesses of our own country, who declared that they had seen him alive after his death, and that they heard him discoursing with his disciples, and saw him ascending into the height of the heavens, and entering into. **And we saw two witnesses**, whose bodies Jesus raised from the dead, who told us of many strange things which Jesus did among the dead, of which we have a written account in our hands.[xlviii]

As you can see, even though this passage from a potentially unreliable apocryphal gospel mentions these two witnesses, there is nothing at all which identifies them.

As we continue in Revelation chapter eleven we see:

> these are the two olive *trees* , and the two lamp-stands that before the God of the earth do stand; and if any one may will to injure them, fire doth proceed out of their mouth, and doth devour their enemies, and if any one may will to injure them, thus it behoveth him to be killed. These have authority to shut the heaven, that it may not rain rain in the days of their prophecy, and authority they have over the waters to turn them to blood, and to smite the land with every plague, as often as they may will. (Rev 11:4-6 YLT)

From these verses we find an indication that the two witnesses are most likely symbolic in nature. The entire passage seems similar to the account in Zechariah chapter four. But in this passage John uses these emblems shows that these two witnesses could be compared to two Olive trees in that they would supply oil to the lamp stands. The end result would be that they would supply light to the churches to which the Revelation was addressed. The hyperbolic language which follows shows that there would be a great plague upon the land as a result of the light shown and the persecution which would be entailed as a result of the desire on the part of those who despised Jesus to suppress this light. As a result of this immense persecution and prior to the siege of Jerusalem, and in many of the surrounding communities, and many Christians were ruthlessly martyred for the sake of the message of the kingdom of God.

> 'And when they may finish their testimony, the beast that is coming up out of the abyss shall make war with them, and overcome them, and kill them, and their dead bodies *are* upon the broad-place of the great city (that is called spiritually Sodom, and Egypt, where also our Lord was crucified,) and

> they shall behold—they of the peoples, and tribes, and tongues, and nations—their dead bodies three days and a half, and their dead bodies they shall not suffer to be put into tombs, and those dwelling upon the land shall rejoice over them, and shall make merry, and gifts they shall send to one another, because these—the two prophets—did torment those dwelling upon the land.' And after the three days and a half, a spirit of life from God did enter into them, and they stood upon their feet, and great fear fell upon those beholding them, and they heard a great voice out of the heaven saying to them, 'Come up hither;' and they went up to the heaven in the cloud, and their enemies beheld them; and in that hour came a great earthquake, and the tenth of the city did fall, and killed in the earthquake were names of men—seven thousands, and the rest became affrighted, and they gave glory to the God of the heaven. The second woe did go forth, lo, the third woe doth come quickly. (Rev 11:7-14 YLT)

In verse seven we are introduced to the Beast which comes out of the abyss and kills the saints. There is much more that will be said about this beast later on. But as to the message in verses seven through eleven, we come up empty. For other than that spoken above, there seems to be no historical evidence of such an event as a literal resurrection and ascension of individuals like this having taken place.

Proceeding onward, in verses twelve through fourteen, we see that there was coming destructive judgment at the hands of God, not only from the Roman armies, but within from the Zealots, who even called upon the Edomites, (Idumeans). Notice how the beginning of these natural means of destruction to come is described by Josephus when the city was being pillaged by the Zealots who called upon the Idumeans for assistance:

> But the shame that would attend them in case they returned

> without doing any thing at all, so far overcame that their repentance, that they lay all night before the wall, though in a very bad encampment; for there broke out a prodigious storm in the night, with the utmost violence**, and very strong winds, with the largest showers of rain, with continued lightnings, terrible thunderings, and amazing concussions and bellowings of the earth, that was in an earthquake**. These things were a manifest indication that some destruction was coming upon men, when the system of the world was put into this disorder; and any one would guess that these wonders foreshowed some grand calamities that were coming.[xlix]

When the Idumeans finally entered the city, this was the horrifying result:

> And now the outer temple was all of it **overflowed with blood**; and that day, as it came on, **they saw eight thousand five hundred dead bodies there.**[l]

Yes, the judgment of the Jewish nation continues! Now we are ready for the seventh trumpet.

The Seventh Trumpet

The blowing of the seventh trumpet signals the announcement of the eternal reign of Christ. This is the notification that the entire Levitical Sacrificial form of government represented by the Old Covenant was about to end forever. The New Covenant is now fully implemented. The full implementation of this New Covenant has been on notice since Jesus declared:

> Truly I say to you, this generation will not pass away until all these things take place. Heaven and earth will pass away, but My words will not pass away. (Matt 24:34,35)

Yes, that generation which was still in existence was about to see the passing away of "heaven and earth," as mentioned earlier. This is a reference to the temple, the Levitical Sacrificial form of

Government and all that it represents in the Jewish system of things.

It is as the writer of Hebrews described:

> For he finds fault with them when he says: "Behold, the days are coming, declares the Lord, when I will establish a **NEW COVENANT** with the house of Israel and with the house of Judah, not like the covenant that I made with their fathers on the day when I took them by the hand to bring them out of the land of Egypt. For they did not continue in my covenant, and so I showed no concern for them, declares the Lord. For this is the covenant that I will make with the house of Israel after those days, declares the Lord: I will put my laws into their minds, and write them on their hearts, and I will be their God, and they shall be my people. And they shall not teach, each one his neighbor and each one his brother, saying, 'Know the Lord,' for they shall all know me, from the least of them to the greatest. For I will be merciful toward their iniquities, and I will remember their sins no more." **In speaking of a new covenant, he makes the first one OBSOLETE. And what is becoming obsolete and growing old is ready to vanish away.** (Hebrews 8:8-13)

The end of the age **was about to occur! Now the ETERNAL kingdom of God would reign forever.**

> And the seventh messenger did sound, and there came great voices in the heaven, saying, 'The kingdoms of the **WORLD** did become *those* of our Lord and of His Christ, and **he shall reign to the ages of the ages!'** (Rev 11:15)

I would like to point out here that when this verse says "The kingdoms of the **WORLD** did become those of our Lord and of His Christ" we see the use of the Greek word **κοσμος (kosmos).** This is **NOT** making reference to the realm of the local area, and proceeding to the area of the entire world, as this word indicates. In fact its meaning is "the orderly arrangement," and is sometimes used to indicate the entire universe.

Continuing, we see:

> and the twenty and four elders, who before God are sitting upon their thrones, did fall upon their faces, and did bow before God, saying, 'We give thanks to Thee, O Lord God, the Almighty, who art, and who wast, and who art coming, because Thou hast taken Thy great power and didst reign; and the nations were angry, and Thine anger did come, and the time of the dead, to be judged, and to give the reward to Thy servants, to the prophets, and to the saints, and to those fearing Thy name, to the small and to the great, and to destroy those who are **destroying the LAND**.' And opened was the sanctuary of God in the heaven, and there was seen the ark of His covenant in His sanctuary, and there did come lightnings, and voices, and thunders, and an earthquake, and great hail. (Rev 11:16-19 YLT)

So now we are about to see yet another perspective of the judgment upon the land of Israel. These are represented in the 16th chapter of the book. I would like to reiterate what I said before concerning these judgments. **These judgments received by the apostle were indeed just different depictions of the same event.** How do we know this? **Because the seventh angel stated that at the blowing of the seventh trumpet, the mystery of God is finished!** But there are still more judgments described in this book. If indeed they were separate judgments, the angel would not make the statement that after this vision **the mystery of God is FINISHED, for it would be a false statement.**

Before we get to what are described as the seven vials or bowls, we must examine the next vision given to John. As we shall see, it contains much more vivid symbolic imagery.

Chapter 11

The Fourth Vision

The Woman, Israel

> And a great sign was seen in the heavens, a woman having been clothed with the sun, and the moon was underneath her feet; and on her head a crown of twelve stars; and having *a babe* in womb. She cries, being in labor, and having been distressed to bear. (Rev 12:1,2)

Here we see a symbolic representation of faithful Israel, who is shown with an exalted status. Israel is frequently labeled as a woman by the prophets. Notice Isaiah 54:5-6:

> "For your husband is your Maker, Whose name is the LORD of hosts; And your Redeemer is the Holy One of Israel, Who is called the God of all the earth. "For the LORD has called you, Like a wife forsaken and grieved in spirit, Even like a wife of one's youth when she is rejected," Says your God. (Isa 54:5,6)

She is also labeled as a harlot. This will be significant later:

> "Moreover, you played the harlot with the Assyrians because you were not satisfied; you played the harlot with them and still were not satisfied. "You also multiplied your harlotry with the land of merchants, Chaldea, yet even with this you were not satisfied."'" (Ezekiel 16:28,29 See also Jeremiah 3:6-8)

She has also been pictured by the prophets as a mother giving birth. Notice the words of the prophet Isaiah:

> As the pregnant woman approaches the time to give birth, She writhes and cries out in her labor pains, Thus were we before You, O LORD. We were pregnant, we writhed in labor, We gave birth, as it seems, only to wind. We could not accomplish deliverance for the earth, Nor were inhabitants of the world born. (Isaiah 26:17,18) See also Isaiah 66:7-12.

Yes, throughout the centuries, the history of the nation of Israel has been very much sorted. God has loved them at times, and then judged them for their unfaithfulness. But unquestionably, this woman had been distressed for centuries as she waited for the promised Messiah **to crush Satan** and bring in the everlasting Kingdom of God! But the dreadful enemy is lurking.

The Great Red Dragon

> And another sign was seen in the heavens. And, behold, a great red dragon having seven heads and ten horns! And on his heads were seven diadems, and his tail drew the third *part* of the stars of the heaven, and he throws them to the earth. And the dragon stood before the woman being about to bear, so that when she bears he might devour her child. And she bore a son, a male, who is going to shepherd all the nations with an iron staff. And her child was caught away to God, and *to* His throne. And the woman fled into the wilderness, where she had a place, it having been prepared from God, that there they might nourish her a thousand two hundred and sixty days. (Rev 12:1-6 From the Rotherham Emphasized Bible)
>
> Note: This entire chapter (Chapter 12) will be quoted from the Rotherham Emphasized Bible 1902.

Centuries ago the prophet Isaiah mentions the dragon:

> In that day the LORD will punish Leviathan the fleeing serpent, With His fierce and great and mighty sword, Even Leviathan

> the twisted serpent; And **He will kill the dragon who lives in the sea.** (Isa 27:1 NASB)

Yes, here we find the great dragon, the deceiver, who will manifest his power through the use of the beast (more on this later). But try though he may, there was no way that this dragon was going to thwart the promise of God **to deliver the promised Messiah,** and in exactly the right time according to the prophets.

Satan Thrown Down to Earth

> And war occurred in Heaven, Michael and his angels making war against the dragon. And the dragon and his angels made war, but they did not have strength, nor yet was place found for them in Heaven. And the great dragon was cast out, the old serpent being called devil, and, Satan; he deceiving the whole habitable world was cast out onto the earth, and his angels were cast out with him. (Rev 12:7-9)

So here we have the great dragon Satan, who has pulled out all stops, but has been unable to stop the birth and appearance of the promised Messiah. And now he has been kicked out of heaven and thrown to the earth. Can you imagine the **horrendous fury** of that dragon as he has been **denied the power** to stop the presence of the coming Messiah, and **denied the ability to reside in heaven?** We will soon see the manifestation of that fury. Now let's continue:

> And I heard a great voice saying in Heaven, Now has come the salvation and power and the kingdom of our God, and the authority of His Christ, because the accuser of our brothers is thrown down, the one accusing them before our God day and night. And they overcame him because of the blood of the Lamb, and because of the Word of their testimony. And they did not love their soul even until death. (Rev 12:10-11)

What a powerful proclamation is made by these verses. Through all of his lies and deceit, Satan has been completely foiled. These verses declare the **Lamb of God to be victorious over His greatest adversary**! It gives the credit where it belongs. The Lamb of God is **now ready to fulfill the prophetic statement of John the Baptist** when he said:

> "Behold, the Lamb of God who takes away the sin of the world! (John 1:29 NASB)

Now in heaven, the King of Kings has displayed His awesome power! It is just as the Apostle Paul prophesied under the inspiration of the Holy Spirit:

> The God of peace will soon crush Satan under your feet. (Romans 16:20)

It's time to oust that dreadful adversary from heaven so that the Kingdom of God can reside with no interference from these forces of evil. Those mentioned in verse eleven were willing to die for the sake of Christ, and now they were rewarded. As we continue:

> Because of this, be glad, the heavens and those tabernacling in them. Woe to the ones dwelling on the earth, and in the sea, because the devil came down to you having great anger, knowing that he has a little time! And when the dragon saw that he was cast out onto the earth, he pursued the woman who bore the male. And two wings of the great eagle were given to the woman, that she might fly into the wilderness, to her place, where she is nourished there a time, and times, and half a time, away from the serpent's face. And the serpent threw water out of his mouth like a river after the woman, that he might cause her to be carried off by the river. And the earth helped the woman, and the earth opened its mouth and swallowed the river which the dragon threw out of his mouth. And the dragon was enraged over the woman, and

> went away to make war with the rest of her seed, those keeping the commandments of God, and having the testimony of Jesus Christ. (Rev. 12:12-17)

Old Covenant Israel has not changed. She has been used of God to fulfill his promises, but has been for the most part unfaithful. She has now colluded with Satan to destroy God's chosen ones. She will soon become a thing of the past as Isaiah noted centuries earlier when he wrote:

> It will come about that he who is left in Zion and remains in Jerusalem will be called holy--everyone who is recorded for life in Jerusalem. When the Lord has washed away the filth of the daughters of Zion and purged the bloodshed of Jerusalem from her midst, by the spirit of judgment and the spirit of burning, (Isaiah 4:3-4 NASB)

The target of the horrendous fury of Satan is revealed. It is his desire to pour out his wrath on the remnant of Israel who were faithful to the Christ.

The Introduction of the Beast

Now as we enter the thirteenth chapter of the book we see a most fascinating character introduced. Notice the passage:

> And the dragon stood on the sand of the seashore. Then I saw a beast coming up out of the sea, having ten horns and seven heads, and on his horns were ten diadems, and on his heads were blasphemous names. And the beast which I saw was like a leopard, and his feet were like those of a bear, and his mouth like the mouth of a lion. And the dragon gave him his power and his throne and great authority. (Rev 13:1,2 NASB)

Does the description of this beast sound familiar? It should. With seven heads and ten horns, we see that it is very similar to the dragon mentioned in chapter 12. Now that the great dragon Satan has failed at his direct attempt to stop the presence of the Messiah, we see a transfer of power to this gruesome beast. In chapter two of this book, we identified this beast as having a twofold identity. This would be both Rome, and Caesar Nero. If you would like to review the reasons for this, please reread Chapter two. But for now we will proceed with this assumption. Continuing in chapter thirteen we find:

> I saw one of his heads as if it had been slain, and his fatal wound was healed (vs 3 NASB).

It is as if the Apostle John digresses momentarily to identify the time frame. This occurred after the death of Nero on June 9, of AD 68. General Galba was briefly in control as a civil war erupted in the Roman Empire. But the civil war was short-lived and Vespasian emerged as the emperor. However, the chapter reverts back to the time prior to the death of Nero as it continues.

> And the whole earth was amazed and followed after the beast; they worshiped the dragon because he gave his authority to the beast; and they worshiped the beast, saying, "Who is like the beast, and who is able to wage war with him?" There was given to him a mouth speaking arrogant words and blasphemies, and authority to act for forty-two months was given to him. And he opened his mouth in blasphemies against God, to blaspheme His name and His tabernacle, that is, those who dwell in heaven. It was also given to him to make war with the saints and to overcome them, and authority over every tribe and people and tongue and nation was given to him. All who dwell on the earth will worship him, everyone whose name has not been written from the foundation of the world in the book of life of the Lamb who has been slain. If anyone has an ear, let him hear. If anyone is destined for captivity, to captivity he goes; if anyone kills with the sword, with the sword he must be killed. Here is the perseverance and the faith of the saints. (Rev 13:3-10 NASB)

The time frame here is AD 64 through the midpoint of the year in AD 68. At that time, Emperor Nero was the emperor of Rome. He was worse than a barbarian. He is properly labeled as the beast. Notice what Josephus says about him:

> NOW as to the many things in which **Nero acted like a madman**, out of the extravagant degree of the felicity and riches which he enjoyed, and by that means **used his good fortune to the injury of others**; and after what manner **he slew his brother, and wife, and mother,** from whom his barbarity spread itself to others that were most nearly related to him; and how, at last, he was so distracted that **he became an actor in the scenes,** and upon the theater, - I omit to say any more about them, because there are writers enough upon those subjects everywhere; but I shall turn myself to those actions of his time in which the Jews were concerned.[li]

Here is a man who murdered his family to reduce any potential threats against his reign. After the burning of Rome, Nero sought to blame the Christians. Thus, he made it a point to single out the Christians for intense persecution. He loved to torture them in the most barbaric ways possible. Notice what Fox's book of Martyrs says:

> This dreadful conflagration continued nine days; when Nero, finding that his conduct was greatly blamed, and a severe odium cast upon him, determined to lay the whole upon the Christians, at once to excuse himself, and have an opportunity of glutting his sight with new cruelties. This was the occasion of the first persecution; and the barbarities exercised on the Christians were such as even excited the commiseration of the Romans themselves. Nero even refined upon cruelty, and contrived all manner of punishments for the Christians that the most infernal imagination could design. In particular, **he had some sewed up in skins of wild beasts, and then worried by dogs until they expired; and others dressed in shirts made**

> **stiff with wax, fixed to axletrees, and set on fire in his gardens, in order to illuminate them**. This persecution was general throughout the whole Roman Empire; but it rather increased than diminished the spirit of Christianity. In the course of it, St. Paul and St. Peter were martyred.[lii]

This barbarism was a part of the Roman Empire for these years, thus properly labeling Nero and the Roman Empire in general as "the beast." As we shall see in the next verses, the Apostle **John confirms the dual nature of the beast** with the following words:

> Then I saw another beast coming up out of the earth, and he had two horns like a lamb and spoke like a dragon. And he exercises all the authority of the first beast in his presence, and causes the earth and those who dwell in it to worship the first beast, whose deadly wound was healed. He performs great signs, so that he even makes fire come down from heaven on the earth in the sight of men. And he deceives those who dwell on the earth—by those signs which he was granted to do in the sight of the beast, telling those who dwell on the earth to make an image to the beast who was wounded by the sword and lived. **He was granted *power* to give breath to the image of the beast, that the image of the beast should both speak and cause as many as would not worship the image of the beast to be killed.** He causes all, both small and great, rich and poor, free and slave, to receive a mark on their right hand or on their foreheads, and that no one may buy or sell except one who has the mark or the name of the beast, or the number of his name. Here is wisdom. Let him who has understanding calculate the number of the beast, for it is the number of a man: His number *is* 666. (Rev 13:11-18 NKJV)

Through the use of much symbolic language in these verses, we see that this beast was given the power to execute God's judgment upon that unfaithful nation.

We must remember that besides the torture and execution of the Christians, it was Emperor Nero who commissioned General Vespasian to bring the Jews under control. Vespasian took this to mean that he should bring war against the Jews, thus history and the Jewish Historian Josephus recorded the horrors of this war in his volumes of "The Wars of the Jews"." However we must remember that behind this all was the powerful judgment prophesied by Jesus in Matthew 24, Mark 13, and Luke 21.

Note: As I have already reviewed the proof of Nero and the Roman Government's role in Revelation 13 (Chapter 2), I will now move on to chapter 14.

The Lamb of God and the 144,000 Rejoicing on Mount Zion

As we approach chapter fourteen, we see a familiar scene. The one hundred and forty-four thousand are pictured again. We must remember that Jesus preached first to the Jews. Here we see a preview of the fulfillment of the promise that these chosen ones, His servants would be protected. Once again, I would like to point out the fact that when these verses in chapter 14 mention "the earth," the Greek word used here is **NOT κοσμος (kosmos). Kosmos** is the word used to encompass the entire globe. The word chosen by the Apostle John under the inspiration of the Holy Spirit to describe the region of this event is the Greek word **γε (ge)** which is indicative of a smaller area, in this case, the region of Judea. This point is crucial in the understanding of these verses.

> "But when these things begin to take place, straighten up and lift up your heads, because your redemption is drawing near." (Luke 21: 28)

Now pictured as under the protection of the Lamb of God (with a certain future in heaven), notice the overwhelming joy of the saints as we read these verses:

> And I saw, and lo! the Lamb, standing upon the mount Zion,—and, with him, a hundred and forty-four thousand, having his name and his Father's name written upon their foreheads. And I heard a sound out of heaven, as the sound of many waters, and as the sound of, loud thunders; and, the sound which I heard, was as of harp-singers harping with their harps, And **they sing as it were a new song before the throne**, and before the four living creatures and the elders. And, no one, was able to learn the song, save the hundred and forty-four thousand, who had been **redeemed from the earth**. These, are they, who with women, were not defiled, for they are, virgin. These, are they who follow the Lamb whithersoever he is going. These, were **redeemed from mankind, as a firstfruit unto God** and the Lamb; and, in their mouth, was found no falsehood,—faultless, they are. (Rev 14:1-5 Rotherham)

What joy is displayed here! They were the first-fruits to God, and to the Lamb, spoken of as His choice ones. Here we see the chosen ones, redeemed from the earth. Their praises were as melodious as the sound of many waters as well as being loud like thunder as they were pictured standing before the throne. They were singing the song of the New Covenant as they were now declared as faultless under the loving grace of the Lamb of God **soon to be victorious,** as prophesied by John the Baptist (John 1:29). This will happen soon at the destruction of Babylon the Great as we shall see.

The Message of the Three Angels

The First Angel

> And I saw another messenger, flying in mid-heaven, having an

> age-abiding glad-message to announce unto them who are dwelling upon the earth, even unto every nation and tribe and tongue and people, saying with a loud voice,—Fear God and give him glory, because **THE HOUR OF HIS JUDGING IS COME;** and do homage unto him that made heaven and the earth and sea and fountains of waters. (Rev 14:6,7 Rotherham)

The first Angel was making an announcement to those in the entire region upon which this judgment was being executed. Did you notice what that judgment was? He said:

"THE HOUR OF HIS JUDGING IS COME"

Do you understand the ***profound significance*** of this statement? Remember that this was written **to the seven churches** mentioned in the beginning of this prophecy. This was **NOT** an event which was to happen in the distant future, it was **ABOUT TO HAPPEN** very soon! This "hour of judging" was now about to bring a **certain catastrophe** for those enemies of God in the wicked city of Jerusalem and the surrounding area.

The Second Angel

> And, another, a second messenger followed, saying—Fallen! fallen! is Babylon the great, who, of the wine of the wrath of her lewdness, hath caused all the nations to drink. (Rev 14:8 Rotherham)

Who is this city named "Babylon the Great?" It could not be literal Babylon because that was destroyed centuries ago. This city named "Babylon the Great" was acting as a harlot in conjunction with the surrounding nations as we shall see when we identify this entity in the ensuing chapters of this Revelation given to John. Yes! This Babylon and Jerusalem are the very same entity.

The Third Angel

> And, another, a third messenger, followed them, saying with a loud voice—**If anyone doeth homage unto the beast and his image**, and receiveth a mark upon his forehead, or upon his hand, he also, **shall drink of the wine of the wrath of God**, which is prepared, unmixed, in the cup of his anger;—and he shall be tormented with fire and brimstone, before holy messengers and before the Lamb; And, the smoke of their torment, unto ages of ages, ascendeth; And they have no rest day or night, who do homage unto the beast and his image, or if anyone receiveth the mark of his name. Here, is, the endurance of the saints,—they who keep the commandments of God and the faith of Jesus. And I heard a voice out of heaven, saying—Write! Happy, the dead who, in the Lord, do die, from henceforth. Yea! (saith the Spirit) that they may rest from their toils, for, their works, do follow with them. (Rev 14:9-13 Rotherham)

The message from the third angel was clear. Those who are a part of this system of ungodly "Babylon the Great" will "drink the wine of the wrath of God." Their judgment will be devastating, giving them no rest, and will last unto the "ages of ages." As we noticed in the message given by the second angel, **this wrath was now upon them.**

The Harvest of the "Son of Man" on the Cloud

> And I saw, and lo! a white cloud, and, upon the cloud, one sitting like unto a son of man, having, upon his head, a crown of gold, and, in his hand, a sharp sickle. And, another messenger, came forth out of the sanctuary, crying out with a loud voice, unto him that was sitting upon the cloud—Thrust in thy sickle, and reap; because the hour to reap is come, because the harvest of the earth is ripe. And he that was sitting upon the cloud, thrust in, his sickle upon the earth; and the earth was reaped. And, another messenger, came forth

> out of the sanctuary that is in heaven,—he also, having a sharp sickle. And, another messenger, came forth out of the altar, who hath authority over the fire,—and called out with a loud voice, unto him who had the sharp sickle, saying—Thrust in thy sharp sickle, and gather the clusters of the vine of the earth; because the grapes thereof are fully ripe. And the messenger, thrust in, his sickle into the earth, and gathered the vine of the earth, and cast it into the great wine-press of the wrath of God. And the wine-press was trodden outside the city, and there came forth blood out of the wine-press, even unto the bits of the horses, at a distance of a thousand six hundred furlongs. (Rev 14:14-20)

Now we see the "Son of Man" in His glory. This is the image that Jesus wanted Caiaphas and the kangaroo court in Jerusalem to remember. This occurred at His illegal "trial" to remember when He told them:

> But I tell you, from now on you will see the Son of Man seated at the right hand of Power and coming on the clouds of heaven." (Matt 26:64 ESV)

First, I would like to reiterate the point that **He never told them** that He would come back to the earth **in the flesh** as some would have you to believe. He very specifically told them that He would be coming "on the clouds of heaven." Now as we look at verse 1 we notice that He had in His hand a sharp sickle. This was for reaping, and cutting down, ending the growth process. In this case, it meant devastation. He was about to cut down, and **totally devastate** those mentioned who were under judgment. As we see at the end of this passage, blood was everywhere, "even unto the bits of the horses" symbolic of an amount of destruction that was unparalleled in the history of the region. When grapes are put into a winepress, they are done so with the purpose of extracting as much wine as possible. This was the effect of the judgment upon the nation. The devastation would be complete, and over a million would lose their lives. Notice the death toll mentioned by Josephus in the "Wars of the Jews:"

> Now the number (32) of those that were carried captive during this whole war was collected to be ninety-seven thousand; as was **the number of those that perished during the whole siege eleven hundred thousand, the greater part of whom were indeed of the same nation [with the citizens of Jerusalem],** but not belonging to the city itself; for they were come up from all the country to the feast of unleavened bread, and were on a sudden shut up by an army, which, at the very first, occasioned so great a straitness among them, that there came a pestilential destruction upon them, and soon afterward such a famine, as destroyed them more suddenly.[liii]

With this event, the fourth vision given to the Apostle John is ended, and a new vision begins.

Let us proceed.

Chapter 12

The Fifth Vision

The Bowl Judgments

The fifth vision begins with a scene from heaven. The seven judgments to follow are another representation of the previous judgments, highlighting some different nuances as to their nature. Notice the scene in heaven:

> And I saw another sign in heaven, great and marvellous,—seven messengers having seven plagues, the last, because, in them, was ended the wrath of God. And I saw as a glassy sea mingled with fire, and them who escape victorious from the beast, and from his image, and from the number of his name, standing upon the glassy sea, having harps of God; and they sing the song of Moses the servant of God and the song of the Lamb, saying—Great and marvelous, are thy works, Lord, God, the Almighty! Righteous and true, are thy ways, O King of the ages! Who shall in anywise not be put in fear, O Lord, and glorify thy name,—because, alone, full of lovingkindness; because, all the nations, will have come, and will do homage before thee, because, thy righteous deeds, were made manifest? And, after these things, I saw, and the sanctuary of The Tent of Witness in heaven, was opened; And the seven messengers who had the seven plagues, came forth, out of the sanctuary clothed with a precious stone, pure, bright, and girt about the breasts with girdles of gold. And, one of the four living creatures, gave, unto the seven messengers, seven golden bowls, full of the wrath of God who liveth unto the

> ages of ages. And the sanctuary was filled with smoke by reason of the glory of God, and by reason of his power; and, no one, was able to enter into the sanctuary, until the seven plagues of the seven messengers should be ended. (Revelation 15:1-8 Rotherham)

Once again we see the number seven. This number is symbolic, picturing completeness. Tying this in with the previous chapter, we see assurances that the enemies of God would be cut off, and that the Kingdom of God would be triumphant. This chapter makes a four-fold statement which will be described in detail in the subsequent chapters through the judgment of the seven vials (or bowls).

1. Seven angels appear. These angels would bring with them another view of these same judgments. These would detail a different depiction of the complete wrath of God upon the beast mentioned earlier. This would result in complete devastation.
2. Next we notice that it mentions those who escape from the beast standing on a sea of glass mingled with fire, celebrating the victory through joyful music.
3. We see the interior of the temple in heaven opened up, with the seven angels getting ready to pour out the seven plagues upon the land. They are adorned with pure white linen and girded with gold. One of the four living creatures gives the seven golden bowls to them. As verse seven notes: these bowls are full of the wrath of God, once again bringing the prophesied destruction upon the land.

4. No one was able to enter into the sanctuary until these seven plagues were ended. This is indicative of the fact that once these judgments were ended, Jesus, now as both a King and a Priest according to the "rank of Melchizedek" could come into the Holy of Holies in heaven and present His sacrificial blood, thus redeeming mankind. (Heb 7:15-28)

Thus we can say that chapter fifteen is an introductory chapter. It magnificently and solemnly sets the stage for another depiction of the same massive judgments upon the nation of Israel. In this depiction we will see much more detail about why this devastating judgment is necessary.

As proof that these judgments are the same as the trumpet judgments, J. Stuart Russell in his book "The Parousia" notes the following for the sake of comparison[liv]

The Trumpets	The Bowls (Vials)
Plagues poured out on the land	Plagues poured out on the land
Affects the sea, which becomes as blood	Affects the sea, which becomes as blood
Affects the rivers and fountains of waters	Affects the rivers and fountains of waters
Affects the sun, moon, and stars	Affects the sun
The abyss (the seat of the beast) opened. Men	Poured out on the seat of the beast (the abyss). Men

tormented	tormented.
The angels of the great river Euphrates loosed. Muster of hordes of cavalry.	Poured out on the great river Euphrates. Hosts muster for the battle of the great day.
Catastrophe; judgment; the kingdom proclaimed. Terrible natural phenomena – voices, thunderings, and an earthquake.	Catastrophe; proclamation of the end. Terrible natural phenomena – voices, thunderings, and an earthquake.

The Pouring out of the Seven Bowls (Vials)

As we open this chapter, we see what Russell was talking about right away. We also notice why it was **necessary to show the effect of these plagues from a different perspective** than that of the Trumpet plagues. We will be looking at this chapter from Young's Literal Translation. Notice verses one and two:

> And I heard a great voice out of the sanctuary saying to the seven messengers, 'Go away, and **pour out the vials of the wrath of God to the earth**;' and the first did go away, and **did pour out his vial upon the land**, and there came **a sore—bad and grievous—to men**, those having the mark of the beast, and those bowing to his image. (Rev. 16:1, 2 YLT)

As Russell stated above, we see the first bowl poured out upon the land. However, whereas the first Trumpet showed the effect upon the vegetation of the earth, this plague shows the effect upon men. The Historian Josephus recognized that the plagues visible upon the people of Israel were similar to the plagues upon Egypt. Notice the following words written by him:

> Shall I say nothing, or shall I mention the removal of our fathers into Egypt, who, (17) when they were used tyrannically, and were fallen under the power of foreign kings for four hundred years together, and might have defended themselves by war and by fighting, did yet do nothing but commit themselves to God! Who is there that does not know that Egypt was overrun with all sorts of wild beasts, and consumed by all sorts of distempers? how their land did not bring forth its fruit? how the Nile failed of water? how the ten plagues of Egypt followed one upon another? ... It was God who then became our General, and accomplished these great things for our fathers ...[lv]

There was among other things a siege going on in which people were being slaughtered in mass as well as starving to death. Those inside the city of Jerusalem were so very hungry as we have already seen that some of them were even cooking and eating their own children. But this gave cause to other terrible things that happened to men's bodies. Make no mistake about it the plague upon the city was so terrible that these people wanted out, no matter what the cost. Here is an example of this in the writings of Josephus:

> Hereupon some of the deserters, having no other way, leaped down from the wall immediately, ... and they met with a quicker despatch from the too great abundance they had among the Romans, than they could have done from the famine among the Jews; **for when they came first to the Romans, they were puffed up by the famine, and swelled like men in a dropsy;**
>
> **after which they all on the sudden overfilled those bodies that were before empty, and so burst asunder,** excepting such only as were skillful enough to restrain their appetites, and by degrees took in their food into bodies unaccustomed

> thereto. Yet did another plague seize upon those that were thus preserved; for there was found among the Syrian deserters **a certain person who was caught gathering pieces of gold out of the excrements of the Jews' bellies; for the deserters used to swallow such pieces of gold,** as we told you before, when they came out, and for these did the seditious search them all; … So the multitude of the Arabians, with the Syrians, cut up those that came as supplicants, and searched their bellies. Nor does it seem to me that any misery befell the Jews that was more terrible than this, since in one night's time about two thousand of these deserters were thus dissected. … **but in reality it was God who condemned the whole nation, and turned every course that was taken for their preservation to their destruction**.[lvi]

They were so famished that they gorged themselves to the point where their bowels burst open! Some were swallowing gold and when the enemy found out about it cut them open to get the gold. What could be worse than this plague? Maybe the second one as described here:

> And the second messenger did pour out his vial to the sea, and there came blood as of *one* dead, and every living soul died in the sea. And the third messenger did pour out his vial to the rivers, and to the fountains of the waters, and there came blood, and I heard the messenger of the waters, saying, 'righteous, O Lord, art Thou, who art, and who wast, and who shalt be, because these things Thou didst judge, because blood of saints and prophets they did pour out, and blood to them Thou didst give to drink, for they are worthy;' and I heard another out of the altar, saying, 'Yes, Lord God, the Almighty, true and righteous *are* Thy judgments.' (Rev 16:3-7 YLT)

Josephus also records the following horrific events:

> And for such as were drowning in the sea**, if they lifted their heads up above the water,** they were either **killed by darts**, or caught by the vessels; but if, in the desperate case they were

> in, they attempted to swim to their enemies**, the Romans cut off either their heads or their hands;** and indeed they were destroyed after various manners every where, till the rest being put to flight, were forced to get upon the land, while the vessels encompassed them about [on the sea]: but as many of these were repulsed when they were getting ashore, **they were killed by the darts upon the lake; and the Romans leaped out of their vessels, and destroyed a great many more upon the land**: one might then see the lake all bloody, and full of dead bodies, for not one of them escaped. **And a terrible stink, and a very sad sight there was on the following days over that country; for as for the shores, they were full of shipwrecks, and of dead bodies all swelled; and as the dead bodies were inflamed by the sun, and putrefied, they corrupted the air**, insomuch that the misery was not only the object of commiseration to the Jews, but to those that hated them, and had been the authors of that misery.[lvii]

The plague of the waters was extreme. It resulted in mass destruction and pollution of the waters to an extent never before seen, even under the plagues upon the Egyptians.

> And the fourth messenger did pour out his vial upon the sun, and there was given to him to scorch men with fire, and men were scorched with great heat, and they did speak evil of the name of God, who hath authority over these plagues, and they did not reform—to give to Him glory. (Rev 16:8,9 YLT)

We have already seen the report of Josephus in Book 4, Chapter 8, Section 1 that there was mass destruction in the land by fire. Here are more of the miseries that the Roman armies brought with fire as recorded by the historian:

> . . . and if at any time he was freed from those that were above him, which happened frequently, from their being drunk and tired, he sallied out with a great number upon Simon and his party; and this he did always in such parts of the city as he could come at, till **he set on fire those houses that**

> **were full of corn, and of all other provisions**. (4) The same thing was done by Simon, when, upon the other's retreat, he attacked the city also; as if they had, on purpose, done it to serve the Romans, by destroying what the city had laid up against the siege, and by thus cutting off the nerves of their own power. Accordingly, it so came to pass**, that all the places that were about the temple were burnt down, and were become an intermediate desert space**, ready for fighting on both sides of it; and that **almost all that corn was burnt**, which would have been sufficient for a siege of many years. So they were taken by the means of the famine, which it was impossible they should have been, unless they had thus prepared the way for it by this procedure.[lviii]

Now as we continue in chapter 16 we find:

> And the fifth messenger did pour out his vial upon the throne of the beast, and his kingdom did become darkened, and they were gnawing their tongues from the pain, and they did speak evil of the God of the heaven, from their pains, and from their sores, and they did not reform from their works. (Rev 16:10,11 YLT)

The darkness of the horrors of the wars grew worse every day. For each day brought more pain, death, and destruction. These people could see the devastating judgment was upon them. God had indeed deserted them and they could see it, cursing God in the process.

History records the following:

> **THUS did the miseries of Jerusalem grow worse and worse every day**, and the seditious were still more irritated by the calamities they were under, even while the famine preyed upon themselves, after it had preyed upon the people. **And indeed the multitude of carcasses that lay in heaps one upon another was a horrible sight, and produced a pestilential stench,** which was a hinderance to those that would make sallies out of the city, and fight the enemy: but as those were

> to go in battle- array, who had been already used to ten thousand murders, and must tread upon those dead bodies as they marched along, so were not they terrified, nor did they pity men as they marched over them; nor did they deem this affront offered to the deceased to be any ill omen to themselves; but as they had their right hands already polluted with the murders of their own countrymen, and in that condition ran out to fight with foreigners**, they seem to me to have cast a reproach upon God himself, as if he were too slow in punishing them**; for the war was not now gone on with as if they had any hope of victory; for they gloried after a brutish manner in that despair of deliverance they were already in.[lix]

Now as we continue the record of the Apostle John and the bowl judgments we see:

> And the sixth messenger did pour out his vial upon the great river, the Euphrates, and dried up was its water, that the way of the kings who are from the rising of the sun may be made ready; and I saw *come* out of the mouth of the dragon, and out of the mouth of the beast, and out of the mouth of the false prophet, three unclean spirits like frogs— for they are spirits of demons, doing signs—which go forth unto the kings of the earth, and of the whole world, to bring them together to the battle of that great day of God the Almighty; — 'lo, I do come as a thief; happy *is* he who is watching, and keeping his garments, that he may not walk naked, and they may see his unseemliness,' — and they did bring them together to the place that is called in Hebrew Armageddon. (Rev 16:12-16)

At first look, this seems out of place. The reason is that most of the forces employed in the destruction of Jerusalem came from the West, and not from the Northeast, which is the location of the Euphrates. However, this idea is disputed by Russell. Of this passage, J. Stuart Russell says in his book, The Parousia, the following:

> The drying up of the Euphrates seems plainly to signify its being crossed with ease and speed; and this, taken in connection with the corresponding symbol under the sixth trumpet, viz. the loosing of the four angels bound at the Euphrates, points to the drawing of troops from that quarter for the invasion of Judea. This we know to be a historical fact. Not only Roman legions from the frontier of the Euphrates, but auxiliary kings whose dominions lay in that region, such as Antiochus of Commagene and Sohemus of Sophene, most properly designated 'kings from the east,' followed the eagles of Rome to the siege of Jerusalem.[lx]

I would also like to point out that once again we are misled by the English translation of verse 16 where it says:

> for they are spirits of demons, doing signs—which go forth unto the kings of the earth, and of the whole world, to bring them together to the battle of that great day of God the Almighty; (Rev 16:14)

Once again we see the words "**kings of the earth**" but the word used for earth here is the Greek word ***ge*** which in this context means "***land.***" Also we see the expression "**and of the whole world.**" The Greek word used here is the word ***oikoumenes*** which has reference to the entire Roman Empire in this context. (Source: Strong's Hebrew and Greek Dictionaries) For more on these words, please go back to chapter 7 which discusses these words in great detail.

As Bible history has shown, God uses ungodly nations to perform His judgments, and by using "three unclean spirits like frogs— for they are spirits of demons, doing signs" we see the same pattern in how God does His judgments. The reference to Armageddon is symbolic of the "plain of Megiddo" where battles were fought in the Old Testament. Unger's Bible Dictionary notes the following about this place:

> Megiddo occupied a very marked position on the southern rim of the plain of Esdraelon, the great battlefield of Palestine. It was famous for two great victories: of Barak over the Canaanites (Judg. 4:15), and of Gideon over the Midianites (Judg. 7); and for two great disasters: the deaths of Saul (1 Sam. 31:8) and of Josiah (II Kings 23:29, 30; II Chron. 35:22). Armageddon becomes a poetical expression for terrible and final conflict.[lxi]

Now as we move on to the seventh bowl (vial) we see:

> Then the seventh angel poured out his bowl upon the air, and a loud voice came out of the temple from the throne, saying, "It is done." And there were flashes of lightning and sounds and peals of thunder; and there was a great earthquake, such as there had not been since man came to be upon the earth, so great an earthquake was it, and so mighty. The great city was split into three parts, and the cities of the nations fell. Babylon the great was remembered before God, to give her the cup of the wine of His fierce wrath. And every island fled away, and the mountains were not found. And huge hailstones, about one hundred pounds each, came down from heaven upon men; and men blasphemed God because of the plague of the hail, because its plague was extremely severe. (Rev 16:17-21 NASB)

Here we see that the message is given in hyperbolic language. This is done to make a point of the severity of this judgment. The writer of Hebrews spoke of this time in Hebrews chapter 12 when he said:

> And His voice shook the earth then, but now He has promised, saying, "YET ONCE MORE I WILL SHAKE NOT ONLY THE EARTH, BUT ALSO THE HEAVEN." (Heb 12:26 NASB)

Speaking of the judgment on Jerusalem once again, with its temple (referred to as heaven and earth by Jesus at Matt 5:17, 18), this prophecy outlines the complete devastation of the city of

Jerusalem which is "Babylon the Great." Why is it referred to as Babylon the Great? It is because it is now the great city that Babylon was at one time. Both cities killed and persecuted the prophets. Both cities were so completely destroyed that it was as if there was nothing there that would indicate that there had been a city there. As for the huge hailstones raining down on the city, this is a reference to the stones catapulted upon the city during the destruction by Vespasian and Titus of the Roman armies. We find the explanation of this in the writings of Josephus:

> Vespasian then **set the engines for throwing stones and darts round about the city. The number of the engines was in all a hundred and sixty,** and bid them fall to work, and dislodge those that were upon the wall. At the same time such engines as were intended for that purpose threw at once lances upon them with a great noise, **and stones of *<u>the weight of a talent</u>* were thrown by the engines that were prepared for that purpose, together with fire, and a vast multitude of arrows,** which made the wall so dangerous, that the Jews durst not only not come upon it, but durst not come to those parts within the walls which were reached by the engines; for the multitude of the Arabian archers, as well also as all those that threw darts and slung stones, fell to work at the same time with the engines.[lxii]

Jesus confirmed the destruction of all of this, including the temple when He said in the Sermon on the Mount:

> Do not think that I came to abolish the Law or the Prophets; I did not come to abolish but to fulfill. For truly I say to you, **until heaven and earth pass away**, not the smallest letter or stroke shall pass from the Law until all is accomplished." (Matt 5:17-18)

Yes! When Jesus said heaven and earth, He **meant the temple**, and here's why. Now if we look at what Jesus said here, we know that we absolutely **cannot** take it in the literal sense. Let's read verse 18 again:

> "For truly I say to you, **until heaven and earth pass away**, not the smallest letter or stroke shall pass from the Law until **ALL** is accomplished."

Now just think about this for a minute. If this **IS** literal, it means that until the **literal** heaven and the **literal** earth pass away, **that we are still, and will always be** under the Law of Moses!

Chapter 13

The Sixth Vision

The Great Harlot

As we approach the seventeenth chapter of the prophecy given to John, we see the description of a great harlot. The harlot is riding the beast spoken of in chapter twelve of this prophecy. This beast is none other than the great deceiver, Satan. Notice how this chapter opens:

> And one of the seven messengers who had the seven bowls came, and spake with me, saying—Hither! I will point out to thee **the judgment of the great harlot**, who sitteth upon many waters, **with whom the kings of the earth committed lewdness,**—and they who were dwelling upon the earth were made drunk with the wine of her lewdness. And he carried me away into a desert, in spirit. And I saw a woman, sitting upon a scarlet wild-beast full of names of blasphemy, having seven heads and ten horns. And, the woman, was arrayed with purple and scarlet, and decked with gold and precious stone and pearls,—having a cup of gold in her hand, full of abominations and the impurities of her lewdness; and, upon her forehead**, a name written, a secret: Babylon the great, the Mother of the Harlots** and of the Abominations of the earth. And I saw the woman, **drunk with the blood of the saints**, and **with the blood of the witnesses of Jesus.** And I was astonished, when I beheld her, with great astonishment. (Rev 17:1-6 Rotherham)

There is great precedence in the Old Testament for the identification of this great harlot. And now I will digress to make a very important point. There is a definite pattern here that has continued for centuries, and the Apostle John shows it once again. The prophet Ezekiel spoke similarly of a harlot in his day. I would like to take relevant verses here to show how God identified that harlot in Ezekiel's day. Notice the words of the prophet:

> Again the word of the LORD came to me: "Son of man, make known to Jerusalem her abominations, (Ezek 16:1,2 ESV)

Here we see that harlot identified as Jerusalem in the Old Testament. Now the prophet elaborated on the love shown by God prior to her harlotry.

> I made you flourish like a plant of the field. And you grew up and became tall and arrived at full adornment. Your breasts were formed, and your hair had grown; yet you were naked and bare. "When I passed by you again and saw you, behold, you were at the age for love, and I spread the corner of my garment over you and covered your nakedness; I made my vow to you and entered into a covenant with you, declares the Lord GOD, and you became mine. (Ezek 16:7,8 ESV)

The love God had for the city of Jerusalem was very clear as the eloquent words of the prophet bear out. These words describe a deep and abiding love, full of protection against all enemies. But then the prophet showed how the harlot threw all of this love aside in order to purvey her harlotry.

> "But you trusted in your beauty and played the whore because of your renown and lavished your whorings on any passerby; your beauty became his. You took some of your garments and made for yourself colorful shrines, and on them played the whore. The like has never been, nor ever shall be. You also took your beautiful jewels of my gold and of my silver, which I

> had given you, and made for yourself images of men, and with them played the whore. And you took your sons and your daughters, whom you had borne to me, and these you sacrificed to them to be devoured. Were your whorings so small a matter that you slaughtered my children and delivered them up as an offering by fire to them? (Ezek 16:15-21 ESV)

After the prophet described how this was done, he gave them a listing of those with whom the harlot was unfaithful.

> You also played the whore **with the Egyptians**, your lustful neighbors, multiplying your whoring, to provoke me to anger. You played the whore also **with the Assyrians**, because you were not satisfied; yes, you played the whore with them, and still you were not satisfied. You multiplied your whoring also **with the trading land of Chaldea**, and **even with this you were not satisfied**. "How sick is your heart, declares the Lord GOD, because you did all these things, the deeds of a brazen prostitute, (Ezek 16:26-30 ESV)

And as a result of this, the prophet told them that the penalty for their sins was coming soon.

> You bear the penalty of your lewdness and your abominations, declares the LORD. "For **thus says the Lord GOD: I will deal with you as you have done, you who have despised** the oath in breaking the covenant, (Ezek 16:58,59 ESV)

This penalty would eventually involve the destruction of Jerusalem the first time. But as I stated earlier, this was a pattern of action that would show itself again, even though God forgave them for their earlier sins and promised to keep His covenant with them. But now the promised Messiah has been delivered, and ***even He*** **was rejected**. This was the last straw for the great harlot! She was drunk with the blood of the saints, having been the chief persecutor and enemy of the servants of God.

Yes, this great harlot who is adorned with a robe of purple and scarlet, decked with gold and precious stones is **none other than the city of Jerusalem** who played the harlot just as she did in the past. Even the prophet Isaiah confirms the mention of Jerusalem in connection with the term harlot when he states:

> How the faithful city has become a harlot, She who was full of justice! Righteousness once lodged in her, But now murderers. (Isa 1:21 NASB)

Chapter 17 continues:

> And the messenger said unto me—Wherefore wast thou astonished? I, will tell thee the secret of the woman, and of the wild-beast that carrieth her, which hath the seven heads and the ten horns. The wild-beast which thou sawest, was, and is not, and is about to come up out of the abyss, and into, destruction, goeth away. And they who are dwelling upon the earth whose name is not written upon the book of life from the foundation of the world, will be astonished, when they see the wild-beast, because it was, and is not, and shall be present. (Rev 17: 7,8 Rotherham)

Once again I must point out that this was not a worldwide event. The Greek word for earth in verse 8 is not ***kosmos*** which has a global connotation, but the Greek word ***ge*** which is local by nature. The Apostle John is speaking of the Jewish people, not all people of the planet Earth. Next, from a series of descriptions, he identifies the beast. Why does he not come right out with it? Remember that the followers of Christ were enduring much persecution here and this type of description was necessary at that time. Notice what is written:

> Here, is the mind that hath wisdom. The seven heads, are, seven mountains, whereupon the woman sitteth; and they are, seven kings: **the five, have fallen, the one, is, the other,**

> **hath not yet come;** and, whensoever he shall come, a little while, must he remain, and the wild-beast which was and is not. And he, is an eighth, and is, of the seven,—and, into destruction, goeth away. And, the ten horns which thou sawest, are, ten kings,—who, indeed, have not received, sovereignty, as yet, but, authority, as kings, for one hour, shall receive, with the wild-beast. These, have, one mind, and, their power and authority, unto the wild-beast, they give. These, with the Lamb, **will make war; and, the Lamb, will overcome them, because he is, Lord of lords, and King of kings**,—and, they who are with him, are called and chosen and faithful. And he saith unto me—The waters which thou sawest, where the harlot sitteth, are, peoples and multitudes, and nations and tongues. **And the ten horns which thou sawest, and the wild-beast, these, shall hate the harlot, and, desolate, shall make her, and naked, and, her flesh, shall they eat, and, herself, shall they burn up with fire.** For, God, hath put into their hearts, to do his mind, and to do one mind,—and to give their sovereignty unto the wild-beast, until the words of God shall be completed. And, **the woman whom thou sawest, is the great city**, which hath sovereignty over the kings of the earth. (Rev 17:7-18 Rotherham)

Although I have already covered this at length in Chapter 2, once again, let me reiterate the **incredible specificity** of this! The Apostle mentions seven kings. Five have fallen, and one is still reigning. The seventh is said to have not yet arrived, but when he does, his reign will be short-lived. When we examine these specific facts, we see that the angel is telling John that these kings represent the emperors in succession of the Roman Empire. If we look up these emperors according to secular history, we find that they are:

- **Julius Caesar (49 - 44 BC),**
- **Augustus Caesar (31BC – AD 14),**
- **Tiberius Caesar (14 - AD 37),**
- **Gaius Caesar (37 - AD 41),**

- **Claudius (41 - AD 54),**
- **Nero (54 - AD 68),**
- **Galba (June AD 68 – January AD 69)**

The five that have fallen:

Julius, Augustus, Tiberius, Gaius, and Claudius.

One is:

Nero

One is yet to come:

Galba (only a little while)

Notice **how precisely** the succession of emperors is described in the book! There is no way this could be a coincidence! All of them reigned over a period of years with the exception of Galba who only reigned for about 6+ months. The reason Galba reigned such a short period of time is because it was the beginning of a civil war in Rome, and amazingly, this exact scenario was described **precisely** in verse 10 of chapter 17. And once again, we have also established with profound accuracy the timing of the writing of this book. The book of Revelation **had to be written prior to June 8, AD 68**, the day that Nero committed suicide.

The time was now at hand! Jesus spoke of this harlot also when he said:

> "O Jerusalem, Jerusalem, the city that **kills the prophets** and stones those sent to her! How often I wanted to gather your children together, just as a hen gathers her brood under her wings, and you would not have it! "**Behold, your house is left to you desolate**; and I say to you, you will not see Me until the time comes when you say, 'BLESSED IS HE WHO COMES IN THE NAME OF THE LORD!'" (Luke 13:34,35)

It was now time for that desolation to take place. As verse 16 pronounces, the beast will make her naked and burn her with fire. History records that this is exactly what happened. From the pen of Josephus we read:

> I shall therefore speak my mind here at once briefly: - That **neither did any other city ever suffer such miseries,** nor did any age ever breed a generation more fruitful in wickedness than this was, from the beginning of the world. Finally, they brought the Hebrew nation into contempt, that they might themselves appear comparatively less impious with regard to strangers. They confessed what was true, that they were the slaves, the scum, and the spurious and abortive offspring of our nation, while they overthrew the city themselves, and forced the Romans, whether they would or no, to gain a melancholy reputation, by acting gloriously against them, and did almost draw that fire upon the temple, which they seemed to think came too slowly; and indeed **when they saw that temple burning from the upper city, they were neither troubled at it, nor did they shed any tears on that account**, while yet these passions were discovered among the Romans themselves; which circumstances we shall speak of hereafter in their proper place, when we come to treat of such matters.[lxiii]

In this passage from "The Wars of the Jews," the historian Josephus makes a very profound statement, and that is that **the misery experienced by this city was unparalleled!** His words also show that he agreed with the extreme **wickedness of this generation** as spoken of by our Lord. Indeed the judgment that came upon this city could not have been worse. With the writing of these words, we have **the confirmation of the fulfillment of the clear promise and the prophecy of our Lord Jesus** concerning the judgment of that city!

The Aftermath of the Judgment

As we continue in Chapter 18 we see:

> After these things I saw another angel coming down from heaven, having great authority, and the earth was illumined with his glory. And he cried out with a mighty voice, saying, "Fallen, fallen is Babylon the great! She has become a dwelling place of demons and a prison of every unclean spirit, and a prison of every unclean and hateful bird. "For all the nations have drunk of the wine of the passion of her immorality, and the kings of the earth have committed acts of immorality with her, and the merchants of the earth have become rich by the wealth of her sensuality." (Rev 18:1-3 NASB)

Once again, I must reiterate that the Greek word for earth used here is ***ge***, not ***kosmos.*** Therefore the best translation of that word in this situation would be **land.** Thus, it is speaking of the kings in the area **of the land of the Roman Empire**. With Jerusalem having fallen, it was cursed by God, a place where fowl birds such as vultures would soon consume the flesh of the dead bodies. The judgment is now being executed precisely as foretold by Jesus. As we finish the chapter, we see the lamenting of the aftermath by the Apostle.

> And I heard another voice from heaven saying, "**Come out of her, my people, lest you share in her sins, and lest you receive of her plagues**. For her sins have reached to heaven, and God has remembered her iniquities. Render to her just as she rendered to you, and repay her double according to her works; in the cup which she has mixed, mix double for her. In the measure that she glorified herself and lived luxuriously, in the same measure give her torment and sorrow; for she says in her heart, 'I sit *as* queen, and am no widow, and will not see sorrow.' **Therefore her plagues will come in one day—death and mourning and famine. And she will be utterly burned with fire, for strong *is* the Lord God who judges her.** "The

> kings of the earth who committed fornication and lived luxuriously with her will weep and lament for her, when they see the smoke of her burning, standing at a distance for fear of her torment, saying, 'Alas, alas, that great city Babylon, that mighty city! **For in one hour your judgment has come.'** (Rev 18:4-10 NKJV)

The concept of the "the great city," so named for being the seat of the temple, spoken of as "heaven and earth," and the covenantal city of God, which He made with the Israelite people now stands in ruins in this vision. It must have been similar to what Jeremiah felt when he saw the ruins of the city of Jerusalem when it was destroyed by the Babylonians.

> How lonely sits the city *That was* full of people! *How* like a widow is she, Who *was* great among the nations! The princess among the provinces Has become a slave!. . . Jerusalem has sinned gravely, Therefore **she has become vile**. All who honored her despise her Because they have seen her nakedness; Yes, **she sighs and turns away. Her uncleanness *is* in her skirts;** She did not consider her destiny; Therefore her collapse was awesome; She had no comforter. "O LORD, behold my affliction, For *the* enemy is exalted!" (Lam 1:1, 8-9 NKJV)

And now in this vision as the apostle sees the city laid waste, he sees the emptiness of the city compared to its once powerful image as a major source of trade among the nations of the area. He sees the mourning of the merchants because the source of their wealth is now completely reduced to rubbish.

> And the **merchants of the earth weep and mourn over her, because no one buys their cargo any more**— cargo of gold and silver and precious stones and pearls and fine linen and purple cloth and silk and scarlet cloth and all kinds of scented wood and all kinds of ivory goods and all kinds of goods of

> precious wood and bronze and iron and marble and cinnamon and amomum and incense and ointment and frankincense and wine and olive oil and fine wheat flour and wheat and domesticated animals and sheep and horses and carriages and slaves and human lives. "And the fruit your soul desires has departed from you, and all the luxury and the splendor has perished from you, and they will never find them any more." **The merchants of these *things*, who became rich from them, will stand far off, weeping and mourning because of the fear of her torment, saying, "Woe, woe, the great city, dressed in fine linen and purple cloth and scarlet cloth, and adorned with gold and precious stones and pearls, because in one hour such great wealth has been laid waste!"** And every shipmaster and every seafarer and sailors and all those who labor on the sea stood far off and began to cry out *when they* saw the smoke of her burning, saying, "Who *is* like the great city?" And they threw dust on their heads and were crying out, weeping and mourning, saying, "Woe, woe, the great city, in which all those who had ships on the sea became rich from her prosperity, because **in one hour she has been laid waste!"** (Rev 18:11-19 Lexham English Bible)

But even through all of this, the **apostle is told to be joyful, because the vindication of the blood of the saints is now complete!** Remember that the saints in heaven were saying "How long, holy and true Lord, will you not judge and avenge our blood from those who live on the earth?" (Rev 6:10) Notice the words of inspiration given to John:

> **"Rejoice over her, O heaven, and *you* holy apostles and prophets, for God has avenged you on her!"** Then a mighty angel took up a stone like a great millstone and threw *it* into the sea, saying, "Thus with violence the great city Babylon shall be thrown down, and shall not be found anymore. The sound of harpists, musicians, flutists, and trumpeters shall not be heard in you anymore. No craftsman of any craft shall be found in you anymore, and the sound of a millstone shall not be heard in you anymore. The light of a lamp shall not shine in

> you anymore, and the voice of bridegroom and bride shall not be heard in you anymore. For your merchants were the great men of the earth, for by your sorcery all the nations were deceived. And **in her was found the blood of prophets and saints**, and of all who were slain on the earth." (Rev 18:20-24 NKJV)

As a result of all of this, there was now rejoicing in heaven as we see in the beginning of chapter 19. There is a great shout of praise:

> After this, I heard what sounded like a lot of voices in heaven, and they were shouting, "**Praise the Lord!** To our God belongs the glorious power to save, because his judgments are honest and fair. That filthy prostitute ruined the earth with shameful deeds. But God has judged her and made her pay the price for murdering his servants." Then the crowd shouted, "Praise the Lord! Smoke will never stop rising from her burning body." After this, the twenty-four elders and the four living creatures all knelt before the throne of God and worshiped him. They said, "Amen! Praise the Lord!" From the throne a voice said, "If you worship and fear our God, give praise to him, no matter who you are." (Rev 19:1-5 Contemporary English Version)

Yes! There is much rejoicing! **God has once again kept His promise**! Jesus promised this would happen when He was on the earth. Even regarding the temple He stated: "Not one stone shall be left upon another." Why was it so completely destroyed? It was because there was so much gold in the temple that those pillagers wanted to be sure to get every last piece. There was no longer any need of a temple! The true Lamb of God has now given the perfect sacrifice, rendering any future sacrifices useless and detestable in the sight of God. It was very fitting that heaven should say "Alleluia" rendering magnificent praise to the one who always keeps His promises.

And although there are still more works of judgment to come, first there is an event which is spoken of here by the Apostle John:

> And I heard, as it were, the voice of a great multitude, as the sound of many waters and as the sound of mighty thunderings, saying, "Alleluia! For the Lord God Omnipotent reigns! Let us be glad and rejoice and give Him glory, for the marriage of the Lamb has come, and His wife has made herself ready." And to her it was granted to be arrayed in fine linen, clean and bright, for the fine linen is the righteous acts of the saints. Then he said to me, "Write: 'Blessed *are* those who are called to the marriage supper of the Lamb!' " And he said to me, "These are the true sayings of God." And I fell at his feet to worship him. But he said to me, "See *that you do* not *do that!* I am your fellow servant, and of your brethren who have the testimony of Jesus. Worship God! For the testimony of Jesus is the spirit of prophecy." (Rev 19:6-10 NKJV)

After one more verse of praise and adoration, we see the prophet speaking of a marriage supper that is about to occur. What does this mean? For that answer we have to go back to the Old Testament. The relationship of God to Israel is often spoken of in terms of a marriage. Notice what is said here in the book of Isaiah:

> For your Maker *is* your husband, The LORD of hosts *is* His name; And your Redeemer *is* the Holy One of Israel; He is called the God of the whole earth. For the LORD has called you Like a woman forsaken and grieved in spirit, like a youthful wife when you were refused," Says your God. (Isaiah 54:5-6 NKJV)

But Israel was also like an unfaithful wife as noted by the prophet Jeremiah:

> "Return, O backsliding children," says the LORD; "**for I am married to you**. I will take you, one from a city and two from a family, and I will bring you to Zion. (Jer 3:14 NKJV)

Yes, Israel was constantly backsliding. It got so bad that God commissioned the prophet Hosea to a very special calling. The prophet Hosea is called by God to marry a prostitute. Why would God call a prophet to do such a thing? It was for the purpose of showing the nation how they were acting:

> When the LORD began to speak by Hosea, the LORD said to Hosea: "Go, take yourself a wife of harlotry And children of harlotry, **For the land has committed great harlotry *By departing* from the LORD."** So he went and took Gomer the daughter of Diblaim, and she conceived and bore him a son. (Hosea 1:1-2 NKJV)

With each succeeding child, judgment was pronounced, but later mercy and salvation are also promised. Finally we notice in chapter 1 of Hosea's prophecy the following:

> "Yet the number of the children of Israel Shall be as the sand of the sea, Which cannot be measured or numbered. And it shall come to pass In the place where it was said to them, 'You *are* not My people,' *There* it shall be said to them, '*You are* sons of the living God.' Then the children of Judah and the children of Israel Shall be gathered together, And appoint for themselves one head; And they shall come up out of the land, For great *will be* the day of Jezreel! (Hosea 1:10-11 NKJV)

This prophecy was to proclaim the conversion of the Gentiles and the calling of the Jews together in the last days under the glorious reign of the Savior. But how is this possible since God called for a divorce? Notice the words of the prophet:

> Say to your brethren, 'My people,' And to your sisters, 'Mercy *is shown*.' "Bring charges against your mother, bring charges; **For she *is* not My wife, nor *am* I her Husband**! Let her put away her harlotries from her sight, And her adulteries from between her breasts; (Hosea 2:1-2)

Yet later on the prophet also said that God would show mercy:

> "And it shall be, in that day," Says the LORD, "*That* you will call Me 'My Husband,' And no longer call Me 'My Master,' For I will take from her mouth the names of the Baals, And they shall be remembered by their name no more. In that day I will make a covenant for them With the beasts of the field, With the birds of the air, And *with* the creeping things of the ground. Bow and sword of battle I will shatter from the earth, To make them lie down safely. "I will betroth you to Me forever; Yes, I will betroth you to Me In righteousness and justice, In lovingkindness and mercy; I will betroth you to Me in faithfulness, And **you shall know the LORD**. (Hosea 2:16-20)

Yes, as the prophet was pointing out, there would be judgment, but mercy. The judgment would be on unfaithful Israel to whom Jesus declared:

> Therefore, indeed, I send you prophets, wise men, and scribes: ***some* of them you will kill and crucify,** and ***some* of them you will scourge** in your synagogues and persecute from city to city, **that on you may come all the righteous blood shed on the earth**, from the blood of righteous Abel to the blood of Zechariah, son of Berechiah, whom you murdered between the temple and the altar. Assuredly, I say to you, all these things will come upon this generation. (Matt 23:34-36 NKJV)

As the Apostle John stated in Revelation, this Great Harlot has now been put away for good:

> For true and righteous *are* His judgments, because He has judged the great harlot who corrupted the earth with her fornication; and He has avenged on her the blood of His servants *shed* by her." Again they said, "Alleluia! Her smoke rises up forever and ever!" (Rev 19:2-3 NKJV)

But because of His great mercy, there would now be a marriage with the faithful remnant of Israel as spoken of above in Revelation 19:6-10. But as John also noted there is more work to do. There are also other enemies of God which must be disposed of.

> And I saw heaven opened, and behold, a white horse, and He who sat on it is called Faithful and True, and in righteousness He judges and wages war. His eyes are a flame of fire, and on His head are many diadems; and He has a name written on Him which no one knows except Himself. **He is clothed with a robe dipped in blood, and His name is called The Word of God. And the armies which are in heaven, clothed in fine linen, white and clean, were following Him on white horses.** From His mouth comes a sharp sword, so that with it He may strike down the nations, and He will rule them with a rod of iron; and He treads the wine press of the fierce wrath of God, the Almighty. And on His robe and on His thigh He has a name written, "KING OF KINGS, AND LORD OF LORDS." Then I saw an angel standing in the sun, and he cried out with a loud voice, saying to all the birds which fly in midheaven, "Come, assemble for the great supper of God, so that you may eat the flesh of kings and the flesh of commanders and the flesh of mighty men and the flesh of horses and of those who sit on them and the flesh of all men, both free men and slaves, and small and great." And I saw the beast and the kings of the earth and their armies assembled to make war against Him who sat on the horse and against His army. **And the beast was seized, and with him the false prophet** who performed the signs in his presence, by which he deceived those who had received the mark of the beast and those who worshiped his image; **these two were thrown alive into the lake of fire** which burns with brimstone. And **the rest were killed with the sword which came from the mouth of Him who sat on the horse**, and all the birds were filled with their flesh. (Rev 19:11-21 NASB)

The rider of the white horse is identified as the same one who was called "The Word" in John's Gospel. (John 1:1, 14) The judgment performed on these enemies of the Christ, who was waging this war from the heavenly realm would be lasting and sure. The beast and the false prophet would be gone forever. The blood of the saints has been avenged. That is why there was so much praise and adoration in the heavenly realm! But there is yet more to come for the enemies of Christ!

The Judgment of the Dragon

We now come to a section in the prophecy given to John over which there has been much speculation, and many differing ideas as to the meaning thereof. It has even been the cause of much division throughout the history of the Christian church. In fact entire systems of eschatological views have been built on the speculation of the meaning of the following short verses. Notice the words as we begin chapter twenty:

> Then I saw an angel coming down from heaven, holding in his hand the key to the bottomless pit and a great chain. And he seized the dragon, that ancient serpent, who is the devil and Satan, and bound him for a thousand years, and threw him into the pit, and shut it and sealed it over him, so that he might not deceive the nations any longer, until the thousand years were ended. After that he must be released for a little while. (Rev 20:1-3 ESV)

The thousand years mentioned here is where the term "millennial" was born. But actually, this term "millennial" is **never found in the Bible**. Even the term "millennial kingdom" is a complete misnomer, **not being found anywhere in the Bible**. Concerning this term, Henry Chadwick, the author of the book ***The Early Church***, had this to say:

> "Millenarian belief **originated in a fusion of various strands. Babylonian astrology contributed the notion of millennial periods under the seven planets.** Psalm 89:4 (A day with the Lord is as a thousand years) provided a key for the interpretation of the seven days of creation in Gen. i; and the

> epistle to the Hebrews (iv, 4-9) interpreted the sabbath as symbol of heavenly rest. By putting these elements together it was natural to form the notion, found in Irenaeus and Hippolytus, that world history will last 6,000 years leading up to a seventh millennium under the reign of Christ. After Clement of Alexandria and Origen, for whom it was a fundamental error to treat the Apocalypse as providing any basis for chronological calculations, **very few Greek Fathers accepted the millennial hope,** but it survived longer in the West.[lxiv]

From this it appears that any notion of a "millennial reign of Christ" was born out of the throes of a pagan concept. Therefore, when we think of any of the forms of this concept, such as amillennialism, premillennialism, or postmillennialism, we must think of the origin of the concept. **The concept is of PAGAN ORIGIN. It even seems to have originated in Babylon!** If this is true, and there is no basis in the Bible for a concept of a millennial kingdom, then I must ask, **why would we want to believe such a notion?**

But church historian Eusebius believed that the prophecy given by Christ in Matthew 24, Mark 13, and Luke 21 were fulfilled during the time of the destruction of Jerusalem. Notice the following quote from Eusebius' writings:

> But the number of calamities which everywhere fell upon the nation at that time; the extreme misfortunes to which the inhabitants of Judea were especially subjected, the thousands of men, as well as women and children, that perished by the sword, by famine, and by other forms of death innumerable—all these things, as well as the many great sieges which were carried on against the cities of Judea, and the excessive sufferings endured by those that fled to Jerusalem itself, as to a city of perfect safety, and finally the general course of the whole war, as well as its particular occurrences in detail, and **how at last the abomination**

> **<u>of desolation</u>, proclaimed by the <u>prophets</u>, <u>Daniel 9:27</u> stood in the very <u>temple of God</u>,** so celebrated of old, **the <u>temple</u> which was now awaiting its total and final destruction by fire** — all these things any one that wishes may find accurately described in the history written by <u>Josephus</u>.[lxv]

When we look at the prophecies of the Old Testament, there is a passage in the book of Daniel that must be considered when we speak of this period of "a thousand years" as spoken of in Rev 20: 2-3. That passage is found in Daniel chapter 12. Look at this passage:

> "But you, Daniel, shut up the words and seal the book, until the time of the end. Many shall run to and fro, and knowledge shall increase." Then I, Daniel, looked, and behold, two others stood, one on this bank of the stream and one on that bank of the stream. And someone said to the man clothed in linen, who was above the waters of the stream, "How long shall it be till the end of these wonders?" And I heard the man clothed in linen, who was above the waters of the stream; he raised his right hand and his left hand toward heaven and **swore by him who lives forever that it would be for a time, times, and half a time, and that when the *<u>shattering of the power of the holy people</u>* comes to an end *<u>ALL THESE THINGS WOULD BE FINISHED</u>*.** (Dan 12:4-7 ESV)

With this passage, we know for a certainty that the "thousand years" must be a **symbolic** period of time. This means that whenever **this symbolic** period of "a thousand years" began, **it had to come to an end before the time of the destruction of the temple and the city of Jerusalem**. There is no question that the "power of the holy people" was shattered at that time. It brought an end to the temple, the priesthood, and the entire system of Levitical sacrificial worship, and scattered the Jews in many directions! The Jews would never come together again to form anything resembling that system of government and worship. That **forces this time frame** to be about the same length of time (a generation) as Jesus spoke of in the Olivet Discourse. Thus, that time frame **must by necessity be** a period of time lasting forty years that would end just prior to the destruction of Jerusalem.

Considering the fact that Satan is said in verse three to have been "loosed for a little while," it had to have occurred prior to the destruction of Jerusalem, because according to Daniel's prophecy, "when the shattering of the power of the holy people comes to an end ***ALL THESE THINGS WOULD BE FINISHED!"*** Thus we have an end bookmark for the end of the period known as "a thousand years." Now we continue with chapter twenty:

> Then I saw thrones, and seated on them were those to whom the authority to judge was committed. Also I saw the souls of those who had been beheaded for the testimony of Jesus and for the word of God, and those who had not worshiped the beast or its image and had not received its mark on their foreheads or their hands. They came to life and reigned with Christ for a thousand years. The rest of the dead did not come to life until the thousand years were ended. This is the first resurrection. Blessed and holy is the one who shares in the first resurrection! Over such the second death has no power, but they will be priests of God and of Christ, and they will reign with him for a thousand years. (Rev 20:4-6 ESV)

These saints who are mentioned here reigning with Christ are **the same saints** mentioned in Revelation chapter 6 who were given white robes and told to rest "a little longer." This period designated as "a little longer" is the same period which is symbolically designated as the "thousand years." The saints here were told to "rest a little longer until the number of their fellow servants and their brothers should be complete, who were to be killed as they themselves had been." (Revelation 6:11) If indeed this period sometimes designated as "the Millennium" was an actual thousand year period, how could it be that God would tell the saints in chapter six that they needed to rest a **LITTLE** longer. That would make no sense.

Now I want you to **look closely to what I am about to say. It gets a little complex**. Let's take this passage apart. As such, I will digress from the Revelation momentarily to discuss the resurrection as it relates to this passage. However, a complete discussion of the resurrection is beyond the scope of this work.

Revelation 20:4-5 tells us that there are two groups who participate in the first resurrection. I have highlighted these groups in bold letters in the passage. Notice what it says:

> Then I saw thrones, and seated on them were those to whom the authority to judge was committed. Also I saw **the souls of those who had been beheaded for the testimony of Jesus** and for the word of God, and those who had not worshiped the beast or its image and had not received its mark on their foreheads or their hands. They came to life and reigned with Christ for a thousand years. **The rest of the dead did not come to life until the thousand years were ended**. This is the first resurrection. (Revelation 20:4-5 ESV)

Upon first reading verse 5, it seems very confusing. It appears that there have been two separate and distinct groups being mentioned here, which we would think indicates two resurrections. The above is the verse as translated in the English Standard Version. Now **notice the difference** between this and the New International Version:

Rev 20:5 (**The rest of the dead did not come to life until the thousand years were ended**.) This is the first resurrection. (**NIV)**

Do you see the difference?

1. In the ESV, the passage **must be taken as follows**: "The rest of the dead (in Christ) did not come to life until the thousand years were ended." (This makes them a part of the first resurrection.)
2. In the NIV, the presence of the parentheses is an indication that those words in parentheses are a side note. (In other words, these ones are not a part of the first resurrection, but belong to the second resurrection.)

This passage has to be taken in one of these two ways in order to make sense. Otherwise we have to separate verse 5 as a second resurrection, which is contrary to what it says. As such, there would have to be a third resurrection, but this does not agree with how the verse is written.

I believe that the ESV has translated it correctly, and here is why.

Now in order to put this in perspective, we must remember the prophecy of Daniel 12:1-7 which tells us when the resurrection would occur. I know that this is a repetition of what I said above, but let's read this again:

"At that time shall arise Michael, the great prince who has charge of your people. And there shall be a time of trouble, such as never has been since there was a nation till that time. But at that time your people shall be delivered, everyone whose name shall be found written in the book. **And many of**

> **those who sleep in the dust of the earth shall awake, some to everlasting life, and some to shame and everlasting contempt.** (Daniel 12:1-2 ESV)

This is the resurrection. But let us continue:

> And those who are wise shall shine like the brightness of the sky above; and those who turn many to righteousness, like the stars forever and ever. But you, Daniel, shut up the words and seal the book, until the time of the end. Many shall run to and fro, and knowledge shall increase." Then I, Daniel, looked, and behold, two others stood, one on this bank of the stream and one on that bank of the stream. And someone said to the man clothed in linen, who was above the waters of the stream, "How long shall it be till the end of these wonders?" And I heard the man clothed in linen, who was above the waters of the stream; he raised his right hand and his left hand toward heaven and swore by him who lives forever that it would be for a time, times, and half a time, and **that when the shattering of the power of the holy people comes to an end all these things would be finished.** (Dan 12:3-7 ESV)

Once again I will ask: Did you notice the specificity of this verse? It says: "when the **shattering of the power of the holy people** comes to an end **ALL** these things would be **finished."**

This had to be at the destruction of Jerusalem in AD 70. This was the complete end of the Old Covenant and the Jewish Levitical system of worship. The power of God's heretofore holy people was completely shattered. This system of worship was no longer possible! It also had to be the end of the period sometimes referred to as the Millennium; because Rev. 20:5 plainly states that those dead in Christ did not come to life "until the thousand years were ended."

Also we must realize that Revelation 20:4 tells us that this resurrection includes not only:

1. The saints who were beheaded, but also,
2. Those who had not worshiped the beast or received the mark. Therefore, these are people who are still alive.

If the resurrection included both those dead at the time, and those alive, then we know that **it meant that all believers** were resurrected at that time, both those who were physically dead, and those who were physically alive. Thus, the first resurrection is by nature a **spiritual resurrection**, but at AD 70 it also included those who were removed from "paradise" in Hades, and were taken to heaven. This was the resurrection that Paul was speaking of in the passage in 1 Corinthians 15:42-44. Thus, **we as believers are a part of the first resurrection.**

The picture Paul painted in Romans 6:4 applies to us. **We were buried with Christ**. This put away our sin. **Then we were resurrected** to walk in the newness of life! **We are already part of the first resurrection!** What a blessing! As Rev 20:6 says, **the second death has no authority over us**, and this is in harmony with what Paul said:

> But God, being rich in mercy, because of the great love with which he loved us, even when we were dead in our trespasses, made us alive together with Christ—**by grace you have been saved**— and **raised us up with him and seated us with him in the heavenly places** in Christ Jesus, so that in the coming ages he might show the immeasurable riches of his grace in kindness toward us in Christ Jesus. For by grace you have been saved through faith. And this is not your own doing; it is the gift of God, (Ephesians 2:4-8 ESV)

Do you see the powerful significance of what Paul said? Those saints who were still alive on earth were also seated "with Him in the heavenly places." Their resurrection from spiritual death was complete, and the second death now had no power over them. The only way for man to be restored to that right relationship with God was for Him to also die to the flesh. This is done by belief in Christ as Lord and Savior. It is pictured perfectly by the baptism analogy.....**buried with Christ.......raised to walk in the newness of life.** (Romans 6:3-4) That new life is a spiritual one. When we accept Christ as Savior, we begin a new spiritual life with Christ, and we will never die again (spiritually). That is what Jesus meant when He said:

> Jesus said to her, "**I am the resurrection and the life**. Whoever believes in me, though he die, yet shall he live, and **everyone who lives and believes in me <u>shall never die</u>**. Do you believe this?" (John 11:25-26 ESV)

Now that this concept is covered, back to the Revelation. Let's look at verse 6 again:

> Blessed and holy is the one who shares in the first resurrection! Over such the second death has no power, but they will be priests of God and of Christ, and they will reign with him for a thousand years. (Revelation 20:6 ESV)

What a blessing this was for those who were a part of the first resurrection. Even while they were on the earth, they were reigning with him!

The Loosing and Defeat of Satan

Now the vision given to the Apostle John focuses on Satan at the end of the "thousand year" period. From Young's Literal Translation we read:

> And when the thousand years may be finished, the Adversary shall be loosed out of his prison, and he shall go forth to lead the nations astray, that are in the four corners of the earth—Gog and Magog—to gather them together to war, of whom the number *is* as the sand of the sea; and they did go up over the breadth of the land, and did surround the camp of the saints, and the beloved city, and there came down fire from God out of the heaven, and devoured them; and the Devil, who is leading them astray, was cast into the lake of fire and brimstone, where *are* the beast and the false prophet, and they shall be tormented day and night—to the ages of the ages. (Rev 20:7-10 YLT)

Satan's loosing and misleading the nations is a message similar to what the Apostle Paul sent to the Thessalonian Church when he wrote:

> The coming of the lawless one is by the activity of Satan with all power and false signs and wonders, and with all wicked deception for those who are perishing, because they refused to love the truth and so be saved. Therefore God sends them a strong delusion, so that they may believe what is false, in order that all may be condemned who did not believe the truth but had pleasure in unrighteousness. (2 Thes 2:9-12 ESV)

I would like to add that the loosing of Satan does not mean that he was given complete freedom to do what he wanted. Jesus already stated that Satan had fallen from heaven, and that he was powerless to act against His disciples. On the occasion when the seventy-two that he sent out came back and said:

> The seventy-two returned with joy, saying, "Lord, even the demons are subject to us in your name!" And he said to them, "**I saw Satan fall like lightning from heaven**. Behold, **I have given you authority** to tread on serpents and scorpions, and **over all the power of the enemy, and nothing shall hurt you.** Nevertheless, do not rejoice in this, that the spirits are subject to you, but rejoice that your names are written in

> heaven." (Luke 10:17-20 ESV)

Now the apostle has been given the vision to see that Satan is given a limited amount of freedom to deceive the enemies of God. But as with what happened with the seventy-two, His power is limited and this time **he will suffer a crushing defeat.** This was promised by the prophet Isaiah! Notice the words:

> In that day the LORD with his hard and great and strong sword will punish Leviathan the fleeing serpent, Leviathan the twisting serpent, and **he will slay the dragon that is in the sea**. (Isaiah 27:1 ESV)

This was also prophesied by the Apostle Paul when he told the Roman Christians:

> The God of peace will soon crush Satan under your feet. (Rom 16:20 ESV)

This passage shows that **this was in fact the final blow against Satan.** He was crushed and imprisoned as Young's translations states "to the ages of the ages." Satan is crushed! We have nothing to fear from him. Just as in the case of the seventy-two recorded by Luke in chapter 10, **Christians will never be harassed by Satan again.**

The Great White Throne Judgment

Now as we continue chapter 20 of the book of Revelation we note that the Apostle John was shown the following in this scene:

> Then I saw a great white throne and him who was seated on it. From his presence earth and sky fled away, and no place was found for them. And I saw the dead, great and small, standing before the throne, and books were opened. Then another book was opened, which is the book of life. And the dead were judged by what was written in the books, according to

> what they had done. (Rev 20:11-12)

This vision given to John was very similar to the vision given to Daniel in Daniel chapter seven. And it is almost universally agreed that Daniel chapter seven is placed in the time frame of the Roman Empire. Notice the amazing similarity in this passage in Daniel seven:

> "As I looked, thrones were placed, and the Ancient of Days took his seat; his clothing was white as snow, and the hair of his head like pure wool; his throne was fiery flames; its wheels were burning fire. A stream of fire issued and came out from before him; a thousand thousands served him, and ten thousand times ten thousand stood before him; the court sat in judgment, and the books were opened. (Dan 7:9-10)

We even see the destruction of the beast, which as we have discussed has a dual nature being the Roman Empire and the Emperor Nero. The brutal person of the beast, the great persecutor of Christians, Nero is dead as a victim of his own madness, when he committed suicide. He did this as General Galba was about to capture him. He is long gone and has been replaced. The one who replaced him also fulfilled prophecy by being there for a very short while as we discussed earlier (Revelation 17:10). But the beast was revived under the reign of Vespasian (Revelation 13:3). The Roman Empire has now been used by God to bring judgment on the Harlot! Bible prophecy and the Vision given to John are right on track. Thus, we have proof, both Biblically and historically that this time frame was within the generation that Jesus said would see the total destruction of Jerusalem! But now we see that with the completion of this vision's fulfillment, we will also bring about the fulfillment of what John was given earlier in Revelation 15:8:

> and the sanctuary was filled with smoke from the glory of God

> and from his power, and **no one could enter the sanctuary until the seven plagues of the seven angels were finished.** (ESV)

Now that the seven plagues are finished, and the Parousia is complete, Christ is now rightfully on the throne in His position of glory. The final judgment is occurring. This is a time of fulfillment of Matt 25:

> "When the Son of Man comes in his glory, and all the angels with him, then he will sit on his glorious throne. Before him will be gathered all the nations, and he will separate people one from another as a shepherd separates the sheep from the goats. (Matt 25:31-32 ESV)

It is also a time of fulfillment of that which was written by the writer of Hebrews when he recorded:

> And just as it is appointed for man to die once, and after that comes judgment, so Christ, having been offered once to bear the sins of many, **will appear a second time, not to deal with sin but to save those who are eagerly waiting for him**. (Hebrew 9:27-28)

This passage makes it very clear that **it was *only after the Parousia* occurred that all salvation was possible!** That means that **no one's** salvation is complete until the end of the Parousia! But there is yet more in this vision.

> And the sea gave up the dead who were in it, Death and Hades gave up the dead who were in them, and they were judged, each one of them, according to what they had done. Then Death and Hades were thrown into the lake of fire. This is the second death, the lake of fire. And if anyone's name was not found written in the book of life, he was thrown into the lake of fire. (Rev 20:13-15)

When this passage says that "the sea gave up the dead who were in it," this is a reference to the resurrection. Death and Hades have given up the dead in them and they were thrown in the lake of fire. This puts an end to Hades and it is no more. The resurrection has occurred and the dead have been judged. We are now at the point of a new creation. This was foretold by the prophet Isaiah when he said:

> "For behold, **I create new heavens and a new earth**, and the former things shall not be remembered or come into mind. But be glad and rejoice forever in that which I create; for behold, I create Jerusalem to be a joy, and her people to be a gladness. **I will rejoice in Jerusalem and be glad in my people; no more shall be heard in it the sound of weeping and the cry of distress**. (Isa 65:17-19)

This will be a time when a New Jerusalem will come into existence, one in which there will no more be weeping and wailing as occurred in the Old Jerusalem. The Saints have been vindicated, the remnant of Israel will be saved, and there is more! Heaven and earth in the form of the temple have now been destroyed. The resurrection has occurred, and the promise of the Lord Jesus is being fulfilled in great detail. But just what are we talking about here? We are talking about a New Covenant. It is not a new physical creation. It is a spiritual creation as we shall see. Let us continue.

Section 3

The Final Vision

The Marriage of the Lamb

Final Judgments

Chapter 14

The Seventh (and final) Vision

The New Heavens and the New Earth

The first and most important thing that must be understood about the "new heavens and the new earth" is the timing. We have already noticed the passage in Daniel that tells us that "**when the shattering of the power of the holy people comes to an end *all these things would be finished*.** (Dan 12:7 ESV)

With this in mind, we also have the words of the prophet Isaiah to confirm this. Notice the words of the prophet:

> "Listen to Me, My people; And give ear to Me, O My nation: For law will proceed from Me, And I will make My justice rest As a light of the peoples. My righteousness *is* near, My salvation has gone forth, And My arms will judge the peoples; The coastlands will wait upon Me, And on My arm they will trust. Lift up your eyes to the heavens, And look on the earth beneath. **For the heavens will vanish away like smoke, The earth will grow old like a garment, And those who dwell in it will die in like manner; *But My salvation will be forever,* And My righteousness will not be abolished**. (Isaiah 51:4-6 ESV)

This salvation spoken of here by the prophet was the New Covenant! It would not be a short-lived covenant like the Old Covenant, but it would last forever! Do you understand the profound nature of these words? They describe a New Covenant in a new creation! It would be a New Heavens and a New Earth which would include a New Jerusalem and would come **after the Millennium**! This is very clearly expressed in Rev 20:7-11. But let us continue in chapter 51 where we find:

> These **TWO THINGS** have come to you; Who will be sorry for you?— **Desolation and destruction, famine and swor**d— By whom will I comfort you? Your sons have fainted, They lie at the head of all the streets, Like an antelope in a net; **They are full of the fury of the LORD,** The rebuke of your God. Therefore please hear this, you afflicted, And drunk but not with wine. Thus says your Lord, The LORD and your God, *Who* pleads the cause of His people: "See, I have taken out of your hand The cup of trembling, The dregs of the cup of My fury; You shall no longer drink it. But I will put it into the hand of those who afflict you, Who have said to you, 'Lie down, that we may walk over you.' And you have laid your body like the ground, And as the street, for those who walk over." (Isa 51:19-23)

Do the words of the prophet look familiar? They should! This specifically describes the destruction of the temple and the city of Jerusalem. This actually happened twice as noted by Bible Commentator John Gill. He notes what was spoken of in the Targum concerning this passage, noting that it is a paraphrase of the words of the prophet:

> **These two things are come unto thee**,.... Affliction from the hand of God, though by means of enemies, and no friends to help, support, and comfort, as before hinted: or else this respects what follows, after it is said,
>
> **who shall be sorry for thee**? lament or bemoan thee? they of the earth will rejoice and be glad, and others will not dare to show any concern outwardly, whatever inward grief may be in their breasts, Rev 11:10,

> **desolation, and destruction, and the famine, and the sword**; which may be the two things before mentioned, for though there are four words, they are reducible to two things, desolation, which is the sword, and by it, and destruction, which is the famine, and comes by that, as Kimchi observes: or the words may be rendered thus, "desolation, and destruction, even the famine and the sword"; so that there is no need of making these things four, and of considering them as distinct from the other two, as the Targum makes them, which paraphrases the whole thus, "**two tribulations come upon thee, O Jerusalem**, thou canst not arise; when four shall come upon thee, spoiling and breach, and **the famine and the sword, there shall be none to comfort thee but I.**"[lxvi]

It happened in judgment upon Jerusalem twice! The last time, the temple would never be built again! It would not be needed anymore! It is very similar to the situation of the lament Jeremiah had as he wrote in Lamentations:

> Jerusalem has sinned gravely, Therefore she has become vile. All who honored her despise her Because they have seen her nakedness; Yes, she sighs and turns away. Her uncleanness *is* in her skirts; She did not consider her destiny; Therefore her collapse was awesome; She had no comforter. "O LORD, behold my affliction, For *the* enemy is exalted!" (Lam 1:8-9)

This firmly established the timeframe. The power of the holy people was broken beyond all possibility of repair! Now as we look at Revelation 21 we find:

> Now I saw a new heaven and a new earth, for the first heaven and the first earth had passed away. Also there was no more sea. Then I, John, saw the holy city, New Jerusalem, coming down out of heaven from God, prepared as a bride adorned for her husband. And I heard a loud voice from heaven saying, "Behold, the tabernacle of God *is* with men, and He will dwell with them, and they shall be His people. God Himself will be with them *and be* their God. (Revelation 21:1-3)

So now we have the fulfillment of the promise given to the faithful Old Covenant saints, i.e. the martyrs who asked "how long O Lord?" These saints were given white robes and told to wait a little longer. **In this passage, the wait is over!** The writer of Hebrews spoke of the shortness of the time in his day when he said:

> Therefore do not throw away your confidence, which has great reward. For you have need of endurance, in order that *after you* have done the will of God, you may receive what was promised. **For yet "a very, very little *while*,** *and* the one who is coming will come and will not delay. (Hebrews 10:35-37 Lexham English Bible)

That very, very little while has now arrived! The resurrection has occurred. The bride of the Lamb, now adorned in righteous attire because of the blood of Jesus has received her promise, as **the New Jerusalem descends from heaven to reside with God's people on earth.** This fulfills the promise made through the prophet Isaiah:

> So the ransomed of the LORD shall return, And come to Zion with singing, With everlasting joy on their heads. They shall obtain joy and gladness; Sorrow and sighing shall flee away. (Isaiah 51:11 NKJV)

It also is a complete and accurate fulfillment of the promise that Jesus made when He said:

> "Do not think that I came to destroy the Law or the Prophets. I did not come to destroy but to fulfill. For assuredly, I say to you, **till heaven and earth pass away, one jot or one tittle will by no means pass from the law till all is fulfilled**. (Matt 5:17-18)

Now that "heaven and earth" have passed away, the Old Covenant Law was now **dead and completely defunct.** Once again, as always, God keeps His promises. Let us continue as we look at this promise given to the Apostle John:

> And God will wipe away every tear from their eyes; there shall be no more death, nor sorrow, nor crying. There shall be no more pain, for the former things have passed away." Then He who sat on the throne said, "Behold, I make all things new." And He said to me, "Write, for these words are true and faithful." And He said to me, "It is done! I am the Alpha and the Omega, the Beginning and the End. I will give of the fountain of the water of life freely to him who thirsts. (Revelation 21:4-6 NASB)

The understanding of this passage is wrapped up in the understanding of the meaning of death as spoken of here. Is the Apostle John speaking of a literal physical death in this passage? NO! The death that is spoken of here is NOT physical death. It is speaking of spiritual death. In order to prove this point, it is necessary that I briefly digress from this passage.

A Brief Discussion of Death and Resurrection

For a more complete discussion of this, I would refer you to the appendix entitled "The Resurrection" at the end of this book. But as relates to this point, I would like to ask, when we think of death, we usually think of a lifeless body. When we think of resurrection, we usually think of bodies coming back to life. But from the standpoint of the eschatology of the Scriptures, this concept is erroneous. Please follow along with me as I develop this point. Let's look at what God told Adam about death in the very beginning.

> And the LORD God commanded the man, saying, "Of every tree of the garden you may freely eat; but of the tree of the

> knowledge of good and evil you shall not eat, for **in the day that you eat of it you shall surely die**." (Gen 2:16-17 NKJV)

Since Adam and Eve did disobey and eat of the fruit, did they actually die a physical death that very day? NO! The Bible records that the physical death occurred some 900 years later. So what God was speaking of with Adam was **spiritual death.** This spiritual death is the death that the entire Bible speaks about. And when we speak of resurrection, we must understand that this also must be part of the discussion. The Apostle Paul gave a perfect picture of both death and resurrection in Romans chapter six.

How many of you believers have been baptized?

I will hold my hand up on that one, but I also realize that some of you who are reading this may have determined from your studies that a baptism in water is not necessary. This is an entirely different discussion, but I for my part come down on the side of the baptism of all Christians. Regardless of your stand on physical baptism in the water, I would like to call your attention to a picture which Paul gives us concerning baptism, and how it relates to resurrection. It is found in Romans Chapter 6 and it reads:

> Do you not know that all of us who have been baptized into Christ Jesus were baptized into his death? We were buried therefore with him by baptism into death, in order that, just as Christ was raised from the dead by the glory of the Father, we too might walk in newness of life. For if we have been united with him in a death like his, we shall certainly be united with him in a resurrection like his. We know that our old self was crucified with him in order that the body of sin might be brought to nothing, so that we would no longer be enslaved to sin. For one who has died has been set free from sin. Now if we have died with Christ, we believe that we will also live with him. (Romans 6:3-8 ESV)

So the apostle said here that we were baptized into His death. But I want to look again at verse four. Notice that in verse four is this beautiful picture of our death and resurrection – **Buried with Christ, raised to walk in the newness of life!**

Do you see the profound significance of this passage? I did NOT see it for many years. I remember when I was baptized in water, well over 30 years ago. As I was going down into the water, the Pastor said those very words: “buried with Christ.” Then when I was coming up out of the water he said: “raised to walk in the newness of life.” The implication by those words in Romans 6:4 are that since we were being buried with Christ **we must have been dead in some manner.** So now as we look back, we see that when Adam was placed in the garden he was in perfect spiritual fellowship with God. His most important assignment was to obey God. When he disobeyed God, **he died that day, spiritually**. He was then separated from God....... no more walks in the Garden together, and no more discussions together. It was over. The Apostle Paul confirmed this line of thinking in the book of Romans when he wrote:

> Wherefore, as by one man sin entered into the world, and death by sin; and so **death passed upon all men, for that all have sinned**: For until the law sin was in the world: but sin is not imputed when there is no law. Nevertheless **death reigned from Adam to Moses**, even over them that had not sinned after the similitude of Adam's transgression, who is the figure of him that was to come. (Rom 5:12-14 ESV)

This raises some questions, but first let’s look at what Paul said to the church at Colossae:

> And you, who were ***dead in your trespasses*** and the uncircumcision of your flesh, God made alive together with him, having forgiven us all our trespasses, by canceling the record of debt that stood against us with its legal demands. **This he set aside, nailing it to the cross**. (Colossians 2:13-14)

Did you notice how Paul defines death in this passage?

He said they were **dead in their trespasses**, but God made them alive with Christ. Were they physically dead? Of course not; It is obvious that Paul was speaking of going from **spiritual death to spiritual life.** So now, the question has to be, if death reigned from Adam to Moses, as Paul said earlier, **did Moses solve the problem of death?** Man has continued to die physically even to this day after Moses came, so we know that this does **not speak of physical death**. So what did this mean?

With Moses came the Old Covenant. The purpose of that Old Covenant was to show man the utter impossibility of keeping the covenant due to his inherited sin. So, in effect, what it actually did was to show man the impossibility of his ability to keep the law. But at the same time, the Old Law Covenant pointed to the Messiah who would actually provide redemption for the sins of man. Paul stated it in this passage to the Roman church:

> Therefore, as **one trespass led to condemnation for all men**, so **one act of righteousness leads to justification** and life for **all** men. For as by the one man's disobedience the many were made sinners, so by the one man's obedience the many will be made righteous. Now **the law came in to increase the trespass, but where sin increased, grace abounded all the more,** so that, as sin reigned in death, grace also might reign through righteousness leading to eternal life through Jesus Christ our Lord. (Romans 5:18-21 ESV)

Thus we see that sin and death are inseparable. Verse 20 shows us that when the law entered, the effect of sin increased to an even greater extent. But physical death did not get any worse in terms of its severity. So the reference here is to spiritual death. This is clearly shown by what Paul later said in Romans 7:

> For I was alive without the law once: but when the commandment came, sin revived, **and I died.** And the commandment, which *was ordained* to life, I **found *to be* unto death.** For sin, seizing an opportunity through the commandment, deceived me and through **it killed me.** So the law is holy, and the commandment is holy and righteous and good. Did that which is good, then, bring death to me? By no means! **It was sin, producing death in me through what is good**, in order that sin might be shown to be sin, and through the commandment might become sinful beyond measure. (Romans 7:9-13 ESV)

Do you see the profound significance of this?

It is obvious that since Paul **had not yet died physically**, he **had to be** speaking of spiritual death. This is **the death which all men experience when they sin against God**. But this death is not something which cannot be reversed. Paul also wrote:

> For as in Adam **all** die, even so in Christ shall **all** be made alive. (1 Corinthians 15:22 ESV)

Did you notice how Paul worded this verse? **Paul did not say**, "even so in Christ all **have been** made alive." He said "even so in Christ **shall all be made alive**." He explains why he said it this way in the next verse. Note his words:

> But every man in his own order: Christ the firstfruits; afterward they that are Christ's **at his coming.** (1 Corinthians 15:23 ESV)

This will not happen in the physical realm. If the death that Adam experienced **was spiritual death**, then **the life that Christ brings is spiritual life!**

Now as we return to Revelation chapter 21, **we must remember that this occurred at the Parousia.** Spiritual life for all men was finally and completely restored. **So if the Parousia has not happened, then our salvation is not complete!**

Back to Revelation 21

So as we look at this passage in Revelation 21:4, we must realize that this verse speaks of the New Creation when it says:

> And God will wipe away every tear from their eyes; there shall be no more death, nor sorrow, nor crying. There shall be no more pain, for the former things have passed away." Then He who sat on the throne said, "Behold, I make all things new." And He said to me, "Write, for these words are true and faithful." (Rev 21:4-5 NASB)

In the vision which John saw here, we have the New Creation being fulfilled in the form of the New Covenant. **With this, we have fulfilled all the promises of Jesus, the Lamb of God! We can rejoice!** There is no need for worry concerning the pain of our fallen humanity! Through the **precious blood of the Lamb** who has now **fulfilled His promise** of the Parousia, and has presented His blood in the Holy of Holies in heaven, **that promise is now complete!**

> **And He said to me, "It is done! I am the Alpha and the Omega, the Beginning and the End.** I will give of the fountain of the water of life freely to him who thirsts. (Revelation 21:6 NASB)

This statement puts the finishing touch on that reality. Now as we continue:

> "He who overcomes will inherit these things, and I will be his God and he will be My son. "But for the cowardly and unbelieving and abominable and murderers and immoral persons and sorcerers and idolaters and all liars, their part will be in the lake that burns with fire and brimstone, which is the second death." (Rev 21:7-8 NASB)

Here we see the judgment for the remaining ones not under the blood of Christ. These are the ones who have rejected Christ, and are not saved by the blood of Christ. For that they must suffer loss. They will be sent to Gehenna. The complete discussion of this subject is beyond the scope of this book. I have written **my opinion** of this subject in my book, ***God's Purpose for Hell, a compelling probe of God's love for the lost.*** (Available at Amazon.com)

The New Jerusalem

As we look at the passage below, it is important to realize that as John is receiving this vision, it is not the first time this is spoken of in Scripture. This vision of a "New Jerusalem" as a part of the "New Heavens and New Earth" was given centuries earlier to the prophet Isaiah in chapter 65 of his prophecy. Now let's look at the words given to the Apostle John which describe this city:

> Then one of the seven angels who had the seven bowls filled with the seven last plagues came to me and talked with me, saying, "Come, I will show you the bride, the Lamb's wife." And he carried me away in the Spirit to a great and high mountain, and showed me the great city, the holy Jerusalem, descending out of heaven from God, having the glory of God. Her light *was* like a most precious stone, like a jasper stone,

> clear as crystal. Also she had a great and high wall with twelve gates, and twelve angels at the gates, and names written on them, which are *the names* of the twelve tribes of the children of Israel: three gates on the east, three gates on the north, three gates on the south, and three gates on the west. Now the wall of the city had twelve foundations, and on them were the names of the twelve apostles of the Lamb. And he who talked with me had a gold reed to measure the city, its gates, and its wall. The city is laid out as a square; its length is as great as its breadth. And he measured the city with the reed: twelve thousand furlongs. Its length, breadth, and height are equal. Then he measured its wall: one hundred *and* forty-four cubits, *according* to the measure of a man, that is, of an angel. The construction of its wall was *of* jasper; and the city *was* pure gold, like clear glass. The foundations of the wall of the city *were* adorned with all kinds of precious stones: the first foundation *was* jasper, the second sapphire, the third chalcedony, the fourth emerald, the fifth sardonyx, the sixth sardius, the seventh chrysolite, the eighth beryl, the ninth topaz, the tenth chrysoprase, the eleventh jacinth, and the twelfth amethyst. The twelve gates *were* twelve pearls: each individual gate was of one pearl. And the street of the city *was* pure gold, like transparent glass. (Rev 21:9-21 NKJV)

This is the city spoken of by the writer of Hebrews when he said:

> But you have come to Mount Zion and to the city of the living God, **the heavenly Jerusalem,** and to innumerable angels in festal gathering, . . . Therefore let us be grateful for receiving a kingdom that **cannot be shaken**, and thus let us offer to God acceptable worship, with reverence and awe, for our God is a consuming fire. . . . For here we have no lasting city, but we seek the city **that is to come**. (Hebrews 12:22, 28-29; 13:14 ESV)

I would like to point out that when that last verse in Hebrews stated "the city that is to come," we find the Greek word μελλουσαν which means **it was imminent, very near, i.e. about to come!**

It was **NOT** something for which they would have to wait thousands of years to become a reality, as some have suggested! The reality was very close. In fact this was a real city which already existed in heaven, but had not yet come to the earth**. This is why it is shown as having real dimensions as given in the vision to John**. Thus, it was already . . . but not yet . . . for those early Christians during the time of the writing of the book of Hebrews.

In fact, in John's day the words of the vision he was given states in verse six: "**it is done**" and in the final chapter of Revelation it reiterates the nearness of the time as we shall see.

The apostle Paul had already declared: "But our citizenship is in heaven, and from it we await a Savior, the Lord Jesus Christ." (Phil 3:20 ESV) Here he is stating that ***they were awaiting the Parousia in order for their salvation to be complete*** as he did when he said: "For salvation is **nearer to us now** than when we first believed; (Rom 13:11 ESV) and when he said: "Behold, now is the favorable time; behold, **now is the day of salvation**. (2 Cor 6:2). The writer of Hebrews also declared this when he said: "so Christ was offered once to bear the sins of many. To those who eagerly wait for Him **He will appear a second time, apart from sin, *for salvation***." (Heb 9:28 NKJV)

This is also the same city spoken of by the Apostle Paul when he recorded his letter to the Galatian Church: "But the Jerusalem above is free, and **she is our mother**." (Gal 4:26 ESV) Yes! The Jerusalem above is the New Jerusalem, **and it extends to the believers on earth**. It is the everlasting Kingdom of God. This was also spoken of by the Apostle Paul in a very powerful passage to the church in Ephesus:

> In him we have redemption through his blood, the forgiveness of our trespasses, according to the riches of his grace, which he lavished upon us, in all wisdom and insight making known to us the mystery of his will, according to his purpose, **which he set forth in Christ as a plan for the fullness of time, to unite all things in him, things in heaven and things on earth.** (Eph 1:7-10 ESV)

Wow! Do you understand the profound nature of what is spoken of here by the Apostle Paul? This is in complete harmony with this vision given to John. **Heaven and earth are reunited in this vision!**

> I saw no temple in it, for the Lord God the Almighty and the Lamb are its temple. And the city has no need of the sun or of the moon to shine on it, for the glory of God has illumined it, and its lamp is the Lamb. The nations will walk by its light, and the kings of the earth will bring their glory into it. In the daytime (for there will be no night there) its gates will never be closed; and they will bring the glory and the honor of the nations into it; and nothing unclean, and no one who practices abomination and lying, shall ever come into it, but only those whose names are written in the Lamb's book of life. (Rev 21:22-27 NASB)

As you will notice in verse 22, there was **no temple!** It was **no longer necessary**. Those who are in the Holy City and are alive on the earth are under the blood of Jesus and are cleansed by that blood, thus being declared as righteous. As such they are written in the Lamb's book of life.

The River of Life

As we look at this chapter, the words of the Apostle Paul from Ephesians chapter one mentioned above **once again ring in our**

ears. What was lost in the Garden of Eden is finally restored. It is obvious that the Kingdom of God is actually a reuniting of heaven and earth. There will be a heavenly portion and an earthly portion of this Kingdom. Notice what is revealed to John:

> And he showed me a pure river of water of life, clear as crystal, proceeding from the throne of God and of the Lamb. In the middle of its street, and on either side of the river, *was* the tree of life, which bore twelve fruits, each *tree* yielding its fruit every month. **The leaves of the tree *were* for the healing of the nations.** And there shall be no more curse, but the throne of God and of the Lamb shall be in it, and His servants shall serve Him. They shall see His face, and His name *shall be* on their foreheads. There shall be no night there: They need no lamp nor light of the sun, for the Lord God gives them light. And they shall reign forever and ever. (Rev 22:1-5 NKJV)

Now just think about this for a moment. Why would there need to be any leaves necessary for the healing of the nations? **It is because outside of the Holy City, sin was still present!** This is proof that this Kingdom of God had a dual nature with the reuniting of heaven and earth. On earth, outside of the Kingdom of God, sin still existed. But God made provision for those who would eventually accept Christ and come under the protection of the precious blood of the Lamb. Here we have the eternal Kingdom of God! Those inside the Kingdom of God are forever safe and secure. Thus, they were healed by the leaves of the tree of life. But those on the outside on the earth are not safe and secure. This is where we Christians come into play. Remember that Jesus told His disciples that they were "the salt of the earth." (Matt 5:13) Then He said they were "the light of the world." (Matt 5:14) He also said "Have salt in yourselves and have peace with one another." (Mark 9:50) We can use **the healing power of our "salt,"** that is the

message of Christ to help heal these weary ones by leading them to come to know Christ as their Savior, and by doing this they will be partaking of the tree of life. When this happens, they will be **healed permanently** and forever, safe in the everlasting arms of Christ!

This is a fulfillment of what the prophet Daniel stated would happen during the reign of the fourth world power, the Roman Empire:

> And in the days of these kings the God of heaven will set up a **kingdom which shall never be destroyed;** and the kingdom shall not be left to other people; it shall break in pieces and **consume all these kingdoms**, and it shall stand forever. (Dan 2:44 NKJV)

When Jesus was on the earth it was that time, the time of the rule of the Roman Empire. He began this Kingdom of God when He made the selection of the Apostles. From that tiny beginning He has built the kingdom described above by the prophet Daniel. Notice Jesus words:

> It is like what happens when a mustard seed is planted in the ground. It is the smallest seed in all the world. But once it is planted, it grows larger than any garden plant. It even puts out branches that are big enough for birds to nest in its shade. (Mark 4:31.32 Contemporary English Version)

This is what the Kingdom of God has become, and our role in this kingdom is vital. Let us not forsake this calling by Christ for the Kingdom of God.

Now as we continue with the conclusion of the Vision in Revelation we read:

> And he said to me, "These words are faithful and true"; and the Lord, the God of the spirits of the prophets, sent His angel to show to His bond-servants the things which **must soon take place**. "And behold, **I am coming quickly**. Blessed is he who heeds the words of the prophecy of this book." I, John, am the one who heard and saw these things. And when I heard and saw, I fell down to worship at the feet of the angel who showed me these things. But he said to me, "Do not do that. I am a fellow servant of yours and of your brethren the prophets and of those who heed the words of this book. Worship God." And he said to me, "**Do not seal up the words of the prophecy of this book, for the time is near**. (Revelation 22:6-10 NASB)

Now I would like to make the point here that by these words, **three times** in the short span of these verses, the angel who has given John this vision has made it perfectly clear that this was **NOT** something which would happen in the distant future! As I have highlighted the words in the verses above, we can see that this Vision was given to John to be given to the churches with urgency! **It was about to happen**. But there is another confirming factor to show the urgency if this. The prophet Daniel was told concerning his prophecy:

> But you, Daniel, shut up the words, and **seal the book until the time of the end**; (Daniel 12:4 NKJV)

That was 500-600 years prior to this vision given to the Apostle John. But John was given the words:

> "**Do not seal up the words of the prophecy of this book, for the time is near**. (Revelation 22:10 NASB)

Is it reasonable to think that we could have gone nearly 2000 years since these words were written, and yet this "time that is near" has not yet happened? The notion of this is preposterous! But there is still even more confirmation of this!

> He who is unjust, let him be unjust still; he who is filthy, let him be filthy still; he who is righteous, let him be righteous still; he who is holy, let him be holy still." "And behold, I am coming quickly, and My reward *is* with Me, to give to every one according to his work. (Rev 22:11,12 NKJV)

Do you understand what He is saying here? He is saying that this time that is spoken of here was so very imminent that there would be **very little time left** for repentance! But to those who have put their trust in him, there would be great reward! Yes - **the time of the end was very much at hand!** But amazingly enough, there is even more repetition of this point as we continue:

> **I am the Alpha and the Omega**, the first and the last, the beginning and the end. Blessed are those who wash their robes, so that they may have the right to the tree of life and that they may enter the city by the gates. Outside are the dogs and sorcerers and the sexually immoral and murderers and idolaters, and everyone who loves and practices falsehood. "I, Jesus, have sent my angel to testify to you about these things for the churches. I am the root and the descendant of David, the bright morning star." The Spirit and the Bride say, "Come." And let the one who hears say, "Come." And let the one who is thirsty come; let the one who desires take the water of life without price. (Rev 22:13-17 ESV)

Here we see Jesus reiterating what we said before. In effect, by making the statement "I am the Alpha and Omega" **Jesus is swearing by himself that those who wash their robes in the precious blood of the lamb will be healed by the leaves, partaking of the tree of life!** They would be the ones of the nations who were healed as spoken of in verse two of this final chapter. They will be the ones inside the Holy City, the New Jerusalem, safe and secure. But those outside **who would not choose** to come under the precious blood of the lamb would be labeled as dogs and sorcerers, sexually immoral, murderers and idolaters. These ones would be fit for destruction at that time.

But here we also find our Precious Lord making His **final plea** to those who would humble themselves in the light of the impending destruction of the city of Jerusalem telling them that His living water is a **FREE GIFT. WOW!** How much more do we see the love of our Savior in these words!

As we conclude this seventh vision which also concludes the last book of the Bible, we see that the angel who was bringing this revelation to John also declared this to not only be a vision, but a prophecy. And as always in Scripture, this one was to be fulfilled exactly as prophesied. Therefore, a stern warning was given for the apostle to pass on to the hearers and readers of this book. He told them NOT to change anything here. Notice the words given to the apostle:

> I testify to everyone who hears the words of the prophecy of this book: if anyone adds to them, God will add to him the plagues which are written in this book; and if anyone takes away from the words of the book of this prophecy, God will take away his part from the tree of life and from the holy city, which are written in this book. (Rev 22:18-19 NASB)

Here I must admit that these words of warning have had a profound effect upon me. Why? Because I find myself writing an interpretation of the prophecy. The words given here should give pause to any and all who would delve into this book. However, even knowing this, I have taken this matter very seriously. But through prayer, and deep concern for truth, I have been pressed to show the most important and noteworthy fact of all and that is that **our Lord Jesus always keeps His promises**. And this final book of the Bible has done just that! However, as I said in the beginning of this undertaking in the writing of this book, what I have written here is my opinion of the meaning of the events spoken of in this book. I have tried my best to see to it that the interpretation given here is one which allows for **the unity and clarity of the entire Bible.** To that end, I have done my best to tie all of the evidence together including the prophetic and the historic, from the words of the prophets to the words of the historians as they have presented the details of what occurred. I have confidence that I have done all that I can to make sure that there has been no manipulation of facts herein. It is my belief that the words written in this final book of the Bible **bring to a conclusion all prophecy** just as spoken by our Lord, and recorded by the physician Luke in his account of the Gospel:

> because these are days of vengeance, **so that *ALL THINGS* which are written will be fulfilled** (Luke 21:22 NASB)

> Assuredly, I say to you, this generation will by no means pass away till **all these things** take place. (Matt 24:34 NKJV)

And also as written by the prophet Daniel:

> Then I heard the man clothed in linen, who *was* above the waters of the river, when he held up his right hand and his left hand to heaven, and swore by Him who lives forever, that *it shall be* for a time, times, and half *a time;* and **when the power of the holy people has been completely shattered, *ALL* these *things* shall be finished**. (Daniel 12:7 NKJV)

This final vision given to the Apostle John shows God bringing to a conclusion all things prophetic, but just to make sure that the readers understand the timing, he states it one more time:

> He who testifies to these things says, "**Yes, I am coming quickly**." Amen. Come, Lord Jesus. The grace of the Lord Jesus be with all. Amen. (Rev 22:20 NASB)

Yes, after receiving all of these prophetic visions, the Apostle John, being in awe of all of this, wrote his own thoughts to show his confidence in the near fulfillment of these things. It was serious and deadly for many, but for those persecuted and beloved followers of Jesus, it was a much needed and hoped for answer to prayer. Thus, his words: “Amen, Come Lord Jesus. The grace of our Lord Jesus be with all, Amen.”

Epilogue

> 1 Peter 1:4 God made great and marvelous promises, **so that his nature would become part of us**. Then we could escape our evil desires and the corrupt influences of this world. (From the Contemporary English Version)

What a wonderful statement recorded by the Apostle Peter!

Is there any doubt that the Bible is a book of promises? God has made these promises to those who believe despite the fact that we do not deserve them. We sing praises to God based on His precious promises. Remember this one?

> Standing on the promises of Christ my King
> Through eternal ages let his praises ring
> Glory in the highest, I will shout and sing
> Standing on the promises of God
> Standing, standing
> Standing on the promises of God my Savior
> Standing, standing
> I'm standing on the promises of God

Yes, we have our faith because of the promises of God. Here are some of them upon which we base our faith:

The promise of God's love: This was defined in the writings of Paul:

> Love is patient, love is kind and is not jealous; love does not brag and is not arrogant, does not act unbecomingly; it does not seek its own, is not provoked, does not take into account a

wrong suffered, does not rejoice in unrighteousness, but rejoices with the truth; bears all things, believes all things, hopes all things, endures all things. Love never fails; (1 Cor 13:5-8)

The Apostle John recorded:

We have come to know and have believed the love which God has for us. God is love, and the one who abides in love abides in God, and God abides in him. (1 John 4:16)

for the Father Himself loves you, because you have loved Me and have believed that I came forth from the Father. (John 6:27)

The promise of faith: This is belief that God is real and God is good!

For in it the righteousness of God is revealed from faith to faith; as it is written, "**BUT THE RIGHTEOUS man SHALL LIVE BY FAITH**." (Rom 1:17)

"And God, who knows the heart, testified to them giving them the Holy Spirit, just as He also did to us; and He made no distinction between us and them, **cleansing their hearts by faith**. (Act 15:8,9)

The promise of hope:

What then shall we say to these things? **If God is for us, who is against us?** He who did not spare His own Son, but delivered Him over for us all, how will He not also with Him freely give us all things? Who will bring a charge against God's elect? God is the one who justifies. (Romans 8:31-33)

Now may **the God of hope** fill you with all joy and peace in believing, so that you will abound in hope by the power of the Holy Spirit. (Rom 15:13)

The promise of eternal life:

> "Truly, truly, I say to you, he who hears My word, and believes Him who sent Me, **has eternal life,** and does not come into judgment, **but has passed out of death into life**. (John 5:24)

These are but a few of the precious promises that God has given us upon which we all have based the Christian Faith! God has promised so much more in His precious word. He gives us the help we need just in the right time:

Taken from an old Gideon Bible, I have found **just a few more** of the **PROMISES** He gives us through His Word:

> **The path to Salvation:** John 14:6; Acts 16:31; Romans 10:9
> **Comfort in a time of Loneliness:** Psalm 23; Isaiah 41:10; Hebrews `13:5,6
> **Relief in a time of Suffering:** 2 Cor 12:8-10;
> Protection in a time of **Danger:** Psalm 91; Psalm 121
> **Courage in a time of Fear:** Hebrews 13:5,6; Ephesians 6:10-18
> **Strength in a time of Temptation:** James 1:12-16; 1 Cor 10:6-13

So now it's time for a little intellectual honesty. With all of these **precious promises** we have from our loving God, **why would any of us think that God failed to deliver on the most important promises** in the form of prophecies which was given to His disciples when He walked the surface of this earth in human form?

Let's take these one by one.

Prior to this, His greatest prophecy, Jesus told His disciples:

> But whenever they persecute you in one city, flee to the next; for truly I say to you, **you will not finish going through the cities of Israel until the Son of Man comes. (**Matt 10:23)

Jesus promised them that He would come again after His death but before they would finish their personal ministry in the cities of Israel. If we believe that Jesus **STILL HAS NOT** fulfilled this promise, then we **MUST believe that Jesus was wrong!** If He was wrong, how could He be the creator of the heavens and the earth? (John 1:1-3; Colossians 1:15,16)

Jesus also told His disciples:

> Truly I say to you, there are some of those who are standing here who **will not taste death** until they see the Son of Man coming in His kingdom. (Matt: 16:28)

Some have tried to say that since He showed them the transfiguration 6 days later that this is what He was talking about. But do you really think that Jesus was saying that **most of them would die** during that six day interval? Isn't that the implication of this statement in Matthew 16:28?

Then what was He talking about? It was the same event which He told the high priest during that "Kangaroo court" that occurred prior to His crucifixion. Here is the conversation between Jesus and Caiaphas:

> And the high priest said to him, "I adjure you by the living God, tell us if you are the Christ, the Son of God." Jesus said to him, "You have said so. But I tell ***YOU***, from now on ***YOU*** will see the Son of Man seated at the right hand of Power and coming on the clouds of heaven." Matt 26:63,64

From the use of the word ***YOU***, it is obvious that Jesus was **NOT** speaking of some future generation. Jesus was **specifically** speaking to the High Priest (Caiaphas) and the other members of the Sanhedrin who were present. Once again, we have to ask: **Was Jesus wrong?**

In answer to the question Jesus was asked by His disciples, Jesus said:

> "Now learn the parable from the fig tree: when its branch has already become tender and puts forth its leaves, you know that summer is near. "Even so, **YOU TOO**, when **YOU** see these things happening, recognize that He is near, right at the door. "Truly I say to **YOU, THIS generation will not pass away** until all these things take place. "Heaven and earth will pass away, but My words will not pass away. (Mark 13:28-31)

Do you believe that generation did pass away before those things took place? Did heaven and earth pass away? (Heaven and earth was a reference to the temple based Jewish system of things) With all of the promises we have been given upon which we have based our Christian faith, do you believe that Jesus kept **THIS** promise, His greatest prophecy, in the time frame in which He promised it? If this prophecy were meant for the distant future, would He not have told them "when **THEY** see these things happening," (meaning some future generation)? Wouldn't He have said "that generation will not pass away?" And would He not have made it **very clear** that this was **NOT** a prophecy for them? Of course He would! But we have seen how this prophecy WAS fulfilled in that generation. Otherwise we have to admit the horrible reality that CS Lewis must have been right when he said that Jesus was wrong about this, and that he clearly did not know what he was talking about when he said these things.

Now, let's look at the book of Revelation. The book of Revelation was written with much symbology. As James Stuart Russell points out:

> Symbol and metaphor belong to the grammar of prophecy, as every reader of the Old Testament prophets must know. Is it

> not reasonable that the doom of Jerusalem should be depicted in language as glowing and rhetorical as the destruction of Babylon, or Bozrah, or Tyre? . . . It will at once be seen that the imagery employed in this passage is almost identical with that of our Lord. If these symbols therefore were proper to represent the fall of Babylon why should they be improper to set forth a still greater catastrophe -- the destruction of Jerusalem?[lxvii]

Let's look again at the message John was given as he recorded it in the opening three verses of the Revelation:

> The Revelation of Jesus Christ, which God gave Him to show to His bond-servants, the things which must **SOON** take place; and He sent and communicated it by His angel to His bond-servant John, who testified to the word of God and to the testimony of Jesus Christ, even to all that he saw. Blessed is he who reads and those who hear the words of the prophecy, and heed the things which are written in it; **FOR THE TIME IS NEAR**. (Rev 1:1-3)

Do you really think that he believed that this was a prophecy for the distant future to be fulfilled by people he would never meet or know anything about?

Jesus also inspired John to write to the seven churches the following words which show that this event was imminent:

> I am coming **SOON**. Hold fast what you have, so that no one may seize your crown. (Rev 3:11 ESV)

> The second woe has passed; behold, the third woe is **SOON** to come. (Rev 11:14 ESV)

And even after these words showing the imminence of the situation, and in order to erase all doubt in anyone's mind, he reiterated it **three more times** in His closing words of the prophecy:

> And he said to me, "These words are trustworthy and true. And the Lord, the God of the spirits of the prophets, has sent his angel to show his servants what must **SOON** take place. And behold, I am coming soon. Blessed is the one who keeps the words of the prophecy of this book." (Rev 22:6, 7 ESV)
>
> Behold, I am coming soon, bringing my recompense with me, to repay each one for what he has done. (Rev 22:12 ESV)
>
> He who testifies to these things says, "Surely I am coming **SOON**." Amen. Come, Lord Jesus! (Rev 22:20 ESV)

Jesus also gave the Apostle John a very specific instruction concerning this Revelation:

> And he said to me, "Do not seal up the words of the prophecy of this book, for the time is **NEAR**. (Rev 22:10 ESV)

John was given this instruction because it was imperative that this Revelation be given to the Christians **as soon as possible**. Their lives were at stake, and they needed to know what was about to occur. Some have said that when He said the time was near that Jesus was making a reference to "God's time," and that this still has not occurred. Please be honest with yourself. Don't you think that the idea that this very specific instruction would have no relevant meaning in that short span of time relative to John's life is unrealistic?

With all of this said, if the events of the Revelation have not already occurred, what options are available to us with regard to the timing of this important revelation to John? **We only have four options about what is written in the Revelation.** These are:

1. Jesus misled John. He was not specific enough to help him understand that this was a prophecy which would happen in the distant future. For this to be true, then these events were not relevant to the lives of these seven churches. They were merely symbols of something which would happen much later in the future.

   My question to you is: If this is so, then why is there so much urgency? **Why did He not make this point very clear?**

2. John didn't get it. He totally misunderstood. There was really no urgency at all concerning these events, they were things which would happen "in God's time."

3. Jesus was just plain wrong. This is impossible with an Omniscient God!

4. Jesus lied. This also is impossible as stated in God's word. (Hebrews 6:18)

So here is the big question regarding this Revelation to John. Can we honestly say that we believe that Jesus **ALWAYS KEEPS HIS PROMISES**, but that these events which were to take place **SOON** have still not come to pass after 2000 years of human history?

Notice what has been recorded by the historians of that time regarding the events that occurred after John was given this revelation from Our Lord. First here is what Christian Historian Eusebius recorded:

> But the number of calamities which everywhere fell upon the nation at that time; the extreme misfortunes to which the inhabitants of Judea were especially subjected, the thousands of men, as well as women and children, that perished by the sword, by famine, and by other forms of death innumerable—all these things, as well as the many great sieges which were carried on against the cities of Judea, and the excessive

sufferings endured by those that fled to Jerusalem itself, as to a city of perfect safety, and finally the general course of the whole war, as well as its particular occurrences in detail, and **how at last the abomination of desolation, proclaimed by the prophets, Daniel 9:27 stood in the very temple of God,** so celebrated of old, the temple which was now awaiting its total and final destruction by fire — all these things any one that wishes may find accurately described in the history written by Josephus.[lxviii]

And then later on in Chapter 7 he states:

Verse 1: It is fitting to add to these accounts the true prediction of our Saviour in which he foretold these very events.....Verse 4: These things took place in this manner in the second year of the reign of Vespasian, in accordance with the prophecies of our Lord and Saviour Jesus Christ, who by divine power saw them beforehand as if they were already present, and wept and mourned according to the statement of the holy evangelists, who give the very words which he uttered, when, as if addressing Jerusalem herself, he said: 5. If you had known, even you, in this day, the things which belong unto your peace! But now they are hid from your eyes. For the days shall come upon you, that your enemies shall cast a rampart about you, and compass you round, and keep you in on every side, and shall lay you and your children even with the ground. 6. And then, as if speaking concerning the people, he says, For there shall be great distress in the land, and wrath upon this people. And they shall fall by the edge of the sword, and shall be led away captive into all nations. And Jerusalem shall be trodden down of the Gentiles, until the times of the Gentiles be fulfilled. And again: When you shall see Jerusalem compassed with armies, then know that the desolation thereof is near. 7. **If any one compares the words of our Saviour with the other accounts of the historian concerning the whole war, how can one fail to wonder, and to admit that the foreknowledge and the prophecy of our Saviour were truly divine and marvelously strange.**[lxix]

Eusebius is referring to the time period between AD 66 -73, a period within the generation of which Jesus spoke.

Jewish Historian Josephus wrote several volumes which are a fulfillment of the greatest prophecy of Jesus. Regarding the destruction of the city of Jerusalem and the temple as prophesied by Jesus, note the following:

> Now as soon as the army had no more people to slay or to plunder, because there remained none to be the objects of their fury, (for they would not have spared any, had there remained any other work to be done,) Caesar gave orders that they should now **DEMOLISH THE ENTIRE CITY AND TEMPLE,** but should leave as many of the towers standing as were of the greatest eminency; that is, Phasaelus, and Hippicus, and Mariamne; and so much of the wall as enclosed the city on the west side. This wall was spared, in order to afford a camp for such as were to lie in garrison, as were the towers also spared, in order to demonstrate to posterity what kind of city it was, and how well fortified, which the Roman valor had subdued; but for all the rest of the wall, *it was so thoroughly laid even with the ground by those that dug it up to the foundation, that* ***THERE WAS LEFT NOTHING*** *to make those that came thither believe it had ever been inhabited*. This was the end which Jerusalem came to by the madness of those that were for innovations; a city otherwise of great magnificence, and of mighty fame among all mankind.[lxx]

Don't you see it clearly? This is a **direct fulfillment** of the prophecy given to John in the Revelation. That despicable immoral city of Jerusalem is not mentioned in the book of Revelation except by its code name which is Babylon the Great which is also called Sodom and Egypt. Now let's tie all of this together. First we have the prophecy of Jeremiah calling Jerusalem Sodom:

> Jeremiah 23:14 "Also among the prophets of Jerusalem I have seen a horrible thing: The committing of adultery and walking in falsehood; And they strengthen the hands of evildoers, So that no one has turned back from his wickedness. **All of them have become to Me like Sodom,** And her inhabitants like Gomorrah.

Next, we see that the prophet Isaiah calls Jerusalem Sodom and a harlot:

> Isaiah 1:9-10 Unless the LORD of hosts Had left us a few survivors, We would be like **Sodom**, We would be like Gomorrah. Hear the word of the LORD, You rulers of **Sodom;** Give ear to the instruction of our God, You people of Gomorrah.
>
> Isaiah 1:21 How the faithful city has become a **harlot**, She who was full of justice! Righteousness once lodged in her, But now murderers.

And in another "cloud judgment" centuries earlier, God told Egypt:

> Isaiah 19:1 The oracle concerning Egypt. Behold, **the LORD is riding on a swift cloud** and is about to come to **Egypt;** The idols of Egypt will tremble at His presence, And the heart of the Egyptians will melt within them.

The prophet Ezekiel calls Jerusalem a harlot:

> Ezekiel 16:35-36 Therefore, **O harlot**, hear the word of the LORD. Thus says the Lord GOD, "Because your lewdness was poured out and your nakedness uncovered through your harlotries with your lovers and with all your detestable idols, and because of the blood of your sons which you gave to idols,

Notice the likenesses to Sodom and Egypt from the Old Testament. The fact that **it is the city of Jerusalem** is marked by what John wrote in chapter 11:

> Rev 11:7-8 When they have finished their testimony, the beast that comes up out of the abyss will make war with them, and overcome them and kill them. And their dead bodies will lie in the street of **the great city which mystically is called Sodom** and Egypt, **where also their Lord was crucified**.

Only one city fits this description at the time this was written and that is the great harlot city of Jerusalem! In researching this, we find 18th century commentator Adam Clarke notes the following from one of his revered predecessors, Professor Johan Wettstein:

> He supposes the book of the Apocalypse to have been written a considerable time before the destruction of Jerusalem. **The events described from the fourth chapter to the end he supposes to refer to the Jewish war**, and to the civil commotions which took place in Italy while Otho, Vitellius, and Vespasian were contending for the empire. These contentions and destructive wars occupied the space of about three years and a half, during which Professor Wetstein thinks the principal events took place which are recorded in this book.[lxxi]

Now notice the judgment given to him by our Lord of which John wrote:

> Rev 14:8 And another angel, a second one, followed, saying, "Fallen, fallen is Babylon the great, she who has made all the nations drink of the wine of the passion of her immorality."

The 18th chapter of the book of Revelation gives the judgment upon this "great city."

> Rev 18:2 And he cried out with a mighty voice, saying, "Fallen, fallen is BABYLON the great! She has become a dwelling place of demons and a prison of every unclean spirit, and a prison of every unclean and hateful bird.
>
> Rev 18:10 ..standing at a distance because of the fear of her torment, saying, 'Woe, woe, the great city, BABYLON, the

> strong city! For in one hour your judgment has come.'
>
> Rev 18:21 Then a strong angel took up a stone like a great millstone and threw it into the sea, saying, "So will BABYLON, the great city, be thrown down with violence, and will not be found any longer.

Yes, this revelation was **URGENTLY** given to John by our Lord Jesus who is referred to in John's gospel as "the Word." Did you notice that while Jesus was on earth He continually was quoting the words of the prophets? All that was written before Him was written for Him and His presence that He might fulfill all that is written. These inspired writings are indeed that which makes up the Word of God, and this is what Jesus came to fulfill. Some have said that the Revelation given to John is unintelligible, and should not even be in the Bible canon. But contrary to this, research has shown that it was a book with a **specific** purpose, sent by John to the churches in Asia Minor, with a very **specific** message to its readers.

They needed to take immediate action! **Is there any hint** in chapters two and three that this prophecy was also for the church that would exist more than 2000 years later?

This urgency upon those addressed was the **ONLY** reason for the Revelation being given to John. If this book was, as many believe, a book for the distant future, then you must ponder the notion that **it had to be irrelevant** to the ones to whom it was written and therefore totally useless to them.

Just think about that for a moment. If the symbols here represented tanks and helicopters and modern day weapons of war, then of what possible use could it have been to the early church?

But when we consider the circumstances of those early Christians in the seven churches, we see that many of them were enduring the bitter hand of persecution from a cruel dictator then known as an emperor. That emperor was none other than Nero, the madman who burned his own city. Notice the horrific treatment of Christians by this maniac:

> Nero tried to counter this downturn in his "public approval ratings" by throwing open his own resources to the homeless. He sponsored a number of religious activities designed to show himself innocent. Nothing worked. And so he determined to find scapegoats. He fastened upon the Christians as most suitable for his diabolical purpose.
> A few who admitted their faith were tortured until they revealed the names of others. Beginning a few weeks after the fire, the city was the scene of every imaginable torment. And not Rome only, for persecution spread throughout the empire. But in the capital Nero held nightly spectacles in which every torture was applied to the suffering saints.
> Some were **burned alive**. Others were **sewn into the skins of wild animals** and given to dogs to tear. Still others were **crucified**. Martyrs were exhibited in the circus with Nero presiding, dressed as a charioteer. The wicked emperor threw open his own gardens to more such spectacles. So many Christians died so brutally that public sympathy swung in their favor.[lxxii]

Is it any wonder then that they were eagerly looking for an approaching hour of deliverance, one which this Revelation told them was now close at hand? John himself was suffering with them, as he testifies in his writings. (Rev 1:9) He said in his first letter: 'Children, it is the last hour." (1 John 2:18) His colleague James wrote: "the Judge is standing right at the door" (James 5:9)

The Apostle Paul wrote: “The God of peace will soon crush Satan under your feet.” (Rom 16:20) All of this was written **to be fulfilled in that very same generation** in which Jesus prophesied.

Therefore, we must make the very obvious consideration that this book **had to have practical significance** to these early Christians in order to truly be a Revelation from God. From what has been documented here, **this is the only reasonable conclusion** we can reach.

But what about us in our day?

Having said all of this, we all are concerned about our day and what we can draw from this Revelation from God. We know that the Apostle Paul correctly stated: “All Scripture is inspired by God and profitable for teaching, for reproof, for correction, for training in righteousness; so that the man of God may be adequate, equipped for every good work.” (2 Timothy 3:16,17)

But first of all under this consideration, we must remember that the destruction of Jerusalem is not just another milestone in the annals of history. **It is the fulfillment of Jesus’ greatest prophecy!** It was the end of an epoch. In Luke’s Gospel he tells us concerning the destruction of that “great city” that: “these are days of vengeance, so that **all things which are written** will be fulfilled.”

Do you understand the **profound significance** of what is recorded here by Luke? He is stating that the fulfillment of this prophecy by Jesus **is the fulfillment of all that is recorded in the Holy Scriptures!**

It was the end of the Jewish economy and the fulfillment of the Old Covenant which God gave to the Israelite people. There was now a New Covenant. The writer of Hebrews records:

> But as it is, Christ has obtained a ministry that is as much more excellent than the old as the covenant he mediates is better, since it is enacted on better promises. For if that first covenant had been faultless, there would have been no occasion to look for a second. For he finds fault with them when he says: "Behold, the days are coming, declares the Lord, when I will establish a new covenant with the house of Israel and with the house of Judah, not like the covenant that I made with their fathers on the day when I took them by the hand to bring them out of the land of Egypt. For they did not continue in my covenant, and so I showed no concern for them, declares the Lord. For this is the covenant that I will make with the house of Israel after those days, declares the Lord: I will put my laws into their minds, and write them on their hearts, and I will be their God, and they shall be my people. (Heb. 8:6-10)

Christ did this for His followers. They were no longer under the ritualistic bindings of the Old Law Covenant. All they needed to do was put their complete trust and confidence in the Savior!

The temple which was the symbol of that Old Covenant was now gone. It was no longer necessary. Animal sacrifices were no longer necessary. This temple which was formerly called "heaven and earth" was now gone! (Deuteronomy 31:28-32:6) There were now a "new heavens and a new earth." With the sacrifice of the "Lamb of God" and His return to heaven to establish the Kingdom of God, this Kingdom predicted long ago was now firmly in place. The same Jesus who uttered the words "my kingdom is not of this world" was now in the heavens, having fulfilled His greatest prophecy. He rode that cloud just as He did in Isaiah 19:1 when He came in judgment on Egypt and destroyed the city of Jerusalem along with the temple and its sacrificial form of worship. It would never be restored. He could now deliver the Kingdom of God to His father.

We are now living under the reign of that kingdom. Humans will continue to live and die on the earth. But notice the following promise! Stated in the Revelation we find the following:

> And I heard a voice from heaven, saying, "Write, 'Blessed are the dead who die in the Lord from now on!'" "Yes," says the Spirit, "so that they may rest from their labors, for their deeds follow with them." (Rev 14:13)

Yes! Those who die in the Lord will be blessed! This means that what is being spoken of in the Revelation is not the end of time. This passage makes that clear. People will rest from their struggles in the Lord against the power of the flesh. This is the fulfillment of Isaiah 65. Notice what it says:

> For behold, I create new heavens and a new earth; And the former things will not be remembered or come to mind. (Isa 65:17)

After this the prophet goes on to say:

> No longer will there be in it an infant who lives but a few days, Or an old man who does not live out his days; For the youth **will die** at the age of one hundred And the one who does not reach the age of one hundred Will be thought accursed. (Isa 65:20)

Notice that there are infants and old men. There are those who are blessed and those who are cursed. And there is physical death! This is all as the prophet Isaiah proclaimed, in the New Heavens and the New Earth!

Do you understand the significance of what the prophet is saying?

This is the time in which we are living **NOW!** We are in the Kingdom of God **NOW!** Even in this time we are living, we have fellowship restored with God. But it is after this that we can attain our true citizenship. It is just as the Apostle Paul stated:

> But **our citizenship is in heaven**, and from it we await a Savior, the Lord Jesus Christ, who will transform our lowly body to be like his glorious body, by the power that enables him even to subject all things to himself. (Philippians 3:20,21)

Christ the King is now on His throne. All that is written has been fulfilled, and we can put our full trust in Him as our Lord and Savior. Yes! **Jesus Christ is King!** He has kept these promises! He has kept **EVERY** promise He ever made. As the Apostle Paul stated:

> Christ says **"Yes" to all of God's promises**. That's why we have Christ to say "Amen" for us to the glory of God. (2 Cor 1:20) (Contemporary English Version)

Oh, what joy awaits us! What anticipation we should have as we contemplate entering the city of our true citizenship in heaven!

Appendix 1
The "Millennium" of Revelation
Is this term Scriptural? If so, what is the meaning of this term?

When looking at Revelation 20:2 and 20:6, it has been common practice in the exposition of Scripture for commentators to refer to this period of time as the "Millennium.' Let's look at these two passages:

> **Rev 20:2** And he laid hold of the dragon, the serpent of old, who is the devil and Satan, and bound him for **a thousand years**;
>
> **Rev 20:6** Blessed and holy is the one who has a part in the first resurrection; over these the second death has no power, but they will be priests of God and of Christ and will reign with Him for **a thousand years**.

It is notable that this is the only place in Scripture where there is a reference to this "thousand-year" period that has captivated the minds of the commentators. But there is **no place in Scripture** where the term "millennium" is used. It is the purpose of this Appendix to show why this term is, considering the definition of the term, unsuitable for use in the exposition of these passages. What we will show is that the Scriptures demand that this is actually symbolism for a short period of time that is the perfect length according to what Jesus himself said.

In his book, "The Revelation Made Easy," Dr. Kenneth Gentry made the following statements:

> Revelation is filled with remarkable symbolism. . . . we noted that John speaks of locusts with men's faces, lions teeth, crowns of gold, and tails like scorpions (Rev 9:6). We witnessed lion-headed, serpent tailed horses belching fire and smoke (9:17). We were amazed at the seven-headed dragon with ten horns and seven crowns who is able to pull down one-third of the stars of heaven (12:3-4). Clearly John does not intend our taking Revelation literally. Perhaps this holds true with the 1000 years.[lxxiii]

Dr. Gentry goes on to show that the figure "1000" is often used symbolically (Exodus 20:6; Deut. 1:11; Psalm 50:10; Psalm 84:10; 2 Peter 3:8). I agree with all these statements. But then he goes on to say:

> The widespread employment of 1000 in Scripture discourages our limiting the value to its actual sum. . . One thousand appears to speak of quantitative perfection (10 x 10 x 10), becoming a number of enormous consequences. I will show that the 1000 years began in the first century, has already consumed 2000 years of time, and is not yet over.[lxxiv]

Although these last statements sound good, they ignore the plain statements in Scripture as we shall show. It is just not possible that this period of "1000 years" could be as Dr. Gentry says without proving false other passages of Scripture.

For example, the prophet Daniel said:

> Then I heard the man clothed in linen, who *was* above the waters of the river, when he held up his right hand and his left hand to heaven, and swore by Him who lives forever, that *it shall be* for a time, times, and half *a time;* and **when the power of the holy people has been completely shattered, all**

> **these *things* shall be finished**. (Daniel 12:7 NKJV)

History very clearly shows **that this did happen**. The Levitical, sacrificial form of worship along with the temple were completely done away with **never to appear again**. Why? It was no longer necessary! The sacrifice of the Lamb of God was good forever! Thus, none of the reasons for the existence of the temple were present any longer. Its reason for existing had reached its complete fulfillment. Jesus made this point when He told His disciples:

> "But when you see Jerusalem surrounded by armies, then know that its desolation is near. Then let those who are in Judea flee to the mountains, let those who are in the midst of her depart, and let not those who are in the country enter her. For these are the days of vengeance, **that all things which are written may be fulfilled**. (Luke 21:20-22 NKJV)

These words are very specific. There is no hyperbole here. Jesus meant it as precisely as He said it.

The Apostle Peter, writing in approximately AD 64-65 just before the destruction of Jerusalem stated:

> They will give an account **to Him who is ready to judge the living and the dead.** For this reason the gospel was preached also to those who are dead, that they might be judged according to men in the flesh, but live according to God in the spirit. But **the end of all things is at hand;** therefore be serious and watchful in your prayers. (1 Peter 4:5-7 NKJV)

Yes, these epistles written just before Peter's crucifixion are very clear. Jesus was about to judge the living and dead **because the end of all things was at hand, not thousands of years into the future!**

The Apostle Paul very clearly stated:

> And the God of peace **will crush Satan under your feet shortly**. The grace of our Lord Jesus Christ *be* with you. Amen. (Romans 16:20)

There is **no possibility** that Paul was wrong here. Satan suffered a **crushing defeat** by the sacrifice of the Lamb of God. And when the blood of the Lamb was presented in the Holy of Holies in heaven, **Satan was reduced to nothing** just as the following passage suggests:

> For this purpose the Son of God was manifested, that **He might destroy the works of the devil.** (1 John 3:8 NKJV)

Just as Jesus himself predicted, **the strong man's house has been plundered** (Matthew 12:29). And as Paul predicted, **all things have been put in subjection**, and **heaven and earth have been united** (Ephesians 1:7-10). But heaven is our primary residence, as Paul also stated:

> But our citizenship is in heaven, and from it we await a Savior, the Lord Jesus Christ, (Philippians 3:20 NASB)

So just from what we have seen so far, it is becoming pretty clear that unless these passages are wrong, the "Millennium" of Revelation 20 **could not be** 1000 actual calendar years.

Yes, Paul made it clear to the church in Philippi that the reward of the saints was to be heavenly. But he also made it clear in that very verse that that promise was not yet fulfilled until the Savior returned. Notice that the writer of Hebrews told those Hebrew Christians something profound concerning this:

> For Christ did not enter a holy place made with hands, a mere

> copy of the true one, **but into heaven itself, now to appear in the presence of God for us**; nor was it that He would offer Himself often, as the high priest enters the holy place year by year with blood that is not his own. Otherwise, He would have needed to suffer often since the foundation of the world; but now once at the consummation of the ages He has been manifested to put away sin by the sacrifice of Himself. And inasmuch as **it is appointed for men to die once and after this comes judgment,** so Christ also, **having been offered ONCE** to bear the sins of many, **will appear a second time for salvation** without reference to sin, **to those who eagerly await Him**. (Hebrews 9:24-28 NASB)

Do you see the profound nature of what is said here? Let's take this apart.

1. Christ would appear in heaven one time to present His sacrifice. This would cover the sins of mankind forever!
2. After Christ appears in the Holy of Holies in heaven to present His sacrifice, He must appear a second time **not to cover sin,** as this has already been covered, **but for salvation**!
3. People die once, and then comes the judgment.

This proves that there will **never again be any need for sacrifices of any kind to God**, thus, never again a need for a temple. The precious blood of the Lamb would cover all mankind being offered one time. The passage also states that the salvation of the saints **would not be complete until Christ appears a second time!**

Putting all this evidence together, we discover that the salvation of the saints is **NOT** complete until:

1. Satan is crushed
2. Christ presents his blood in heaven, once for all
3. The power of the Holy people has been shattered (This occurred at the destruction of the temple and the Holy city of Jerusalem in AD70).
4. Christ appears a second time
5. The final judgment occurs

Then in chapter 11 of Hebrews we find the "faith chapter" which tells us that all the saints through the annals of time would receive their salvation at the same time!

> And all these, having gained approval through their faith, did not receive what was promised, because God had provided something better for us, so that apart from us they would not be made perfect. (Hebrews 11:39-40 NASB)

Do you understand what this means? According to what we have studied in the Revelation to John, we found that the martyred saints were dressed in white robes, became priests, were given authority, and this all happened at the same time. It means that unless Christ has already appeared a second time, none of the saints throughout the ages have received their salvation!

Now tying this together is the fact each and every one of these things are mentioned in **Revelation 20 which is very clear in pointing out that all of this is not complete until the end of the "thousand-year" period!**

This ties precisely with what the Apostle Paul wrote:

> For as in Adam all die, so also in Christ all will be made alive. But each in his own order: Christ the first fruits, after that those who are Christ's at His coming, then comes the end,

> when He hands over the kingdom to the God and Father, when He has abolished all rule and all authority and power. For He must reign until He has put all His enemies under His feet. The last enemy that will be abolished is death. (1 Cor 15:22-26 NASB)

Christ reigned from the time He was anointed until the end of the gentile times which occurred in the year AD70. **We know this to be a fact** because the writer of Hebrews made that exceptionally clear when he wrote:

> YOU HAVE PUT ALL THINGS IN SUBJECTION UNDER HIS FEET." For in that He put all in subjection under him, He left nothing *that is* not put under him. But now we do not yet see all things put under him. (Hebrews 2:8 NKJV)

Thus, as we have noted, since this had to occur prior to the end of the "thousand year" period, then that period of time had to be a symbolic number. It was symbolic of the perfect amount of time (within that same generation) that was prophesied by Christ in the Olivet Discourse.

For a more complete discussion of this subject, I would advise:

The Millennium
Past, Present, or Future?
A Biblical Defense for the 40 year Transition Period

Joseph M. Vincent II
JaDon Publishing, Ardmore OK
Available at:
http://www.store.bibleprophecy.com/category/books-print/

Appendix II

The Resurrection

When we think of the resurrection of the dead, we automatically think of dead bodies physically coming up out of the ground, do we not? But is this really what the Bible says about the resurrection? Before we begin, let me show you a picture given by the Apostle Paul which perfectly describes the nature of the resurrection.

How many of you believers, have been baptized?

I will hold my hand up on that one, but I also realize that some of you who may be reading this may have determined from your studies that a baptism in water is not necessary. This is an entirely different discussion, but I for my part come down on the side of the baptism of all Christians. Regardless of your stand on physical baptism in the water, I would like to call your attention to a picture which Paul gives us concerning Baptism, and how it relates to resurrection. It is found in Romans Chapter 6 and it reads:

> Do you not know that all of us who have been baptized into Christ Jesus were baptized into his death? **We were buried therefore with him by baptism into death, in order that, just as Christ was raised from the dead by the glory of the Father, we too might walk in newness of life.** For if we have been united with him in a death like his, we shall certainly be united with him in a resurrection like his. We know that our old self was crucified with him in order that the body of sin might be brought to nothing, so that we would no longer be enslaved to sin. For one who has died has been set free from sin. Now if

> we have died with Christ, we believe that we will also live with him. (Rom 6:3-8 ESV)

So, the apostle said here that we were baptized into His death. But I want to look again at verse four. Notice that in verse four is this beautiful picture of our death and resurrection – **Buried with Christ, raised to walk in the newness of life!**

Do you see the profound significance of this passage? I did NOT see it for many years. I remember when I was baptized in water well over 30 years ago. As I was going down into the water, the Pastor said those very words: "buried with Christ." Then when I was coming up out of the water he said: "raised to walk in the newness of life." The implication by those words in Romans 6:4 are that since we were being buried with Christ, **we must have been dead in some manner.**

But to get the full understanding of this, we must begin with the question: What is death? This requires that we go back to the book of Genesis. Remember that God told Adam that ***on the day*** he ate of the forbidden fruit of the "tree of knowledge" that he would die. This promise was made to him in Genesis chapter 2. But if you look at the chronological record in Genesis you find that Adam lived over 900 years! So how do we reconcile this? When Adam was placed in the garden he was in perfect spiritual fellowship with God. His most important assignment was to obey God. When he disobeyed God, **he died that day, spiritually**. He was then separated from God....... no more walks in the Garden together, and no more discussions together. It was over. But physically, he lived for over 900 years. Here is the passage:

> And the LORD God commanded the man, saying, "You may surely eat of every tree of the garden, but of the tree of the knowledge of good and evil you shall not eat, for ***in the day that you eat of it you shall surely die."*** (Gen 2:16-17 ESV)

So, the question is: Did God keep his word or not? ***YES, He did!*** On that day, Adam and Eve **lost their relationship** with their heavenly father. The death that they suffered was not physical death, but **spiritual death**. The account of this is recorded for us in Genesis 3:

> But the serpent said to the woman, "You will not surely die. For God knows that when you eat of it ***your eyes will be opened, and you will be like God***, knowing good and evil." So when the woman saw that the tree was good for food, and that it was a delight to the eyes, and that the tree was to be desired to make one wise, she took of its fruit and ate, and she also gave some to her husband who was with her, and he ate. Then the ***eyes of both were opened***, and they knew that they were naked. And they sewed fig leaves together and made themselves loincloths. (Gen 3:4-7 ESV)

Yes! The opening of their eyes in this manner signified their **death to God spiritually speaking**. By disobedience to God (***sin***), they were separated spiritually from God in "death." The record in Genesis tells us that because of this, God cast them out of the garden, with no opportunity to eat of the tree of life. Notice the words in Genesis:

> Then the LORD God said, "Behold, the man has become like one of us in knowing good and evil. Now, lest he reach out his hand and take also of the tree of life and eat, and live forever—" therefore the LORD God **sent him out from the garden** of Eden to work the ground from which he was taken. He drove out the man, and at the east of the garden of Eden

> he placed the cherubim and a flaming sword that turned every way to guard the way to the tree of life. (Gen 3:22-24 ESV)

From this we can see that the relationship between God and Adam ended . . . no more beautiful garden, no more chance to eat from the tree of life. But there was still hope for mankind due to the promise which God made. Here was the promise:

> The LORD God said to the serpent, "Because you have done this, cursed are you above all livestock and above all beasts of the field; on your belly you shall go, and dust you shall eat all the days of your life. I will put enmity between you and the woman, and between your offspring and her offspring; **he shall bruise your head, and you shall bruise his heel."** (Gen 3:14-15 ESV)

From these words by God, there was hope. But the meaning of this passage was that there would arise one who would later be called the "son of man" who would crush Satan, who was the serpent. But for now, the relationship between Adam and God had been destroyed due to man's disobedience. Thus, this spiritual death spread to all of Adam's seed. Centuries later, Jesus himself referred to those who were dead in a similar manner. On the occasion when one of His disciples wanted to delay following him, note Jesus words:

> As they were going along the road, someone said to Him, "I will follow You wherever You go." And Jesus said to him, "The foxes have holes and the birds of the air have nests, but the Son of Man has nowhere to lay His head." And He said to another, "Follow Me." But he said, "Lord, permit me first to go and bury my father." But He said to him, "Allow **the dead** to bury their own dead; but as for you, go and proclaim everywhere the kingdom of God." (Luke 9:57-60 NASB)

It is perfectly clear that Jesus was not speaking of someone who was physically dead burying their dead. Notice how 18th Century Bible Commentator Adam Clark describes this:

> "This does not mean any of the twelve, but one of those who were constant hearers of our Lord's preaching; the name of disciple being common to all those who professed to believe in him, John 6:66. Bury my father: probably his father was old, and apparently near death; but it was a maxim among the Jews, that, if a man had any duty to perform to the dead, he was, for that time, free from the observance of any other precept or duty. The children of Adam are always in extremes; some will rush into the ministry of the Gospel without a call, others will delay long after they are called; the middle way is the only safe one: not to move a finger in the work till the call be given, and not to delay a moment after."[lxxv]

The Apostle Paul confirmed this line of thinking in the book of Romans when he writes:

> Wherefore, as by one man sin entered into the world, and death by sin; and so **death passed upon all men, for that all have sinned**: For until the law sin was in the world: but sin is not imputed when there is no law. Nevertheless **death reigned from Adam to Moses**, even over them that had not sinned after the similitude of Adam's transgression, who is the figure of him that was to come. (Rom 5:12-14)

This raises some questions, but first let's look at what Paul said to the church at Colossae:

> And you, who were ***dead in your trespasses*** and the uncircumcision of your flesh, God made alive together with him, having forgiven us all our trespasses, by canceling the record of debt that stood against us with its legal demands. This he set aside, nailing it to the cross. (Col 2:13-14 ESV)

Did you notice how Paul defines death in this passage? He said they were **dead in their trespasses**, but God made them alive with Christ. Were they physically dead? Of course not; It is obvious that Paul was speaking of going from **spiritual death to spiritual life.** So now, the question has to be, if death reigned from Adam to Moses, as Paul said earlier, did Moses solve the problem of death? Man has continued to die physically even to this day after Moses came, so we know that this does **not speak of physical death**. So, what did this mean?

With Moses came the Old Covenant. The purpose of that Old Covenant was to show man the utter impossibility of keeping the covenant due to his inherited sin. So, in effect, what it did was to show man the impossibility of his ability to keep the law. But at the same time, the Old Law Covenant pointed to the Messiah who would actually provide redemption for the sins of man. Paul stated it in this passage to the Roman church:

> Therefore, as **one trespass led to condemnation for all men**, so **one act of righteousness leads to justification** and life for **all** men. For as by the one man's disobedience the many were made sinners, so by the one man's obedience the many will be made righteous. Now **the law came in to increase the trespass, but where sin increased, grace abounded all the more,** so that, as sin reigned in death, grace also might reign through righteousness leading to eternal life through Jesus Christ our Lord. (Rom 5:18-21 ESV)

Thus, we see that sin and death are inseparable. Verse 20 shows us that when the law entered, the effect of sin increased to an even greater extent. But physical death did not get any worse in terms of its severity. So, the reference here is to spiritual death. This is clearly shown by what Paul later said in Romans 7:

> I was once alive apart from the Law; but when the commandment came, sin became alive **and I died;** and this commandment, which was to result in life, proved to result in

> **death for me;** for sin, taking an opportunity through the commandment, deceived me and through **it killed me.** So then, the Law is holy, and the commandment is holy and righteous and good. Therefore did that which is good become a cause of death for me? May it never be! Rather it was sin, in order that it might be shown to be sin by effecting my death through that which is good, so that through the commandment sin would become utterly sinful. (Romans 7:9-13 NASB)

Do you see the profound significance of this? It is obvious that since Paul **had not yet died physically**, he **had to be** speaking of spiritual death. This is **the death which all men experience when they sin against God**. But this death is not something which cannot be reversed. Paul also wrote:

> For as in Adam **all** die, even so in Christ shall **all** be made alive. (1 Cor 15:22 ESV)

Did you notice how Paul worded this verse? **Paul did not say**, "even so in Christ all **have been** made alive." He said "even so in Christ shall all be made alive." He explains why he said it this way in the next verse. Note his words:

> But each in his own order: Christ the first fruits, after that those who are Christ's **at His coming** (1 Cor 15:23 ESV)

This will not happen in the physical realm. If the death that Adam experienced **was spiritual death**, then **the life that Christ brings is spiritual life!** This is what occurred at the Parousia. Spiritual life for all man was finally and completely restored. So, if the Parousia has not happened, then our salvation is not complete. This is confirmed in Hebrews 9 where it says:

> so Christ, having been offered once to bear the sins of many, will appear a second time, not to deal with sin **but to save those who are eagerly waiting for him.** (Heb 9:28 ESV)

We must remember that physical death is not our enemy. Even Paul said that he longed to "go and be with the Lord." When he did go, he was immediately "in Paradise" as was the thief on the cross who professed Christ. He would then go to heaven at the Parousia, because at that time according to Hebrews 9:28 his salvation was complete. Just like Adam, we all die through sin (spiritually). Thus, we can be made alive spiritually through Christ. Paul also confirmed this when writing to the church in Ephesus:

> And you were **dead in the trespasses and sins** . . . But God, being rich in mercy, because of the great love with which he loved us, even when **we were dead in our trespasses**, made us alive together with Christ—**by grace you have been saved** — and **raised us up with him and seated us with him in the heavenly places** in Christ Jesus, so that in the coming ages he might show the immeasurable riches of his grace in kindness toward us in Christ Jesus. (Eph 2:1,4-7 ESV)

When Paul spoke to the Ephesian Church, he made it clear that these first century Christians **were made alive** in Christ because of their being saved. They had been raised from spiritual death! But Paul was just echoing the words spoken to him by Jesus. For these words of our Lord were recorded by the Apostle John:

> Truly, truly, I say to you, if anyone keeps my word, **he will never see death**. (John 8:51 ESV)

The Jews did not understand that He was speaking of spiritual death either! Notice what they say in response to Jesus:

> The Jews said to him, "Now we know that you have a demon! **Abraham died**, as did the prophets, yet you say, 'If anyone keeps my word, he will never taste death.' (John 8:52 ESV)

Then later Jesus once again confirmed His words:

> Jesus said to her, "**I am the resurrection and the life**. Whoever believes in me, though he die, yet shall he live, and everyone who lives and believes in me **shall never die**. Do you believe this?" (John 11:25-26 ESV)

Do you see the contrast here? Obviously, people have continued to die physically! But by trusting and believing in Him while yet alive, we are raised to spiritual life through Him and will never die! Paul also confirmed this in Romans 6:23:

> For the wages of sin is death, but the free gift of God is eternal life in Christ Jesus our Lord. (Romans 6:23 ESV)

Paul made it clear that this was also **spiritual death and spiritual life.** Make no mistake about it, each one of us will die physically, but once we become believers, and put our trust in Christ, we are made alive in the spirit at the very moment we accept him! The Apostle John confirms this with these words:

> And this is the testimony, that God gave us eternal life, and this life is in his Son. **Whoever has the Son has life**; whoever does not have the Son of God **does not** have life. I write these things to you who believe in the name of the Son of God that you may **know that you have eternal life**. (1 John 5:11-13 ESV)

Do you see the incredible significance of this? If you believe, you have life **NOW!** Just as the Jews in that day were focused on physical death, so are most people today. But this was about spiritual death and spiritual life. Now let's focus on another aspect of this that will look at this from another perspective, and that is that the resurrection was the hope of Israel. This was the original teaching of the prophets. Paul confirmed this in the book of Acts. Paul was teaching what the prophets taught:

> But this I confess to you, that according to the Way, which they call a sect, I worship the God of our fathers, **believing everything laid down by the Law** and written in the Prophets, having a **hope in God**, which these men themselves accept, that there will be a **resurrection of both the just and the unjust**. (Acts 24:14-15 ESV)

What did the prophets say about this? Let's look at a few examples:

> **He will swallow up death forever**, And the Lord GOD will wipe away tears from all faces; The rebuke of His people He will take away from all the earth; For the LORD has spoken. And it will be said in that day: "Behold, this *is* our God; We have waited for Him, and He will save us. This *is* the LORD; We have waited for Him; We will be glad and rejoice in His salvation." (Isa 25:8-9 ESV)

> **I will ransom them from the power of the grave**; I will redeem them from death. O Death, I will be your plagues! O Grave, I will be your destruction! Pity is hidden from My eyes. (Hos 13:14 NKJV)

Daniel shows that the timing of this would be for the last days of the nation of Israel. First of all he predicts that the Messiah would come to put an end to sin, and bring in everlasting righteousness:

> Seventy weeks are determined for your people and for your holy city, To finish the transgression, **To make an end of sins**, **To make reconciliation** for iniquity, **To bring in everlasting righteousness**, To seal up vision and prophecy, And **to anoint the Most Holy.** (Daniel 9:24 NKJV)

Then in chapter 12 we confirm the timing of this:

> At that time Michael shall stand up, The great prince who stands *watch* over the sons of your people; And there shall be a time of trouble, Such as never was since there was a nation, *Even* to that time. And **at that time your people shall be delivered**, Every one who is found written in the book. **And many of those who sleep in the dust of the earth shall awake, Some to everlasting life, Some to shame *and* everlasting contempt.** (Daniel 12:1-2 NKJV)

This was the promised resurrection. Next, we see the exact timing:

> Then I heard the man clothed in linen, who *was* above the waters of the river, when he held up his right hand and his left hand to heaven, and swore by Him who lives forever, that *it shall be* for a time, times, and half *a time;* and **when the power of the holy people has been completely shattered, all these *things* shall be finished.** (Daniel 12:7 NKJV)

The power of the Holy people was shattered at the destruction of Jerusalem and the temple! This ended the Old Covenant and allowed the New Covenant to stand on its own alone. This was the time of the resurrection. Now that we know the timing of this, let's look at what Paul said concerning the resurrection hope of Israel. Let's start with Romans 8:

> And not only the creation, but we ourselves, who have the first fruits of the Spirit, groan inwardly as we wait eagerly for adoption as sons, the redemption of our bodies. For in this hope we were saved. Now hope that is seen is not hope. For who hopes for what he sees? But if we hope for what we do not see, we wait for it with patience. (Romans 8:23-25 ESV)

This was the hope of Israel. Paul confirms this in Romans 9:

> I am speaking the truth in Christ—I am not lying; my conscience bears me witness in the Holy Spirit—that I have

> great sorrow and unceasing anguish in my heart. For I could wish that I myself were accursed and cut off from Christ for the sake of my brothers, my kinsmen according to the flesh. ***They are Israelites, and to them belong the adoption***, the glory, the covenants, the giving of the law, the worship, and the promises. To them belong the patriarchs, and from their race, **according to the flesh**, is the Christ, who is God over all, blessed forever. Amen. (Romans 9:1-5 ESV)

The adoption that Paul is speaking of here is the promise of the resurrection ***made to Israel***. But even though this was made according to the flesh, it does not mean that it was fulfilled in a fleshly manner. This is because when Christ was raised from the dead, even though he was raised from the dead bodily, this body was now somehow changed. Actually, **He was raised into the spirit realm** as shown by Peter in this passage:

> For Christ also suffered once for sins, the righteous for the unrighteous, that he might bring us to God, being **put to death in the flesh** but **made alive in the spirit**, (1 Peter 3:18 ESV)

Thus, our Lord, upon His resurrection was **not going** to fulfill these things in the realm of the flesh, but **He would fulfill these** in the realm of the spirit.

> From now on, therefore, we regard no one **according to the flesh**. Even though we once regarded Christ according to the flesh, **we regard him thus no longer**. (2 Cor 5:16 ESV)

This means that **they regarded Him as in the spirit** in terms of His mode of existence. Paul confirmed the meaning of this in Romans 8 when he said:

> Those who are in the flesh **cannot please God**. (Rom 8:8 ESV)

Does this mean no one alive can please God? Of course not! Notice how he continues in the next verse.

> You, however, **are not in the flesh but in the Spirit**, if in fact the Spirit of God dwells in you. Anyone who does not have the Spirit of Christ does not belong to him. (Rom 8:9 ESV)

So, from this we can see unequivocally that he was speaking of these people who, since they were believers, were living in physical bodies who were alive in the spirit. And we also know that since Christ was the first one raised into the realm of the spirit, he was the "first fruits" of those who have fallen asleep. This is a concept that deals with the harvest in Israel. This is what Paul is saying to the Corinthian church:

> But now Christ is risen from the dead, *and* has become the firstfruits of those who have fallen asleep. (1 Cor 15:20 NKJV)

This idea of the first-fruits is a concept that deals with the harvest in Israel, and subsequently, the harvest had to do with the end of the Old Covenant age in Israel. How do we know this? We can determine this from a parable that Jesus gave in Matthew 13:24-30. In this parable, Jesus spoke of an enemy coming in and sowing tares among the wheat in the field, and that they should be gathered up and separated at the harvest, which would occur at the end of the age. When Jesus interpreted this to the disciples He told them that the wheat was a reference to the true believers, and the tares were those wicked ones sown in among them by the enemy to disrupt the faith.

> Therefore as the tares are gathered and burned in the fire, **so it will be at the end of THIS age**. The Son of Man will send out His angels, and they will gather out of His kingdom all things that offend, and those who practice lawlessness, and will cast

> them into the furnace of fire. There will be wailing and gnashing of teeth. (Matt 13:40-42 NKJV)

The end of the age that Jesus was speaking of was the **end of the age Jesus was living in**, the Jewish age, or the end of the Old Covenant age, in which the city of Jerusalem, the temple, and the entire system of Levitical worship would be destroyed. We can confirm the timeframe as being the end of the Jewish age **because the Christian age in which we are now living has no end:**

> Now to Him who is able to do exceedingly abundantly above all that we ask or think, according to the power that works in us, to Him *be* glory in the church by Christ Jesus **to all generations, forever and ever.** Amen. (Eph 3:20-21 NKJV)

This is the age WITHOUT END, the Christian age. Then Jesus said:

> Then the righteous will shine forth as the sun in the kingdom of their Father. He who has ears to hear, let him hear! (Matt 13:43 NKJV)

This is a direct quote from Daniel 12:3. Notice Daniel's words:

> Those who are wise shall shine Like the brightness of the firmament, And those who turn many to righteousness Like the stars forever and ever. (Daniel 12:3 NKJV)

Remember what we saw earlier concerning the timing of this? The prophet Daniel explicitly told when this would happen:

> Then I heard the man clothed in linen, who *was* above the waters of the river, when he held up his right hand and his left hand to heaven, and swore by Him who lives forever, that *it shall be* for a time, times, and half *a time;* and **when the**

> **power of the holy people has been completely shattered**, all these *things* shall be finished. (Daniel 12:7 NKJV)

The time **when the power of the holy people has been completely shattered** was none other than at the end of the Old Covenant age, or at the destruction of the temple, and the holy city in AD 70. Paul confirmed that this resurrection was to happen **at that time**:

> And *do* this, knowing the time, that **now *it is* high time** to awake out of sleep; for now **our salvation *is* nearer than when we *first* believed**. The night is far spent, the day is at hand. Therefore let us cast off the works of darkness, and let us put on the armor of light. (Romans 13:11-12 NKJV)

Paul also confirmed this would happen soon when he said:

> And the God of peace will **crush Satan under your feet shortly**. The grace of our Lord Jesus Christ *be* with you. Amen. (Rom 16:20 NKJV)

Thus, the spiritual death brought on by Satan was now about to be crushed. The resurrection was to occur at the end of the Jewish age. Jesus said:

> Do not think that I came to destroy the Law or the Prophets. I did not come to destroy **but to fulfill.** For assuredly, I say to you**, till heaven and earth pass away**, one jot or one tittle will by no means pass from the law **till all is fulfilled**. (Matt 5:17,18 NKJV)

The term "heaven and earth" was a description of the temple. The Most Holy represented heaven where God alone dwelled, and the rest represented earth, where man was. The Law that He was speaking of was the Old Testament Law.

Do you see the profound significance of this statement?

That law **had to be completely fulfilled** to become obsolete, and **that law had to fulfill all of those references to the resurrection** within the law and that written by the prophets, including those in the writings of the Major Prophets we have mentioned. Thus, the resurrection is spiritual, not physical. It occurs at the time of being "born again." Once again, I will refer to the picture painted by the Apostle Paul. He describes this perfectly in Romans chapter 6 when he says:

> Or do you not know that as many of us as were baptized into Christ Jesus were **baptized into His death?** Therefore we were buried with Him through baptism into death, that **just as Christ was raised from the dead** by the glory of the Father, **even so we also should walk in newness of life**. (Romans 6:3-4 NKJV)

The newness of life that Paul spoke of was that they were no longer separated from God in their sins, but they were now alive in the spirit, having been resurrected from the spiritual death passed down from Adam. The timing of this is crucial. The fact that this would happen soon is **emphasized by Christ himself** when He said:

> Truly, truly, I say to you, **an hour is coming, and is now here**, when the dead will hear the voice of the Son of God, and those who hear will live. For as the Father has life in himself, so he has granted the Son also to have life in himself. And he has given him authority to execute judgment, because he is the Son of Man. Do not marvel at this, for an hour is coming **when all who are in the tombs will hear his voice and come out**, those who have done good to the resurrection of life, and those who have done evil to the resurrection of judgment. (John 5:25-29 ESV)

This was not something which was to happen thousands of years later. Those who were spiritually dead would hear His voice and would live, and all those in the tombs would soon be resurrected, to either life, or judgment. When would this happen? As we found earlier, **Daniel the prophet unequivocally gave a proclamation of the exact timing:**

> And **many of those who sleep in the dust of the earth shall awake, some to everlasting life, and some to shame and everlasting contempt.** . . . . And I heard the man clothed in linen, who was above the waters of the stream; he raised his right hand and his left hand toward heaven and swore by him who lives forever that it would be for a time, times, and half a time, and that **when the shattering of the power of the holy people comes to an end all these things would be finished**. (Daniel 12:2,7 ESV)

There is no question that the power of the Holy people was shattered at the time of the destruction of Jerusalem, the temple, and the entire Levitical system of worship. This occurred at the hands of the Romans in AD 70.

1 Corinthians 15

Now let's look at what Paul said concerning this resurrection. First, we will look at 1 Corinthians 15. In the first eleven verses of this chapter, we find that Paul speaks of the resurrection of Christ, and confirms the fact that it happened, and was witnessed by Peter, James, and over 500 others. Paul mentions that Christ also appeared to him, and he was called into service. The Corinthian church knew that Christ was raised from the dead, but there seemed to be some here who were questioning the concept of the resurrection. Paul's argument was that since they know Christ was raised, it thus must follow that there is a resurrection from the dead. Note what he says:

> Now if Christ is proclaimed as raised from the dead, how can some of you say that there is no resurrection of the dead? But if there is no resurrection of the dead, then not even Christ has been raised. And if Christ has not been raised, then our preaching is in vain and your faith is in vain. We are even found to be misrepresenting God, because we testified about God that he raised Christ, whom he did not raise if it is true that the dead are not raised. For if the dead are not raised, not even Christ has been raised. And if Christ has not been raised, your faith is futile, and you are still in your sins. Then those also who have fallen asleep in Christ have perished. If in Christ we have hope in this life only, we are of all people most to be pitied. (1 Cor 15:12-19 ESV)

Paul's argument is clear. There **is a resurrection from the dead**, and the resurrection of Christ was the beginning. In another letter to the church at Colossae he said: "He is the beginning, the firstborn from the dead, that in everything he might be preeminent." (Col 1:18) Notice how he brings this together.

> But in fact Christ has been raised from the dead, the firstfruits of those who have fallen asleep. For as by a man came death, by a man **has come** also the resurrection of the dead. For as in Adam all die, so also in Christ **shall all be made alive**. But each in his own order: Christ the firstfruits, then at his coming those who belong to Christ. (1 Cor 15:20-23 ESV)

This illustration of the first fruits was in accordance with Jewish Law. Notice the command:

> "Speak to the people of Israel and say to them, when you come into the land that I give you and reap its harvest, **you shall bring the sheaf of the firstfruits of your harvest to the priest**, (Lev 23:10 ESV)

Thus, the **first fruits and the harvest occurred at the same time**. The first fruits were presented; Christ had already been resurrected from the dead as the first fruits. **That means that the harvest of resurrected ones was about to begin.** But now your question might be, "How can this be since the resurrection of Christ was bodily? There were no bodies coming up out of the graves." You are right! But if you will recall, the Jews always required a sign. Jesus told them the only sign they would receive was the sign of Jonah. What did that mean? He told them:

> For just as Jonah was three days and three nights in the belly of the great fish, so will the Son of Man be three days and three nights in the heart of the earth. (Matthew 12:40 ESV)

Jesus rose from the dead so that people living at that time could witness it, and without question they did. And when Christ rose from the dead, He became the "first-fruits" of the harvest. After His ascension to heaven, He did not stay in the same form. That body of a Jewish man was no longer present. But He was as described as John recorded in Revelation chapter one:

> The hairs of his head were white, like white wool, like snow. His eyes were like a flame of fire, his feet were like burnished bronze, refined in a furnace, and his voice was like the roar of many waters. In his right hand he held seven stars, from his mouth came a sharp two-edged sword, and his face was like the sun shining in full strength. (Rev 1:14-16 ESV)

Jesus had returned to His spiritual body, the body of the son of God, and one with the father. Now as we return to 1 Corinthians, we notice the wording of the verse. As Paul emphasizes in verse 21 the resurrection of the dead **has come (present tense).** There was **not to be a gap** of thousands of years between the first fruit and the final harvest. When Paul wrote this to the church in Corinth, it was only about 15 years away. Once again remember that Daniel said: "**when the shattering of the power of the holy people comes to an end all these things would be finished.**" (Daniel 12:7). The power of the holy people was shattered completely when Jerusalem, the temple, and the entire Levitical system of worship was brought to an end in AD 70. Although Paul knows this is about to occur, he did not know the exact timing. This is the end that he speaks of in the next verse.

> Then comes the end, when he delivers the kingdom to God the Father after destroying every rule and every authority and power. For he must reign until he has put all his enemies under his feet. The last enemy to be destroyed is death. For "God has put all things in subjection under his feet." But when it says, "all things are put in subjection," it is plain that he is excepted who put all things in subjection under him. When all things are subjected to him, then the Son himself will also be subjected to him who put all things in subjection under him, that God may be all in all. (1 Cor 15:24-28 ESV)

Just prior to His ascension into heaven, Jesus said: "All authority in heaven and on earth has been given to me." (Mat 28:18) But after His ascension to heaven, He went into the Holy of Holies in heaven to present His blood of the sacrifice. As the writer of Hebrews noted:

> It was indeed therefore necessary for the glimpses of the things in the heavens with these to be purified; but, the heavenly things themselves, with better sacrifices than these. For, not into a Holy place made by hand, entered Christ,— counterpart of the real Holy place ; but, **into the heaven itself, NOW**, to be plainly manifested before the face of God in our behalf;— (Hebrews 9:23-24 Rotherham)

Thus, from this we see that at the ascension, all authority was given to Christ, but when He went into the Most Holy in heaven and presented the blood of His sacrifice, the prophecy given by the Apostle Paul came true when he said: "The God of peace will **soon crush Satan** under your feet."(Romans 16:20) So then at the Parousia, when Christ came as He promised; and through the use of the Roman armies, He completely destroyed the city of Jerusalem, the temple, and the entire system of Levitical sacrifice and worship. Yes with this, Satan was "crushed." This system and those who posed the most severe opposition to them would be finally crushed. Satan's authority over them would end. Additionally, the last enemy, which was the "death" which Adam experienced in the garden, was destroyed. Now, because of the precious blood of Christ being presented in the Holy of Holies in heaven, man could once again have a restored relationship with God. Now as we return to 1 Corinthians, in verse 29 we see that Paul made a very obscure statement:

> Otherwise, what do people mean by being baptized on behalf of the dead? If the dead are not raised at all, why are people baptized on their behalf? (1 Cor 15:29 ESV)

Commentator Adam Clarke said of this verse: " This is certainly the most difficult verse in the New Testament; for, notwithstanding the greatest and wisest men have labored to explain it, there are to this day nearly as many different interpretations of it as there are interpreters."

Remember that **Paul is speaking in the present tense**. He is not speaking of a future event. So, let's just think about this for a moment in the light of what Paul has said in the past. We know that in Romans chapter 5 Paul said:

> Yet death reigned from Adam to Moses, even over those whose sinning was not like the transgression of Adam, who was a type of the one who was to come. . . . For if, because of one man's trespass, death reigned through that one man, much more will those who receive the abundance of grace and the free gift of righteousness reign in life through the one man Jesus Christ. (Rom 5:14,17 ESV)

The presence of the Old Covenant was a stop gap measure to cover the sin of the people and give them a relationship with God, based on the future blood of Christ. The act of baptism symbolized the spiritual death of the believer, and the coming up out of the water symbolized a new life in Christ. So their status changed from being dead in Adam to being made alive in Christ. Of course, this **would not be complete until the Parousia.**

As the writer of Hebrews said:

> so Christ, having been offered once to bear the sins of many, **will appear a second time**, not to deal with sin **but to save those who are eagerly waiting for him**. (Hebrews 9:28 ESV)

Without a doubt, the writer of Hebrews made his point. The Parousia is the **completion of salvation** for the believer. So in looking at verse 29 once again we realize that perhaps Paul was answering a question or misconception posed regarding this by one of the believers in Corinth in the first half of the verse, in relationship to this. But whatever was meant, the statement is meant to show another proof that those who are spiritually dead are raised. Let us continue:

> Why are we in danger every hour? I protest, brothers, by my pride in you, which I have in Christ Jesus our Lord, I die every day! (1 Cor 15:30-31 ESV)

Paul was continually being exposed to death. But he was proud of the faith of his Corinthian brothers. He was emphasizing that this is the cross that they must bear, the possibility of being killed for the sake of Christ.

> What do I gain if, humanly speaking, I fought with beasts at Ephesus? If the dead are not raised, "Let us eat and drink, for tomorrow we die." Do not be deceived: "Bad company ruins good morals." Wake up from your drunken stupor, as is right, and do not go on sinning. For some have no knowledge of God. I say this to your shame. (1 Cor 15:32-34 ESV)

Paul was once again emphasizing the point he made earlier concerning the resurrection of Christ. If there is no resurrection from the dead, there is no point to our faith. We might as well live it up for otherwise we have nothing. But NO, quit associating with those ones who would deny the resurrection, and the existence of God. They are ruining your faith and will cause you to sin with them.

> But someone will ask, "How are the dead raised? With what kind of body do they come?" You foolish person! What you sow does not come to life unless it dies. And what you sow is not the body that is to be, but a bare kernel, perhaps of wheat or of some other grain. But God gives it a body as he has chosen, and to each kind of seed its own body. (1 Cor 15:35-38 ESV)

If the resurrection of those who have died physically was a bodily resurrection of the same type that goes into the ground, there would be **no purpose for Paul to go into the seed analogy** as he did in this passage. The body that dies and goes into the ground is like a seed. Therefore, the body that comes out of the ground is a different body, suited for the purpose which is chosen by God.

> For not all flesh is the same, but there is one kind for humans, another for animals, another for birds, and another for fish. There are heavenly bodies and earthly bodies, but the glory of the heavenly is of one kind, and the glory of the earthly is of another. There is one glory of the sun, and another glory of the moon, and another glory of the stars; for star differs from star in glory. (1 Cor 15:39-41 ESV)

Continuing with his seed analogy, Paul gives some examples of different types of bodies; each one is individually suited for its own purpose. Additionally, even with the heavenly bodies, each body type has its own glory. For example, the sun has a magnitude of glory that is far greater than the moon.

> So is it with the resurrection of the dead. What is sown is **perishable; what is raised is imperishable.** It is sown in dishonor; it is raised in glory. It is sown in weakness; it is raised in power. **It is sown a natural body; it is raised a spiritual body**. If there is a natural body, there is also a spiritual body. (1 Cor 15:42-44 ESV)

This passage sounds simple, but it must be understood in the context of what the rest of the Scriptures say about the resurrection. Now I want you to **look closely** to what I am about to say. It gets a little complex. Revelation 20:4-5 tells us that there are two groups who participate in the first resurrection. Notice what it says:

> Then I saw thrones, and seated on them were those to whom the authority to judge was committed. Also I saw **the souls of those who had been beheaded for the testimony of Jesus** and for the word of God, and those who had not worshiped the beast or its image and had not received its mark on their

> foreheads or their hands. They came to life and reigned with Christ for a thousand years. **The rest of the dead did not come to life until the thousand years were ended**. This is the first resurrection. (Rev 20:4-5 ESV)

Upon first reading verse 5, it seems very confusing. It appears that there have been two separate and distinct groups being mentioned here, which we would think indicates two resurrections. The above is the verse as translated in the English Standard Version. Now notice the difference between this and the New International Version:

> (The rest of the dead did not come to life until the thousand years were ended.) This is the first resurrection. (Rev 20:5 NIV)

Do you see the difference?

- In the ESV, the passage **must be taken as follows**: "The rest of the dead (in Christ) did not come to life until the thousand years were ended." (This makes them a part of the first resurrection.)
- In the NIV, the presence of the parentheses is an indication that those words in parentheses are a side note. (In other words, these ones are not a part of the first resurrection but belong to the second resurrection.)

This passage has to be taken in one of these two ways in order to make sense. Otherwise we have to separate verse 5 as a second resurrection, which is contrary to what it says. As such, there would have to be a third resurrection, but this does not agree with how the verse is written.

I believe that the ESV has translated it correctly, and here is why.

Now in order to put this in perspective, we must remember the prophecy of Daniel 12:1-7 which tells us when the resurrection would occur. Let's read this again:

> "At that time shall arise Michael, the great prince who has charge of your people. And there shall be a time of trouble, such as never has been since there was a nation till that time. But at that time your people shall be delivered, everyone whose name shall be found written in the book. **And many of those who sleep in the dust of the earth shall awake, some to everlasting life, and some to shame and everlasting contempt.** (Daniel 12:1-2 ESV)

This is the resurrection.

> And those who are wise shall shine like the brightness of the sky above; and those who turn many to righteousness, like the stars forever and ever. But you, Daniel, shut up the words and seal the book, until the time of the end. Many shall run to and fro, and knowledge shall increase." Then I, Daniel, looked, and behold, two others stood, one on this bank of the stream and one on that bank of the stream. And someone said to the man clothed in linen, who was above the waters of the stream, "How long shall it be till the end of these wonders?" And I heard the man clothed in linen, who was above the waters of the stream; he raised his right hand and his left hand toward heaven and swore by him who lives forever that it would be for a time, times, and half a time, and **that when the shattering of the power of the holy people comes to an end all these things would be finished.** (Daniel 12:3-7 ESV)

Did you notice how specific this verse was. It specifically says: **"when the shattering of the power of the holy people comes to an end ALL these things would be finished." This had to be at the destruction of Jerusalem in AD 70.**

This was the complete end of the Old Covenant and the Jewish Levitical system of worship. The power of God's heretofore holy people was completely shattered. This system of worship was no longer possible! **It also had to be the end of the Millennium**, because Rev. 20:5 plainly states that those dead in Christ did not come to life "**until the thousand years were ended**." Also, we must realize that Revelation 20:4 tells us that this resurrection includes not only:

- The saints who were beheaded, but also,
- Those who had not worshiped the beast or received the mark. Therefore, these are people who are still alive.

If the resurrection included both those dead at the time, and those alive, then we know that **it meant that all believers** were resurrected at that time, both those who were physically dead, and those who were physically alive. Thus, the first resurrection is by nature a spiritual resurrection, but at AD 70 it included those who were removed from "paradise" in Hades and were taken to heaven. This was the resurrection that Paul was speaking of in the passage in 1 Corinthians 15:42-44. Thus, **we as believers are a part of the first resurrection.** The picture Paul painted in Romans 6:4 applies to us. **We were buried with Christ**. This put away our sin. **Then we were resurrected to walk in the newness of life! We are already part of the first resurrection!** What a blessing! As Rev 20:6 says, **the second death has no authority over us**, and this is in harmony with what Paul said:

> But God, being rich in mercy, because of the great love with which he loved us, even when we were dead in our trespasses,

> made us alive together with Christ—**by grace you have been saved**— and **raised us up with him and seated us with him in the heavenly places** in Christ Jesus, so that in the coming ages he might show the immeasurable riches of his grace in kindness toward us in Christ Jesus. For by grace you have been saved through faith. And this is not your own doing; it is the gift of God, (Ephesians 2:4-8 ESV)

Do you see the powerful significance of what Paul said? Those saints who **were still alive on earth** were also seated "**with Him in the heavenly places.**" Their **resurrection from spiritual death was complete,** and the second death now had no power over them.

> Thus it is written, "The first man Adam became a living being"; the last Adam became a life-giving spirit. But it is not the spiritual that is first but the natural, and then the spiritual. The first man was from the earth, a man of dust; the second man is from heaven. As was the man of dust, so also are those who are of the dust, and as is the man of heaven, so also are those who are of heaven. Just as we have borne the image of the man of dust, we shall also bear the image of the man of heaven. (1 Cor 15:45-49 ESV)

When Adam was placed in the garden he was in perfect spiritual fellowship with God. His most important assignment was to obey God. When he disobeyed God, **he died that day, spiritually**. He was then separated from God .... no more walks in the Garden together, and no more discussions together. It was over. But physically, he lived for over 900 years. When Jesus died on the cross, he died physically as well, but just as man did, **he also suffered spiritual separation from God**. Paul would later tell the Corinthian church:

> For our sake **he made him to be sin who knew no sin**, so that in him we might become the righteousness of God. (2 Cor 5:21 ESV)

As the Apostle John noted:

> And as Moses lifted up the serpent in the wilderness, so must the Son of Man be lifted up, **that whoever believes in him may have eternal life.** "For God so loved the world, that he gave his only Son, that whoever believes in **him should not perish but have eternal life.** (John 3:14-16 ESV)

The fact of the matter is that if Jesus came to the earth to suffer physical death so that we did not have to die physically, **then this death was ineffective.** Why? Because men have continued to die without ceasing! But Jesus experienced the same alienation from God as man did when He died on that Cross. As Paul said, "**he made Him to be sin who knew no sin**, so that in Him we might become the righteousness of God." The only way for the man to be restored to that right relationship with God was for Him to also die to the flesh. This is done by belief in Christ as Lord and Savior. It is pictured perfectly by the baptism analogy.....**buried with Christ.......raised to walk in the newness of life.** (Romans 6:3-4) That new life is a spiritual one. When we accept Christ as Savior, we begin a new spiritual life with Christ, and we will never die again (spiritually). That is what Jesus meant when He said:

> Jesus said to her, "**I am the resurrection and the life**. Whoever believes in me, though he die, yet shall he live, and **everyone who lives and believes in me shall never die**. Do you believe this?" (John 11:25-26 ESV)

Now as we continue with 1 Corinthians we read:

> I tell you this, brothers: flesh and blood cannot inherit the kingdom of God, nor does the perishable inherit the imperishable. Behold! I tell you a mystery. We shall not all sleep, but we shall all be changed, in a moment, in the twinkling of an eye, at the last trumpet. For the trumpet will sound, and the dead will be raised imperishable, and we shall be changed. For this perishable body must put on the imperishable, and this mortal body must put on immortality. When the perishable puts on the imperishable, and the mortal puts on immortality, then shall come to pass the saying that is written: "Death is swallowed up in victory." (1 Cor 15:50-54 ESV)

The words used by Paul in verse 50 makes it clear that the Kingdom of God is not primarily a physical kingdom. It is a spiritual kingdom. We inherit this kingdom spiritually when we become believers. Thus, when we die physically, we do not actually die, but are changed in the twinkling of an eye. Our spirit still lives, and we will receive a spiritual body, as we read earlier in verse 44, "**It is sown a natural body; it is raised a spiritual body**." Since Paul included himself in with those who would "not sleep," we know that Paul was expecting the return of the Lord at any time. What Paul was emphasizing in verses 51-53 is that soon, at the Parousia (the last trumpet), this would be finalized. Not everyone would die at that time, but would be changed in a moment, in the twinkling of an eye **to complete spiritual life**. Thus, they would never die. This is in harmony with what the writer of Hebrews stated:

> so Christ, having been offered once to bear the sins of many, will appear a second time, not to deal with sin **but to save those who are eagerly waiting for him**. (Heb 9:28 ESV)

This event where Christ appeared "a second time," is called the Parousia, and as stated above, it finalized the salvation for the believer. Did you notice the wording at the end of the verse? They were **eagerly awaiting** this event. The death of Adam, that is, spiritual death, was swallowed up forever. It is as Jesus said:

> Truly, truly, I say to you, whoever hears my word and believes him who sent me has eternal life. He does not come into judgment, **but has passed from death to life**. (John 5:24 ESV)

As we conclude the passage in 1 Corinthians 15, we read:

> "O death, where is your victory? O death, where is your sting?" The sting of death is sin, and the power of sin is the law. But thanks be to God, who gives us the victory through our Lord Jesus Christ. Therefore, my beloved brothers, be steadfast, immovable, always abounding in the work of the Lord, knowing that in the Lord your labor is not in vain. (1 Cor 15:55-58 ESV)

It is no wonder that Paul breaks out in praise here. By the accomplishment of being finally changed to complete spiritual life, those alive at that time would never die, and **those believers who had died physically** would be raised from the "paradise" side of Hades, to life in heaven, and would receive their spiritual body. But it is true of both groups that they would always be with the Lord. What a great chapter of encouragement to those to whom Paul wrote.

Scripture Index

Scripture Index

Scripture Index

Scripture Index

Scripture Index

Scripture Index

Scripture Index

Scripture Index

END NOTES

---

[i] Lindsey Hal, *The Late Great Planet Earth*, Zondervan, 1970 p43
[ii] Ibid p. 137

[iii] *REF: Whisenant, Edgar. 88 Reasons Why The Rapture Will Be In 1988: The Feast of Trumpets (Rosh-Hash-Ana) September 11-12-13 (Kindle Locations 167-176). Kindle Edition.*

[iv] Ibid, *(Kindle Locations 167-192). Kindle Edition.*

[v] Jeremiah, David. Escape the Coming Night (pp. 21-22). Thomas Nelson. Kindle Edition.

[vi] Gentry, Kenneth L, Jr., Th.D. *Before Jerusalem Fell, The Dating of the Book of Revelation,* Victorious Hope Publishing, Fountain Inn, S.C.
[vii] Against Heresies, Book 5, Chapter 30,section 3, By Irenaeus of Lyons, http://www.newadvent.org/fathers/0103530.htm
[viii] Against Heresies, Book 2, Chapter 22, Section 5 by Irenaeus of Lyons, http://www.newadvent.org/fathers/0103222.htm
[ix] Gentry, Kenneth, *Before Jerusalem Fell,* 1998 Victorious Hope Publishing, pp. 45-67, also pp. 105, 106

[x] D. Div., Don K. Preston. Who Is This Babylon? (Kindle Location 927). JaDon Management Inc.. Kindle Edition.

[xi] Adam Clarke's Commentary on the Bible, taken from e-Sword, Version 10.2.1, 2013, Rick Meyers (Free download at www.e-sword.net)

[xii] Welton, Jonathan (2013-11-01). Raptureless: An Optimistic Guide to the End of the World – Revised Edition Including The Art of Revelation (Kindle Locations 4468-4472) BookBaby, Kindle Edition.
[xiii] Albert Barnes Notes on the Bible, Daniel 9:24 (taken from e-sword. Free download at www.e-sword.net)
[xiv] This was added as a footnote in the 1701 KJV

[xv] (from "Observations upon the Prophecies of Daniel and the Apocalypse of St. John (Chapter 10), by Sir Isaac Newton)

http://www.gutenberg.org/files/16878/16878-h/16878-h.htm#DanX

[xvi] Lewis, C.S., ***Mere Christianity***, Touchstone Publishing 1996, p.56
[xvii] Various Authors, ***The World's Last Night and other Essays,***
[xviii] Josephus, The Complete Works, Translated by William Whiston, A.M., 1998 Thomas Nelson Publishers, Taken from The Wars of the Jews, 6.5.3, p890

[xix] ibid
[xx] Ibid
[xxi] http://www.centuryone.com/josephus.html Magen Broshi of The Israel Museum

[xxii] Albert Barnes Notes on the Bible, From Commentary on Matthew 24:31
[xxiii] (Thayer's Greek Lexicon, Feb 2014 printing, p. 112)
[xxiv] Ibid, p. 113
[xxv] Noe, John, Ph.D. Unraveling the End, A balanced scholarly synthesis of four competing and conflicting end time views, 2014, East2West Press, Indianapolis, IN, p. 288
[xxvi] D. Div., Don K. Preston. Who Is This Babylon? (Kindle Locations 145-150). JaDon Management Inc.. Kindle Edition.

[xxvii] Albert Barnes Notes on the Bible, Commentary on Isaiah 13:10
[xxviii] Josephus, The Complete Works, Translated by William Whiston, A.M., 1998 Thomas Nelson Publishers, Taken from The Wars of the Jews, 5.10.5. p863

[xxix] Arndt William F., and Gingrich F. Wilbur, A Translation and adaptation of Bauer's Lexicon, University of Chicago Press, fourth edition 1952 P. 446
[xxx] Ibid p. 136
[xxxi] Ibid, p.564
[xxxii]https://www.preteristarchive.com/1684_lightfoot_works-of-john-lightfoot/?highlight=Lightfoot

[xxxiii] Whiston, Josephus, The Complete Works, 1998, The Wars of the Jews, Book 5, Chapter 11, section 1, pp863,864
[xxxiv] Ibid p. 862
[xxxv] Ibid *The Wars of the Jews,* p. 884
[xxxvi] Ibid, *The Wars of the Jews* 6.9.3., p 898

[xxxvii] This list was taken from Foxes Book of Martyrs, Chapter 1 (e-sword reference library)

[xxxviii] Albert Barnes Notes on the Bible, Commentary on Matthew 24:29, Public Domain

[xxxix] Whiston, 1998, Wars of the Jews, Josephus. Book 6, Chapter 7, Section 3, p.895

[xl] Albert Barnes Notes on the Bible, Commentary on Rev. 7:4, Public Domain

[xli] http://www.newadvent.org/fathers/250103.htm (Eccl. Hist. 3:5:3)

[xlii] Adam Clarke's Commentary on the Bible, Rev 8:7, (taken from e-sword)

[xliii] Josephus Book 6 Chapter 6 section 1

[xliv] Ibid., The Wars of the Jews, 4.6.3., p.818
[xlv] Ibid., The Wars of the Jews, 4.8.1., p.822
[xlvi] Ibid, Wars of the Jews, 4.7.2., p.819
[xlvii] Ibid. The Wars of the Jews, 4.10.3., p. 830

[xlviii] (The Gospel of Nicodemus Chapter 22: 8-9) Wake, William. Forbidden books of the original New Testament (p. 144). Kindle Edition.

[xlix] Whiston, 1998, Josephus, The Wars of the Jews, 4.4.5., p.812
[l] Ibid,. The Wars of the Jews, 4.5.1., p.814
[li] Whiston, 1998, Josephus, The Wars of the Jews, 2.13.1 p736
[lii] Foxes Book of Martyrs, Chapter 2, paragraph 2, (Taken from the e-sword reference library)
[liii] Whiston, 1998, Josephus, The Wars of the Jews, 6.9.3, p.898

[liv] Taken from "The Parousia" J. Stuart Russell. Baker Books, 1999 p. 476. (First Published in 1887)

[lv] Whiston, 1998, Josephus, The Wars of the Jews, 5.9.4.,P.859

[lvi] Ibid., Book 5.13.4,5 pp.869,870
[lvii] Ibid., Book 3.10.9., pp794,795
[lviii] Ibid., Book 5.1.4., pp.836,837
[lix] Ibid., Book 6.1.1., p.872

[lx] Russell, James Stuart. Parousia: The New Testament Doctrine of Our Lord's Second Coming (Kindle Locations 6062-6066). Kindle Edition.

[lxi] Unger's Bible Dictionary, 1966 The Moody Bible Institute of Chicago, Third Printing 1981 p89

[lxii] Whiston, 1998, Josephus, The Wars of the Jews, Book 3.7.9., p.775

[lxiii] Whiston, 1998, Josephus, The Wars of the Jews, Book 5.10.5., p.863

[lxiv] Chadwick, Henry, The Early Church, Penguin books 1993, p78

[lxv] Church History (Eusebius), Book 3, Chapter 5, verse 4.
From http://www.newadvent.org/fathers/250103.htm)

[lxvi] John Gill's Exposition of the Bible,. Isaiah 51:19

[lxvii] Russell, James Stuart. Parousia: The New Testament Doctrine of Our Lord's Second Coming (Kindle Locations 1247-1252). Kindle Edition.

[lxviii] From: Church History (Eusebius), Book 3, Chapter 5, verse 4.
See also http://www.newadvent.org/fathers/250103.htm

[lxix] Ibid., Chapter 7 starting with verse 1.
[lxx] Whiston, 1998, Josephus, The Wars of the Jews, Book 7.1.1., p.900
[lxxi] From Adam Clarkes commentary, an opening description the book of Revelation.

[lxxii]https://www.christianity.com/church/church-history/timeline/1-300/nero-unleashed-first-wave-of-terror-11629580.html

---

[lxxiii] Gentry, Kenneth 2008, ***The book of Revelation made easy,*** Published by The American Vision, Inc. Powder Springs, GA, p.100

[lxxiv] Ibid p. 101

[lxxv] From Adam Clarke's Commentary on the whole Bible (Matt. 8:21)–

ABOUT THE AUTHOR

D. Robert Pike (Rob) is a retired Engineer and husband of his beloved wife Ida. He holds a Bachelor of Science degree from Indiana Wesleyan University, a Master of Arts Degree from Webster University, and a Ph.D in Theology from Trinity College and Seminary.

He is the author of four previous books:

1. **God's Promise of Redemption, a story of fulfilled prophecy**
2. **God's Purpose for Hell, a compelling probe of God's love for the lost**
3. **Jehovah's Witnesses, Modern Day Arians or Not**
4. **The Great American Divide, How we got here and what we can do about it**

All of Rob's Books are available at Amazon.com, or by order at your favorite book store.

Rob is an active member of Gideon's International and often speaks in various churches giving the Gideon message of the power of God's Word. He lives with his wife of 36 years in Southwest Florida in the winter, and central Indiana in the summer. His life verse is Proverbs 3:5,6:

> "Trust in the LORD with all your heart, and do not lean on your own understanding. In all your ways acknowledge him, and He will make straight your paths."

Be sure to visit Rob's website at: www.truthinliving.net.

If you have questions concerning this book, send an email to Rob at robpike@truthinliving.net.

Made in the USA
Monee, IL
03 November 2021